THE ADVENTURES OF ③ BARRY WEEN BOY GENIUS ™

Monkey Tales

THE ADVENTURES OF
BARRY WEEN
BOY GENIUS

3

Monkey Tales

written and illustrated by
Judd Winick

cover colors by
Guy Major

chapter break gray tones by
Arthur Dela Cruz

introduction by
Peter David

book design by
Sabotaged Studios

edited by
James Lucas Jones

original series edited by
Jamie S. Rich

original logo design by **Chris Eliopoulos**

published by **Oni Press, Inc.**
publisher, **Joe Nozemack**
editor in chief, **Jamie S. Rich**

associate editor, **James Lucas Jones**

This collects issues 1-3 of the Oni Press comics series
The Adventures of Barry Ween, Boy Genius 3: Monkey Tales.

ONI PRESS, INC.
6336 SE Milwaukie Avenue, PMB 30
Portland, OR 97202
USA

www.onipress.com
www.barryween.com

First edition: November 2001
ISBN 1-929998-18-X

1 3 5 7 9 10 8 6 4 2

PRINTED IN CANADA.

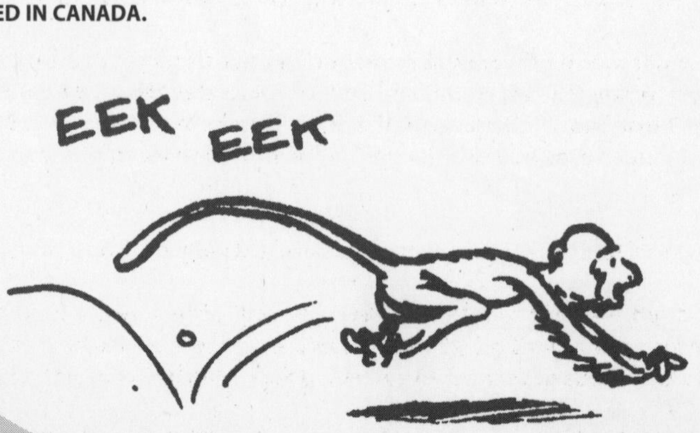
EEK
EEK

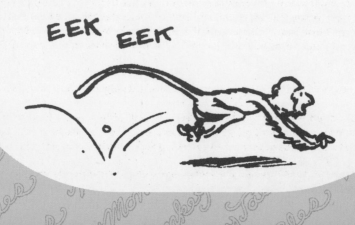

INTRODUCTION

I owe it all to Julie Schwartz.

Backing up a bit: You have to understand that, in any given month, I am hip-deep in comic books. The companies I work for send me comp copies of everything. *Everything*. Plus, whenever I attend a convention, I'm deluged with assorted folks, most of them aspiring artists or writers or artist/writers, all thrusting copies of their latest endeavors into my hands. They do this for a variety of reasons, ranging from "I really love your work and this is my way of saying thanks" to "I was hoping you could plug it in your column." (I must mention that I personally am repulsed by the notion of people trying shamelessly to use whatever means are available to them to plug their creative endeavors. Why, many was the time when I'd be working on comics such as *Supergirl, Young Justice, Captain Marvel, Soulsearchers & Company*, or the newest *Sir Apropos of Nothing* or *New Frontier* novel, and be distracted by my dwelling upon such audacity, such brazen attempts at peddling one's work. Sometimes I even express my ire and disgust in *But I Digress*, my weekly column which runs in *Comics Buyer's Guide*, available in better comic shops or by subscription from Krause Publications, 700 East State Street, Iola, WI 54990).

But enough about just me. Let us instead talk about *The Adventures of Barry Ween, Boy Genius* and me.

My litany above of the free comics I get is hardly going to cause the average wallet-challenged fan to shed a tear on my behalf, but I'm not looking for sympathy. Instead, it's simply an FYI explaining why I'm probably the last person to pick up on a new title. It's because I have no damned time, what with my already drowning in comics on a monthly basis. But one day, as I happened by a comics shop I frequent—Fourth World Comics in Smithtown, NY—I noticed an odd little title with a gorilla on it.

This brings us to the Julie Schwartz part.

For those of you wondering, "Julie Schwartz? Who's she?" I will tell you—after pounding you senseless with a dead mackerel—that Mr. Julius Schwartz is one of the masterminds of the Silver Age of comics. Thanks to Julie Schwartz, fans first encountered such notables as Barry Allen and Hal Jordan who are, respectively, the most famous victim and most famous mass murderer in DC history (and who also had brief careers as superheroes, I think.)

Julie has put forward a number of observations about what makes comics salable, and considering comics were selling a hell of a lot more when he was editing them, it might behoove us to listen to what he had to say. And one of Julie's observations was that if you wanted sales to jump on a comic, stick a gorilla on the cover. Gorillas sold comic books, simple as that. What, you think "Gorilla Grodd" came outta nowhere? You think Superman fought a giant ape or Jimmy Olsen became hirsute out of random chance? Hell no, boys and girls: It was canny marketing. Big monkeys get kids picking up funnybooks. Simple as that.

So imagine my surprise when I discover a huge gorilla adorning the cover of this odd-looking comic. The name of the title was familiar—I'm not *completely* dim. I'd heard good things about *Barry Ween*. I just hadn't chanced to pick it up. But here this Judd Winick guy, who I think had been on *Survivor* or acted in *Wayne's World* or something like that, had stuck a gorilla on the cover.

And I realized that I had to do something I rarely do and actually shell out money for a comic.

I had no choice, really, for one of two things had occurred. Either Winick had followed Julie Schwartz's dictum and put a gorilla on the cover in a shameless endeavor to sell books...in which case I had to buy it out of respect to such bald-faced hucksterism, and also out of deference to someone who revered the word of Schwartz to such a degree. Or else Winick had simply Just So Happened to adorn the cover with an oversized simian, in which case I had to buy it lest Schwartz's dictum be proven wrong. That is to say, Schwartz said people bought comics with gorillas on them, which meant I had to buy it so I wouldn't be dissing Julie, the real Main Man of comics.

So I bought it.

And read it.

And laughed my ass off. And believe me, that is a not-inconsiderable ass we're talking about.

It was my introduction to the world of Barry Ween. Barry has been described in shorthand as *Dexter's Lab* meets *South Park*, and that's true as far as it goes. But the carrot-topped (anti)hero of the following pages is an original nevertheless. Some people rag on Winick for the constant use of profanity. I think that's a pointless criticism. Whether today's kids talk that way or not (and frankly, many of them do) is beside the point. The fact is that *Barry* talks that way, and Jeremy (his best friend, moral base, and conscience), simply picked it up from him. Barry cusses with virtuoso precision, and when he moans a protracted "Fuuuuuck," it's not for shock value; it means he knows that matters have spiraled out of control. If one considers that most airplane black box recorders indicate that the last word of choice is "*Shit!*" (as Bill Cosby commented upon what usually occurs just before a catastrophic vehicular accident, "First you say it, then you do it") that would seem that we should cut the perpetually in-trouble Barry some slack. Besides, if you were Barry Ween—a man who, in the Kingdom of the Blind, possesses not only one eye but two, with more eyes in every nook and cranny of the kingdom—you too would probably be driven to frustrated profanity on a routine basis.

Plus Winick has avoided Barry's turning into a caricature through the simplest means available: Females. Jeremy is obsessed with getting his hands on their bodies, but the intellectually unstoppable Barry endeavors to comprehend their minds, and for the two friends that playing field is frustratingly level. Unlike Clark Kent who once hid his superpowered identity from Lois because he wanted her to love him for the "real him," Barry needs to keep the "real him" under wraps lest his beloved Sara become obsessed with the ultra brilliance that sets Barry apart. But relationships require a foundation of honesty, and so Barry is stymied. It gives us a bit of comfort to know that even a Boy Genius can't sort out a male/female relationship.

In any event, after reading that first issue, I immediately ran out and acquired the earlier trade paperback collections, and found a series filled with relentless invention, hilarity, and occasional poignancy.

But no monkeys.

A ghastly oversight that has, fortunately, now been remedied. And so, with a hearty "Kreegah! Bundolo!" enjoy this trade paperback collection of the first three issues of Barry's adventures with monkeys and other large hairy individuals (including a very charming, big-footed addition to the Barry Ween cast).

May the Schwartz be with you.

--Peter David
Long Island, NY, October 2001

Peter David is the fan-favorite writer of comics like Supergirl *and* Young Justice *for DC Comics, and* Captain Marvel *for Marvel Comics. When he's not writing comics he can be found penning columns for* Comics Buyer's Guide, *novels for popular science fiction franchises like* Star Trek *and* Babylon 5, *and various projects for television.*

For
Eric Ciasullo

Friend, counsel, moral compass, and *oh yeah*,
the guy who married us.

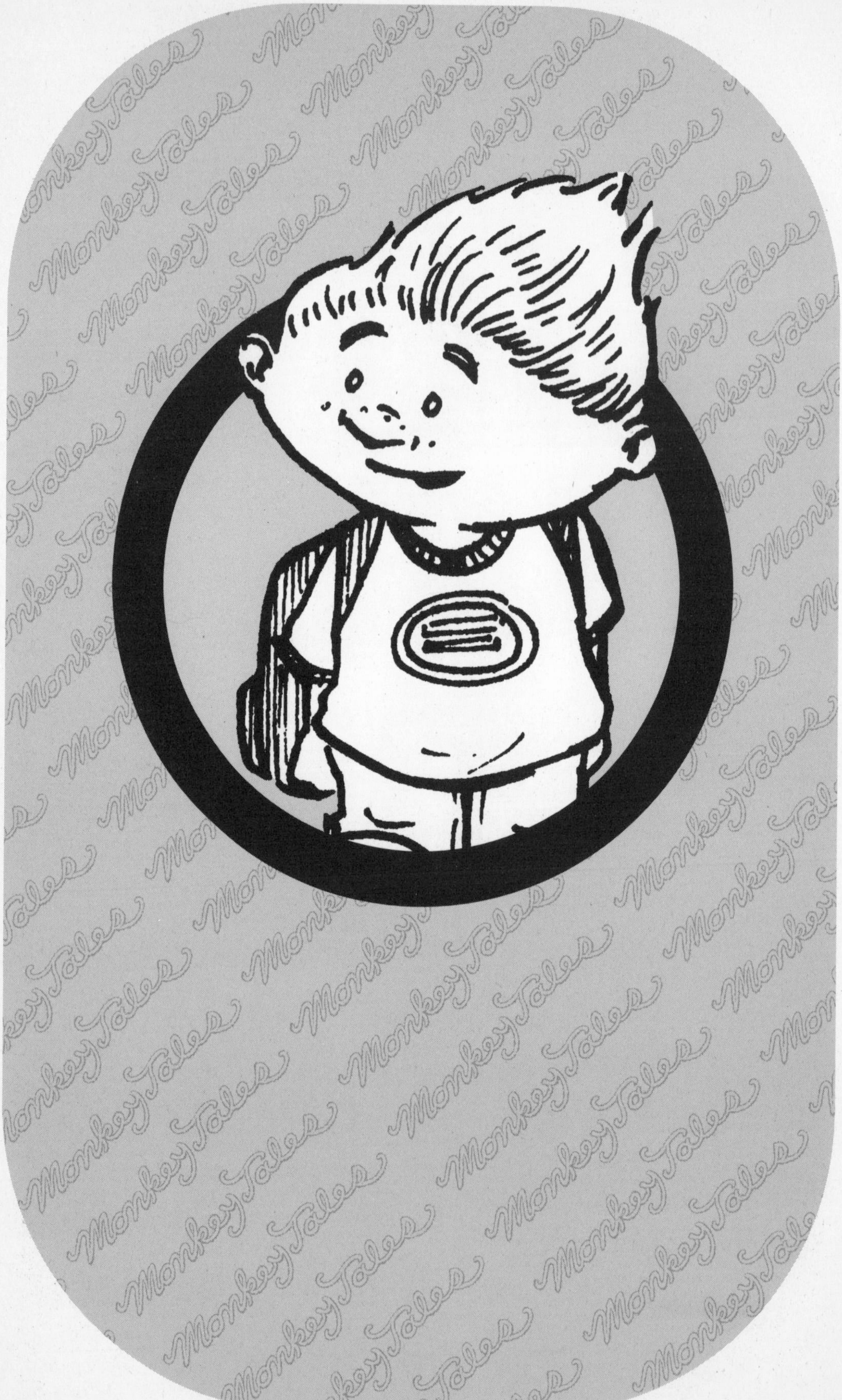
Monkey Tales

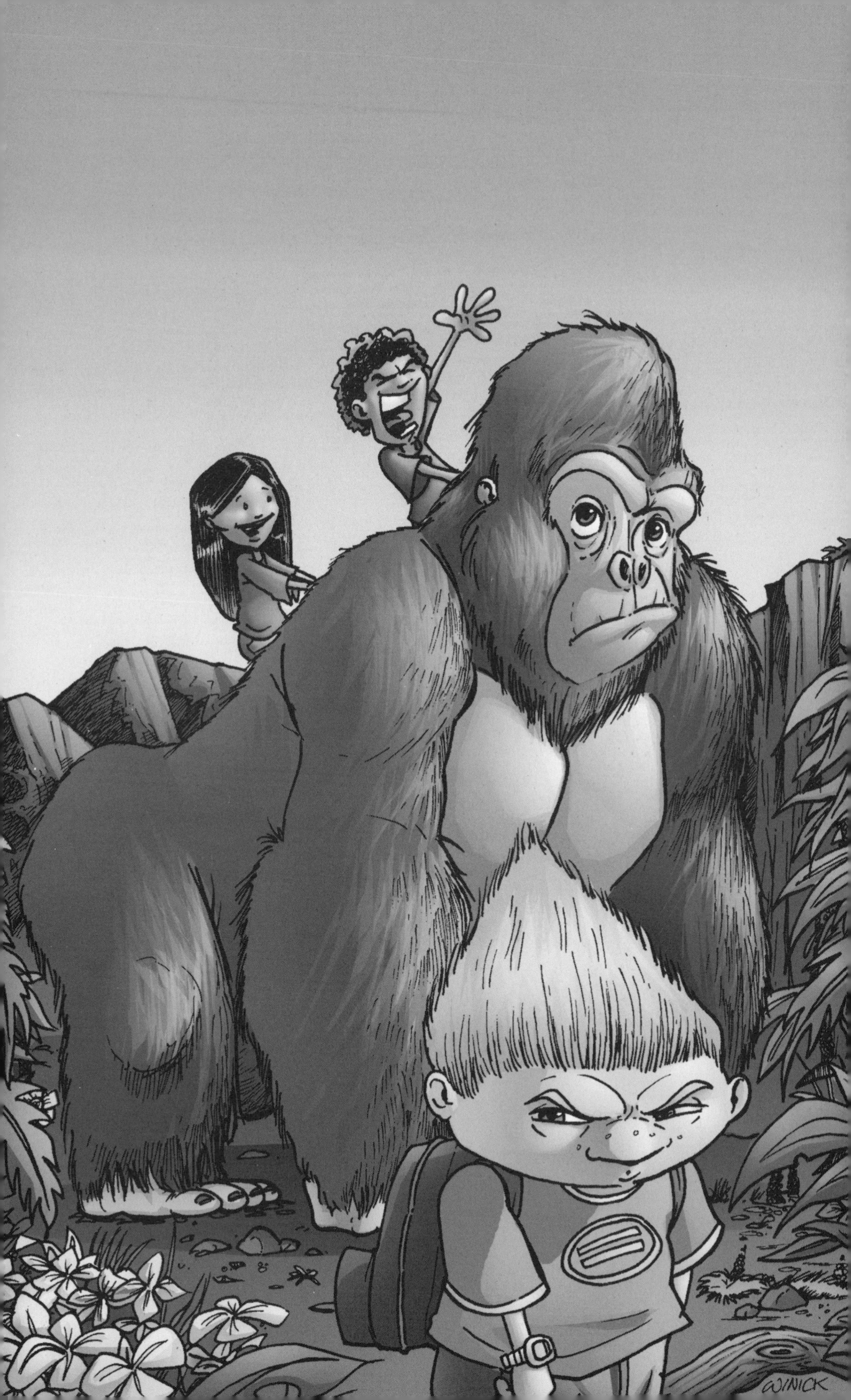
WINICK

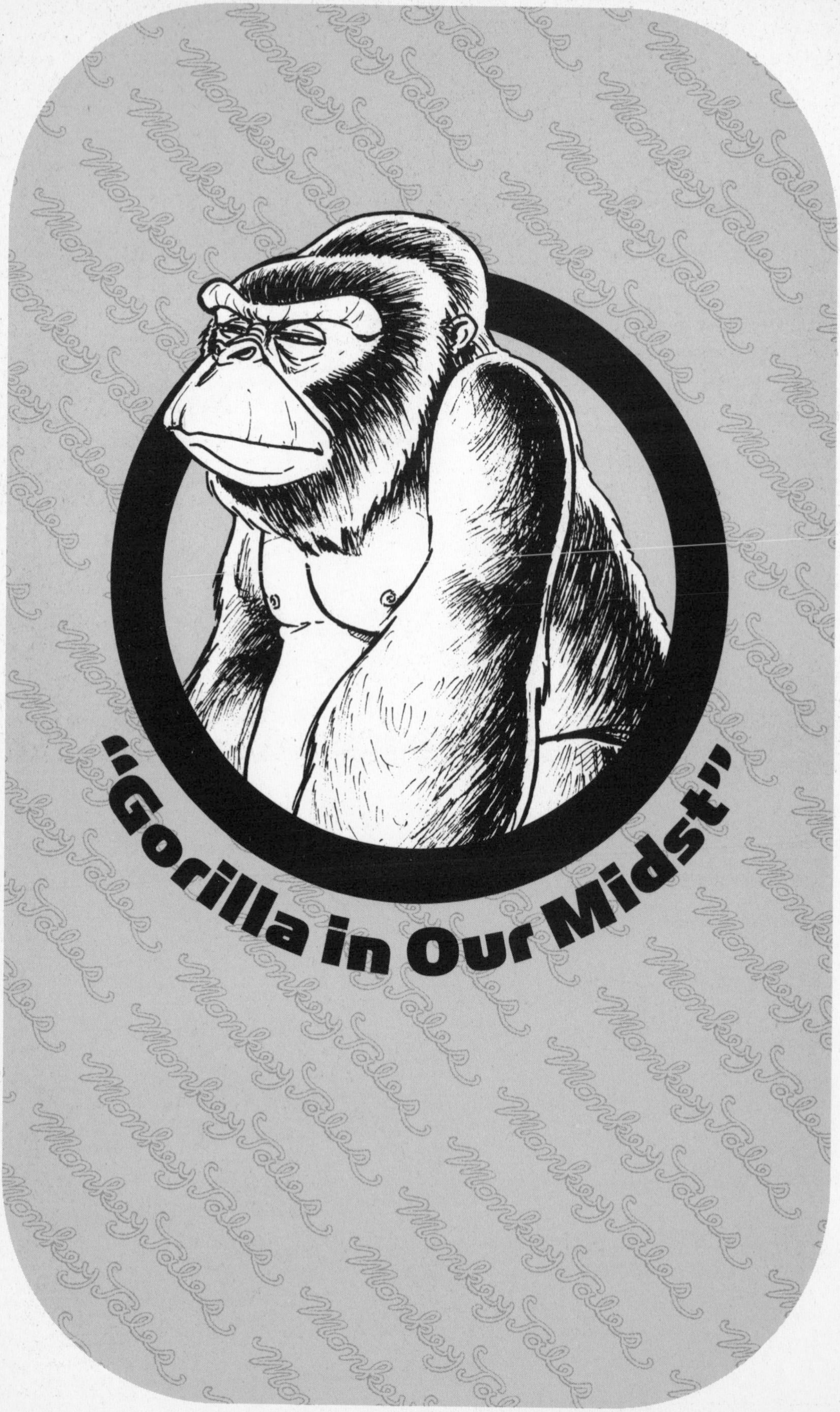
"Gorilla in Our Midst"
Monkey Tales

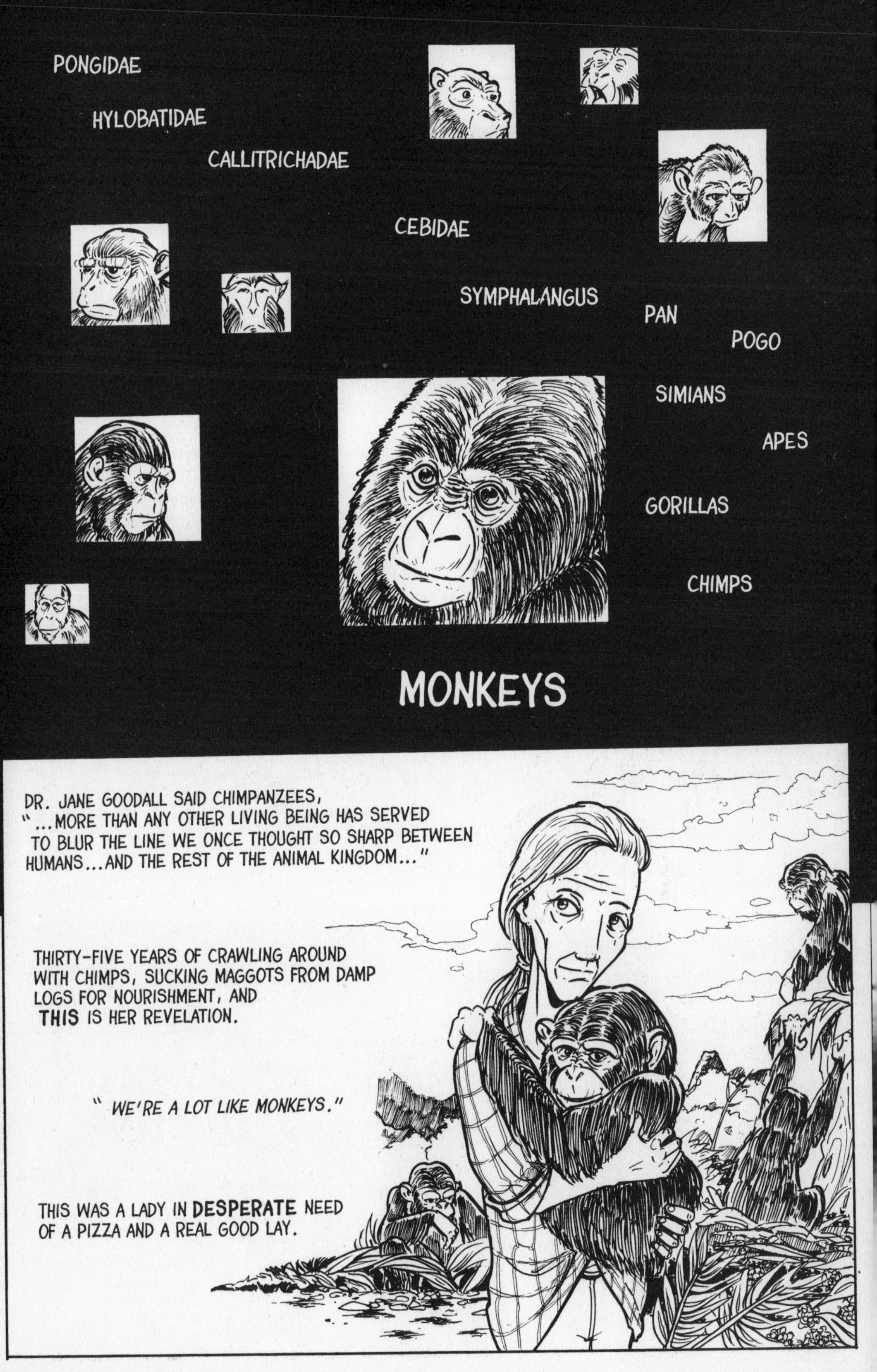
PONGIDAE
HYLOBATIDAE
CALLITRICHADAE
CEBIDAE
SYMPHALANGUS
PAN
POGO
SIMIANS
APES
GORILLAS
CHIMPS
MONKEYS
DR. JANE GOODALL SAID CHIMPANZEES, "...MORE THAN ANY OTHER LIVING BEING HAS SERVED TO BLUR THE LINE WE ONCE THOUGHT SO SHARP BETWEEN HUMANS...AND THE REST OF THE ANIMAL KINGDOM..."
THIRTY-FIVE YEARS OF CRAWLING AROUND WITH CHIMPS, SUCKING MAGGOTS FROM DAMP LOGS FOR NOURISHMENT, AND THIS IS HER REVELATION.
"WE'RE A LOT LIKE MONKEYS."
THIS WAS A LADY IN DESPERATE NEED OF A PIZZA AND A REAL GOOD LAY.

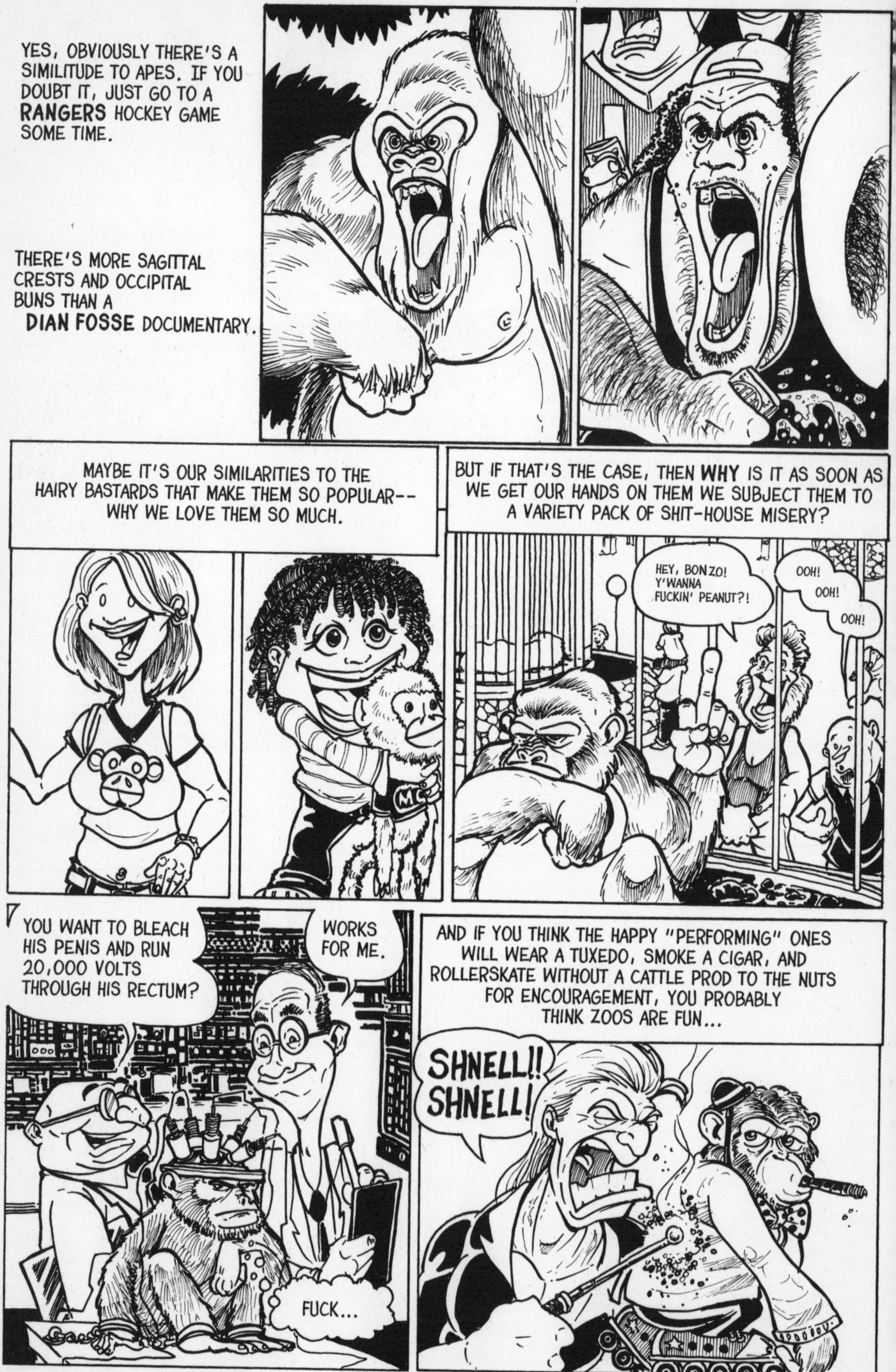
YES, OBVIOUSLY THERE'S A SIMILITUDE TO APES. IF YOU DOUBT IT, JUST GO TO A RANGERS HOCKEY GAME SOME TIME.
THERE'S MORE SAGITTAL CRESTS AND OCCIPITAL BUNS THAN A DIAN FOSSE DOCUMENTARY.
MAYBE IT'S OUR SIMILARITIES TO THE HAIRY BASTARDS THAT MAKE THEM SO POPULAR-- WHY WE LOVE THEM SO MUCH.
MC
BUT IF THAT'S THE CASE, THEN WHY IS IT AS SOON AS WE GET OUR HANDS ON THEM WE SUBJECT THEM TO A VARIETY PACK OF SHIT-HOUSE MISERY?
HEY, BONZO! Y'WANNA FUCKIN' PEANUT?!
OOH!
OOH!
OOH!
YOU WANT TO BLEACH HIS PENIS AND RUN 20,000 VOLTS THROUGH HIS RECTUM?
WORKS FOR ME.
FUCK...
AND IF YOU THINK THE HAPPY "PERFORMING" ONES WILL WEAR A TUXEDO, SMOKE A CIGAR, AND ROLLERSKATE WITHOUT A CATTLE PROD TO THE NUTS FOR ENCOURAGEMENT, YOU PROBABLY THINK ZOOS ARE FUN...
SHNELL!! SHNELL!

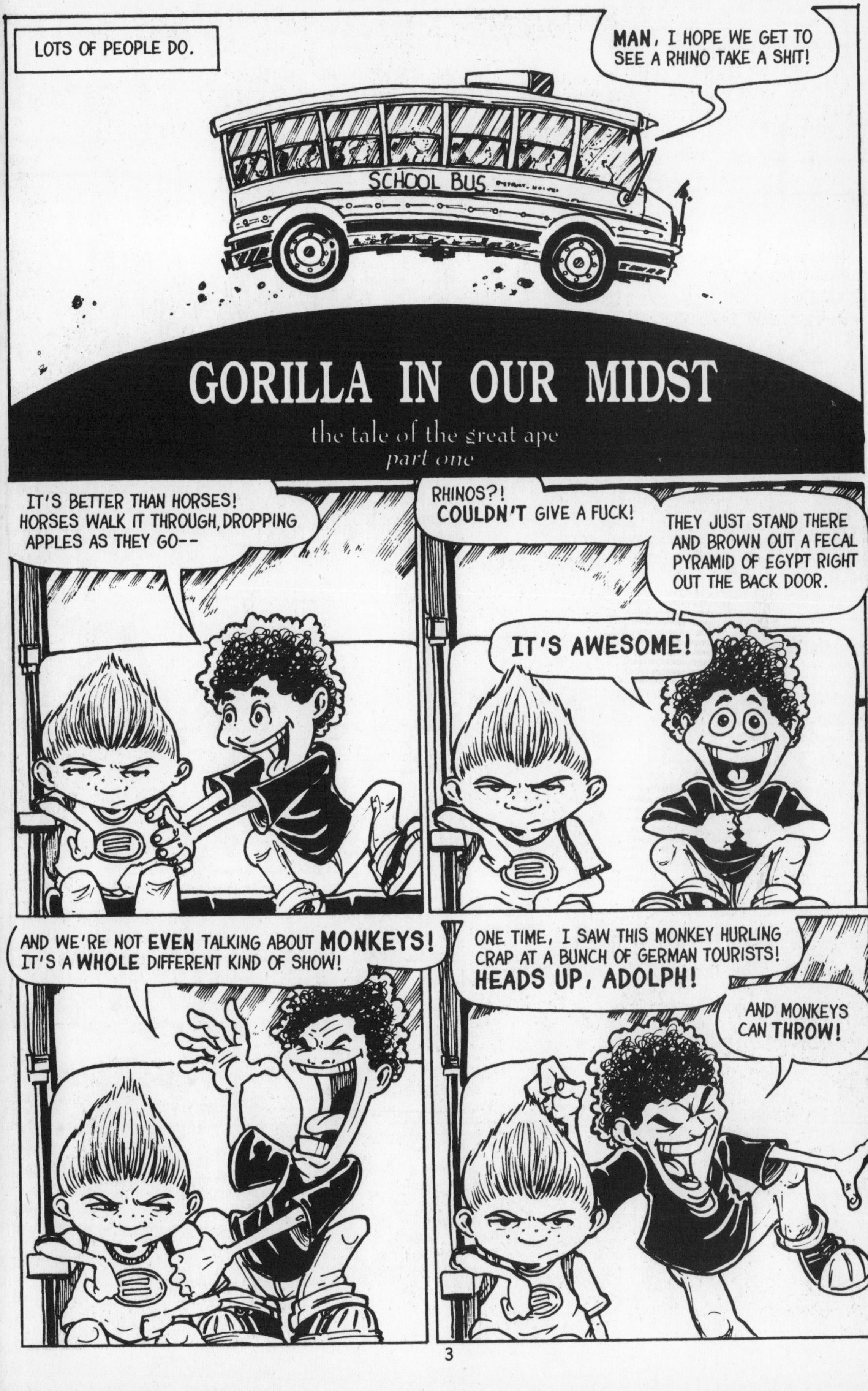
LOTS OF PEOPLE DO.
MAN, I HOPE WE GET TO SEE A RHINO TAKE A SHIT!
SCHOOL BUS
GORILLA IN OUR MIDST
the tale of the great ape
part one
IT'S BETTER THAN HORSES! HORSES WALK IT THROUGH, DROPPING APPLES AS THEY GO--
RHINOS?! COULDN'T GIVE A FUCK!
THEY JUST STAND THERE AND BROWN OUT A FECAL PYRAMID OF EGYPT RIGHT OUT THE BACK DOOR.
IT'S AWESOME!
AND WE'RE NOT EVEN TALKING ABOUT MONKEYS! IT'S A WHOLE DIFFERENT KIND OF SHOW!
ONE TIME, I SAW THIS MONKEY HURLING CRAP AT A BUNCH OF GERMAN TOURISTS! HEADS UP, ADOLPH!
AND MONKEYS CAN THROW!

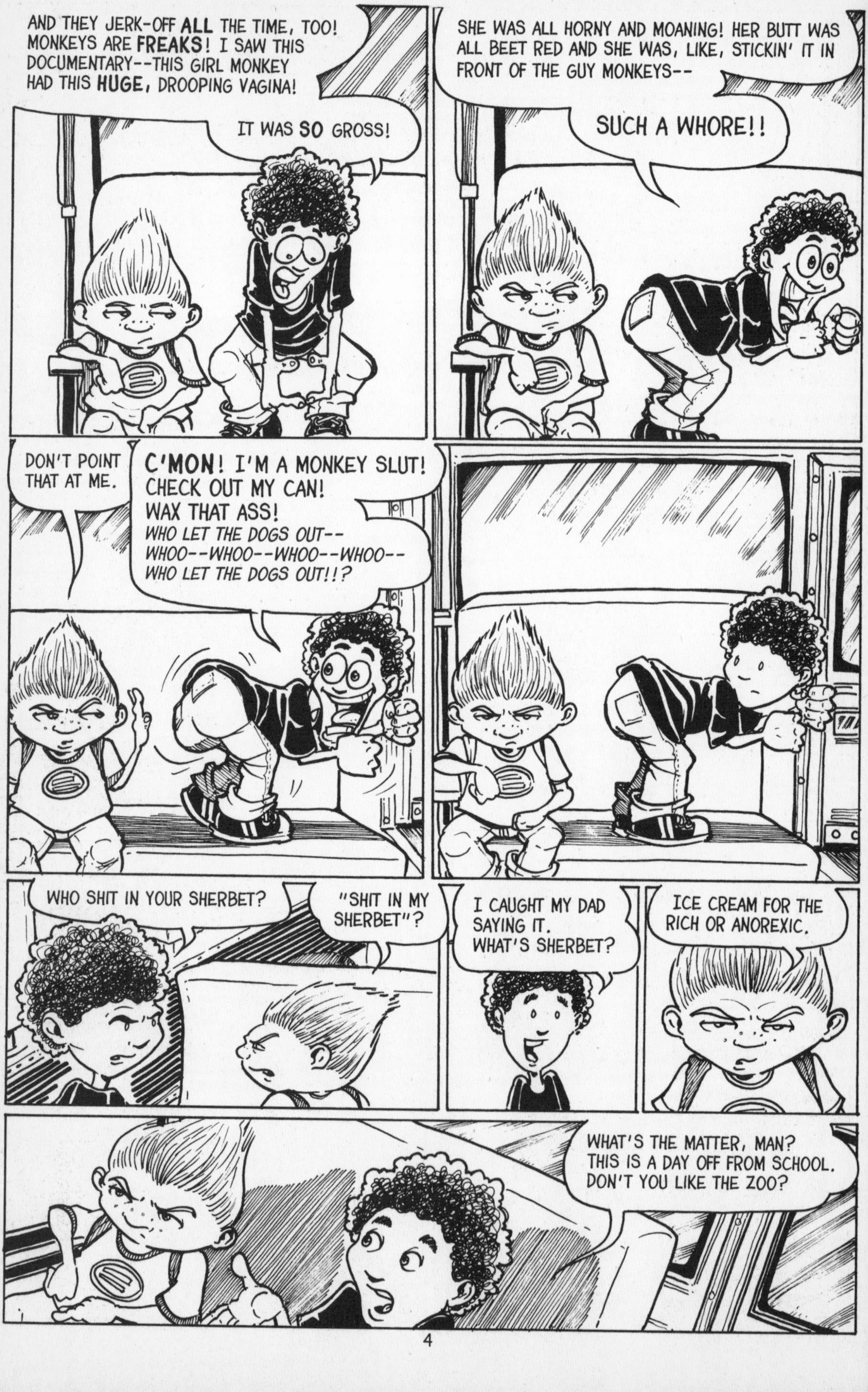
AND THEY JERK-OFF ALL THE TIME, TOO! MONKEYS ARE FREAKS! I SAW THIS DOCUMENTARY--THIS GIRL MONKEY HAD THIS HUGE, DROOPING VAGINA!
IT WAS SO GROSS!
SHE WAS ALL HORNY AND MOANING! HER BUTT WAS ALL BEET RED AND SHE WAS, LIKE, STICKIN' IT IN FRONT OF THE GUY MONKEYS--
SUCH A WHORE!!
DON'T POINT THAT AT ME.
C'MON! I'M A MONKEY SLUT! CHECK OUT MY CAN! WAX THAT ASS! WHO LET THE DOGS OUT-- WHOO--WHOO--WHOO--WHOO-- WHO LET THE DOGS OUT!!?
WHO SHIT IN YOUR SHERBET?
"SHIT IN MY SHERBET"?
I CAUGHT MY DAD SAYING IT. WHAT'S SHERBET?
ICE CREAM FOR THE RICH OR ANOREXIC.
WHAT'S THE MATTER, MAN? THIS IS A DAY OFF FROM SCHOOL. DON'T YOU LIKE THE ZOO?

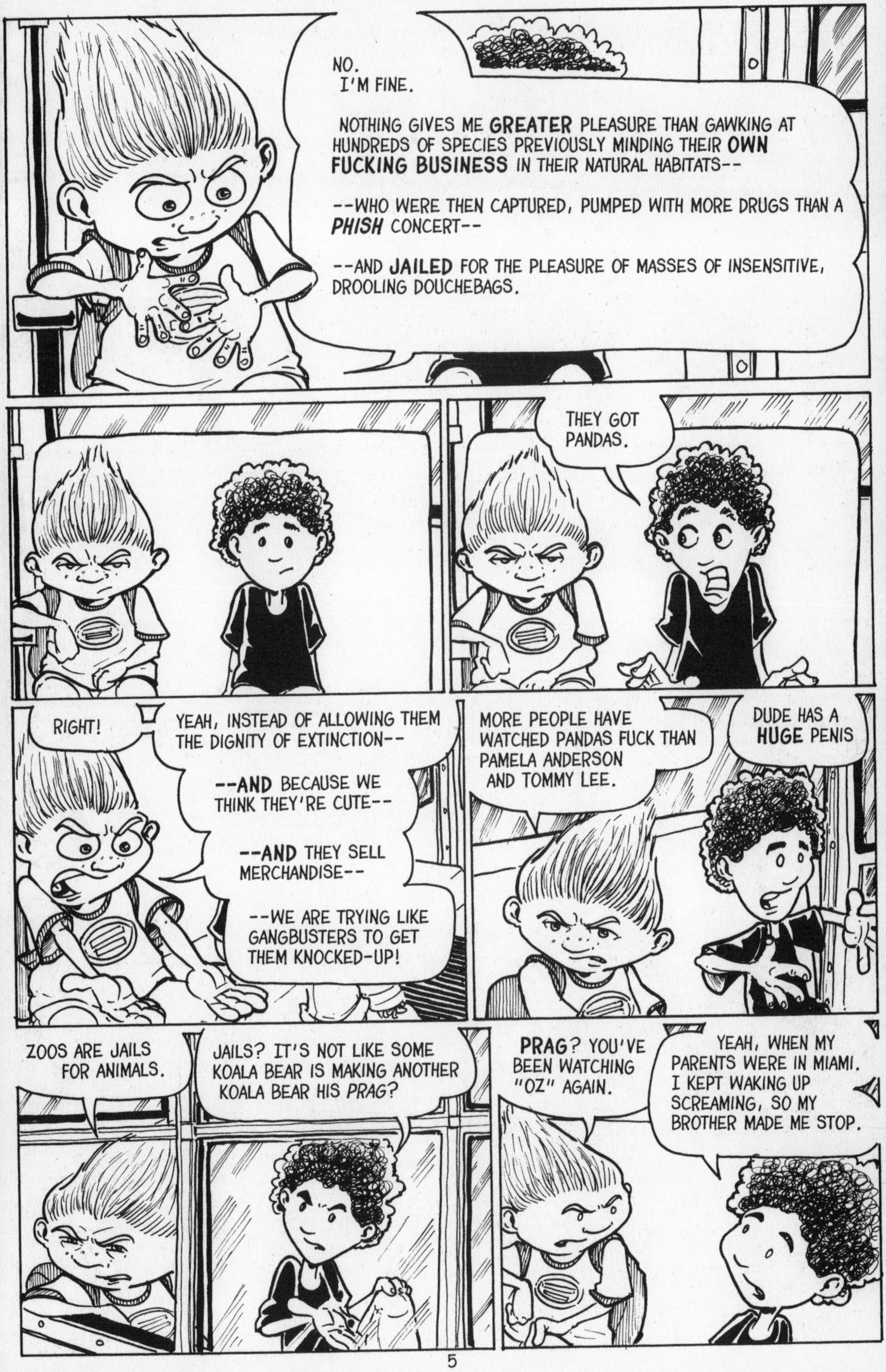

NO.
I'M FINE.
NOTHING GIVES ME GREATER PLEASURE THAN GAWKING AT HUNDREDS OF SPECIES PREVIOUSLY MINDING THEIR OWN FUCKING BUSINESS IN THEIR NATURAL HABITATS--
--WHO WERE THEN CAPTURED, PUMPED WITH MORE DRUGS THAN A PHISH CONCERT--
--AND JAILED FOR THE PLEASURE OF MASSES OF INSENSITIVE, DROOLING DOUCHEBAGS.
THEY GOT PANDAS.
RIGHT!
YEAH, INSTEAD OF ALLOWING THEM THE DIGNITY OF EXTINCTION--
--AND BECAUSE WE THINK THEY'RE CUTE--
--AND THEY SELL MERCHANDISE--
--WE ARE TRYING LIKE GANGBUSTERS TO GET THEM KNOCKED-UP!
MORE PEOPLE HAVE WATCHED PANDAS FUCK THAN PAMELA ANDERSON AND TOMMY LEE.
DUDE HAS A HUGE PENIS
ZOOS ARE JAILS FOR ANIMALS.
JAILS? IT'S NOT LIKE SOME KOALA BEAR IS MAKING ANOTHER KOALA BEAR HIS PRAG?
PRAG? YOU'VE BEEN WATCHING "OZ" AGAIN.
YEAH, WHEN MY PARENTS WERE IN MIAMI. I KEPT WAKING UP SCREAMING, SO MY BROTHER MADE ME STOP.

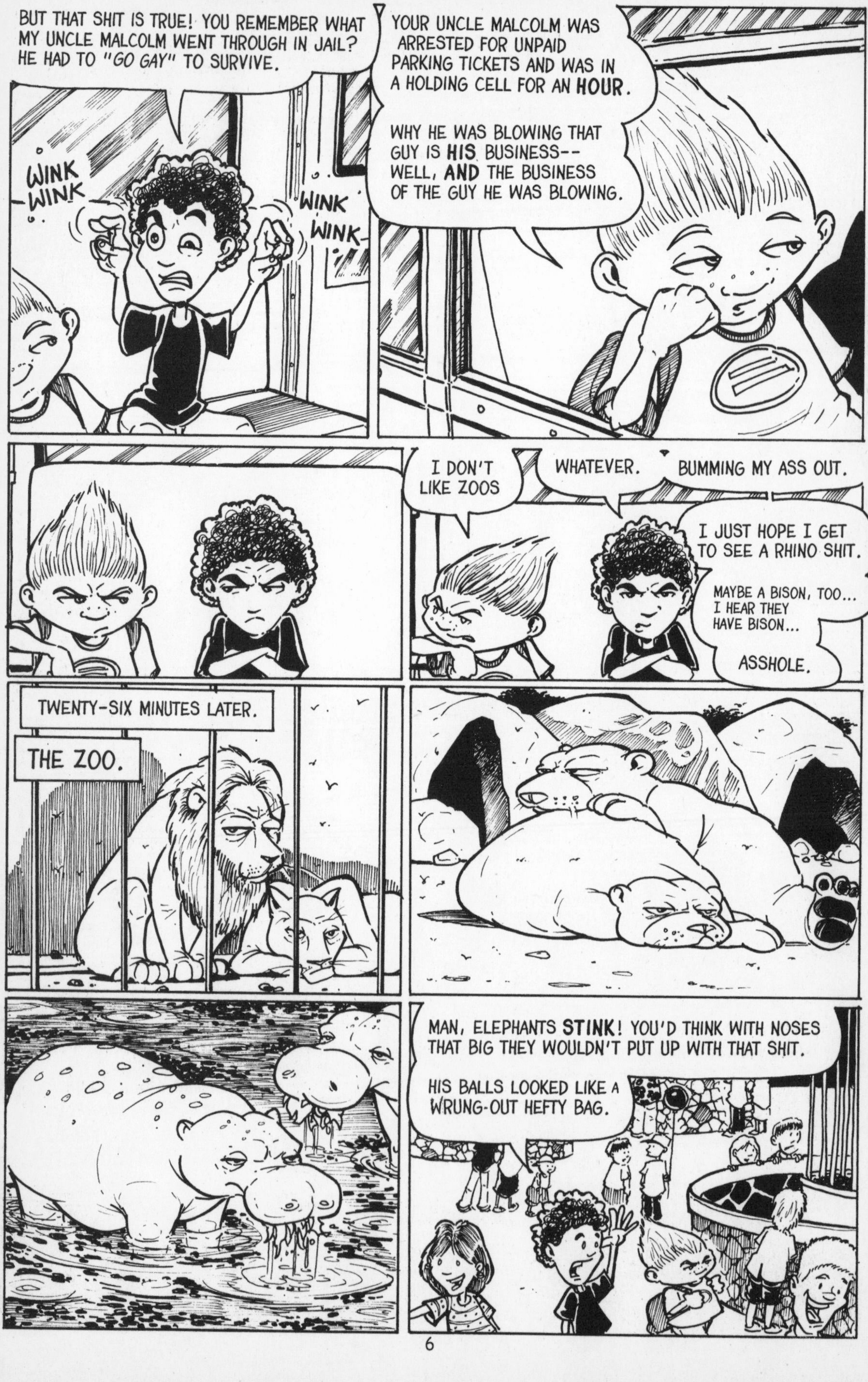

BUT THAT SHIT IS TRUE! YOU REMEMBER WHAT MY UNCLE MALCOLM WENT THROUGH IN JAIL? HE HAD TO "GO GAY" TO SURVIVE.
WINK WINK
WINK WINK
YOUR UNCLE MALCOLM WAS ARRESTED FOR UNPAID PARKING TICKETS AND WAS IN A HOLDING CELL FOR AN HOUR.
WHY HE WAS BLOWING THAT GUY IS HIS BUSINESS-- WELL, AND THE BUSINESS OF THE GUY HE WAS BLOWING.
I DON'T LIKE ZOOS
WHATEVER.
BUMMING MY ASS OUT.
I JUST HOPE I GET TO SEE A RHINO SHIT.
MAYBE A BISON, TOO... I HEAR THEY HAVE BISON...
ASSHOLE.
TWENTY-SIX MINUTES LATER.
THE ZOO.
MAN, ELEPHANTS STINK! YOU'D THINK WITH NOSES THAT BIG THEY WOULDN'T PUT UP WITH THAT SHIT.
HIS BALLS LOOKED LIKE A WRUNG-OUT HEFTY BAG.

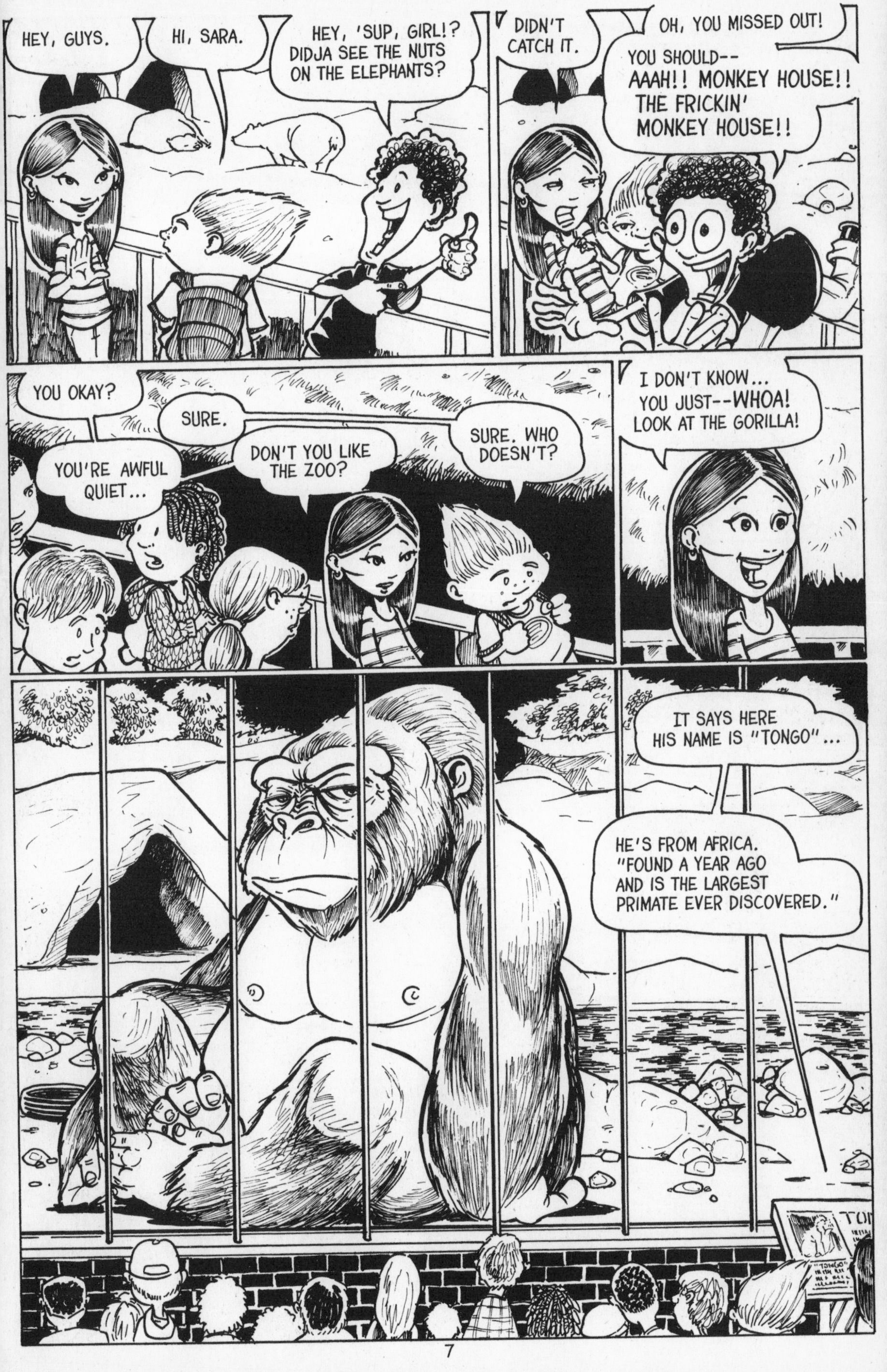
HEY, GUYS.
HI, SARA.
HEY, 'SUP, GIRL!? DIDJA SEE THE NUTS ON THE ELEPHANTS?
DIDN'T CATCH IT.
OH, YOU MISSED OUT!
YOU SHOULD-- AAAH!! MONKEY HOUSE!! THE FRICKIN' MONKEY HOUSE!!
YOU OKAY?
SURE.
YOU'RE AWFUL QUIET...
DON'T YOU LIKE THE ZOO?
SURE. WHO DOESN'T?
I DON'T KNOW... YOU JUST--WHOA! LOOK AT THE GORILLA!
IT SAYS HERE HIS NAME IS "TONGO"...
HE'S FROM AFRICA. "FOUND A YEAR AGO AND IS THE LARGEST PRIMATE EVER DISCOVERED."

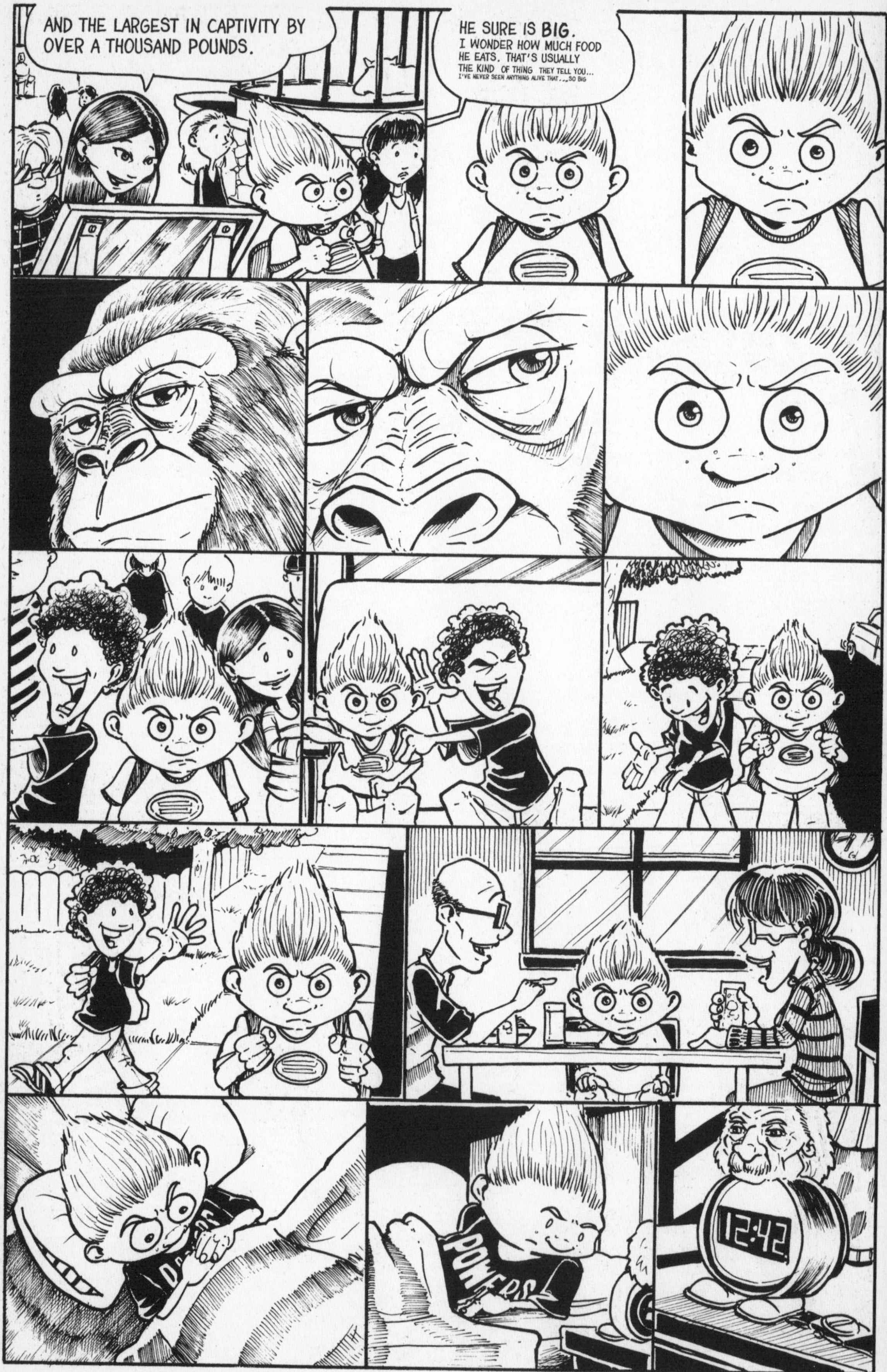
AND THE LARGEST IN CAPTIVITY BY OVER A THOUSAND POUNDS.
HE SURE IS BIG. I WONDER HOW MUCH FOOD HE EATS. THAT'S USUALLY THE KIND OF THING THEY TELL YOU... I'VE NEVER SEEN ANYTHING ALIVE THAT...SO BIG
POWERS
12:42

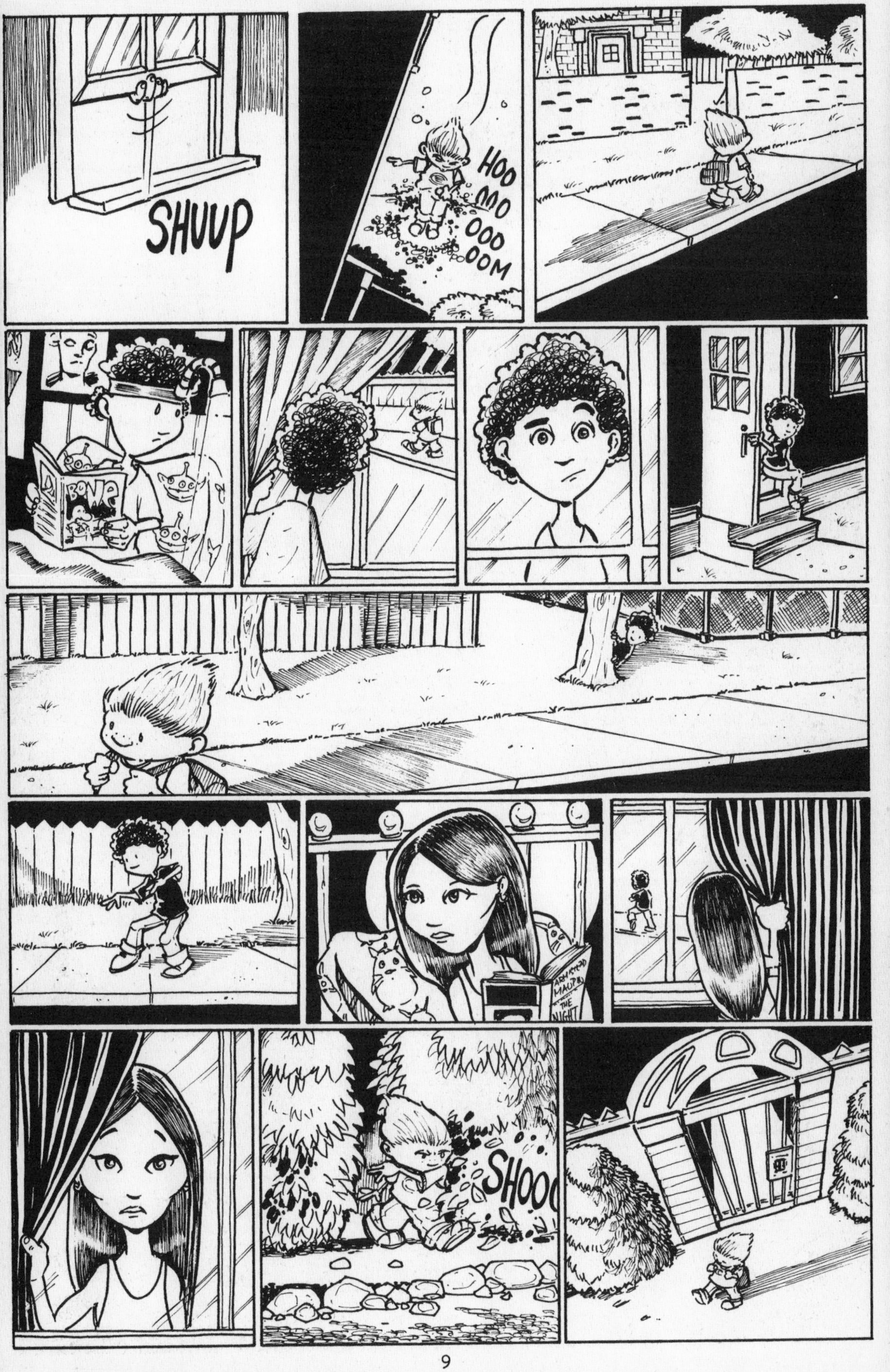
SHUUP
HOOMMOOOOOOM
BONE
ARMISTEAD MAUPIN THE NIGHT
SHOOO

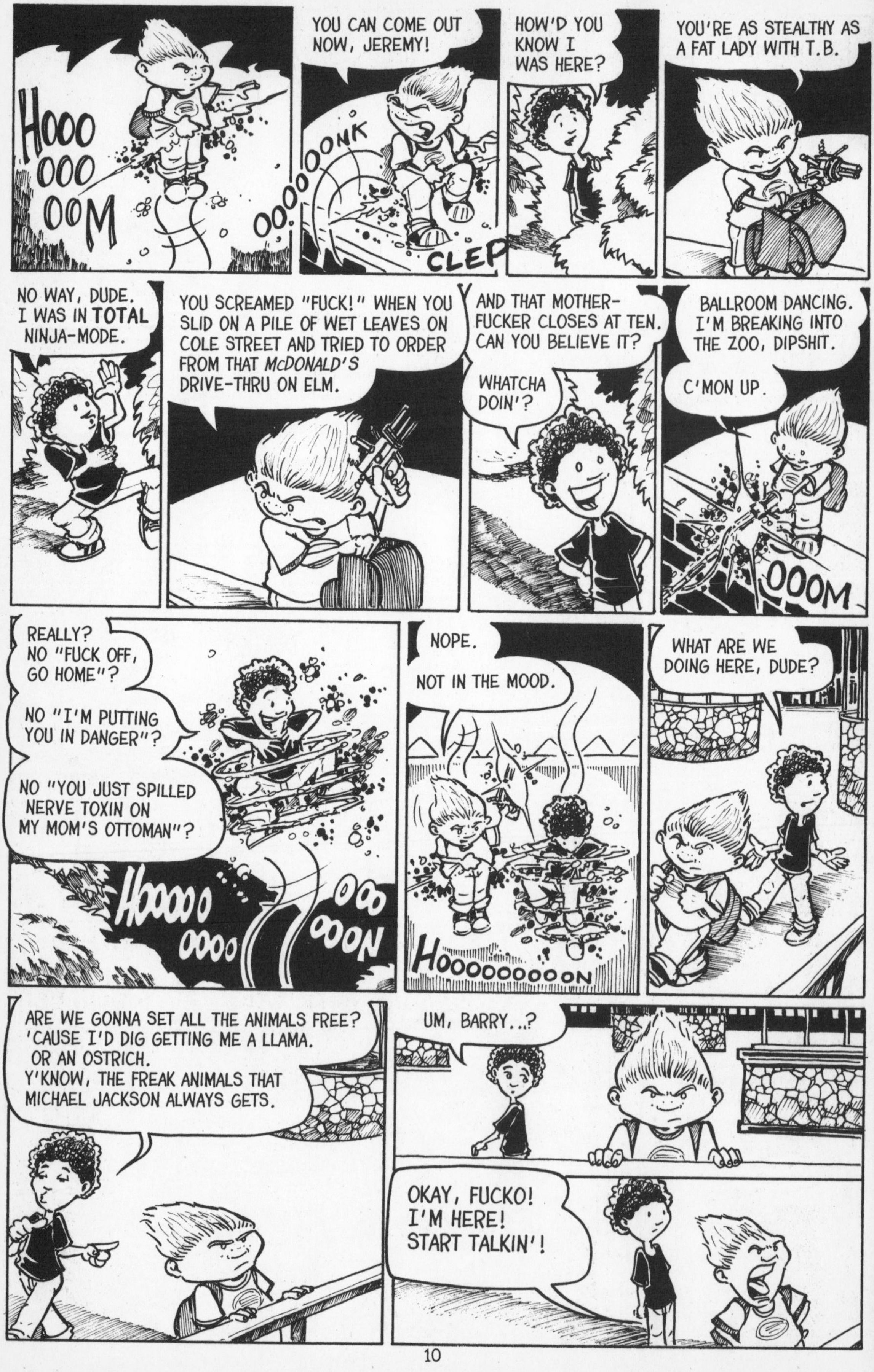
HOOO OOO OOM
YOU CAN COME OUT NOW, JEREMY!
OOOOOONK
CLEP
HOW'D YOU KNOW I WAS HERE?
YOU'RE AS STEALTHY AS A FAT LADY WITH T.B.
NO WAY, DUDE. I WAS IN TOTAL NINJA-MODE.
YOU SCREAMED "FUCK!" WHEN YOU SLID ON A PILE OF WET LEAVES ON COLE STREET AND TRIED TO ORDER FROM THAT McDONALD'S DRIVE-THRU ON ELM.
AND THAT MOTHER-FUCKER CLOSES AT TEN. CAN YOU BELIEVE IT?
WHATCHA DOIN'?
BALLROOM DANCING. I'M BREAKING INTO THE ZOO, DIPSHIT.
C'MON UP.
OOOM
REALLY? NO "FUCK OFF, GO HOME"?
NO "I'M PUTTING YOU IN DANGER"?
NO "YOU JUST SPILLED NERVE TOXIN ON MY MOM'S OTTOMAN"?
HOOOOO OOOO OOO OOON
NOPE.
NOT IN THE MOOD.
HOOOOOOOOOON
WHAT ARE WE DOING HERE, DUDE?
ARE WE GONNA SET ALL THE ANIMALS FREE? 'CAUSE I'D DIG GETTING ME A LLAMA. OR AN OSTRICH. Y'KNOW, THE FREAK ANIMALS THAT MICHAEL JACKSON ALWAYS GETS.
UM, BARRY...?
OKAY, FUCKO! I'M HERE! START TALKIN'!

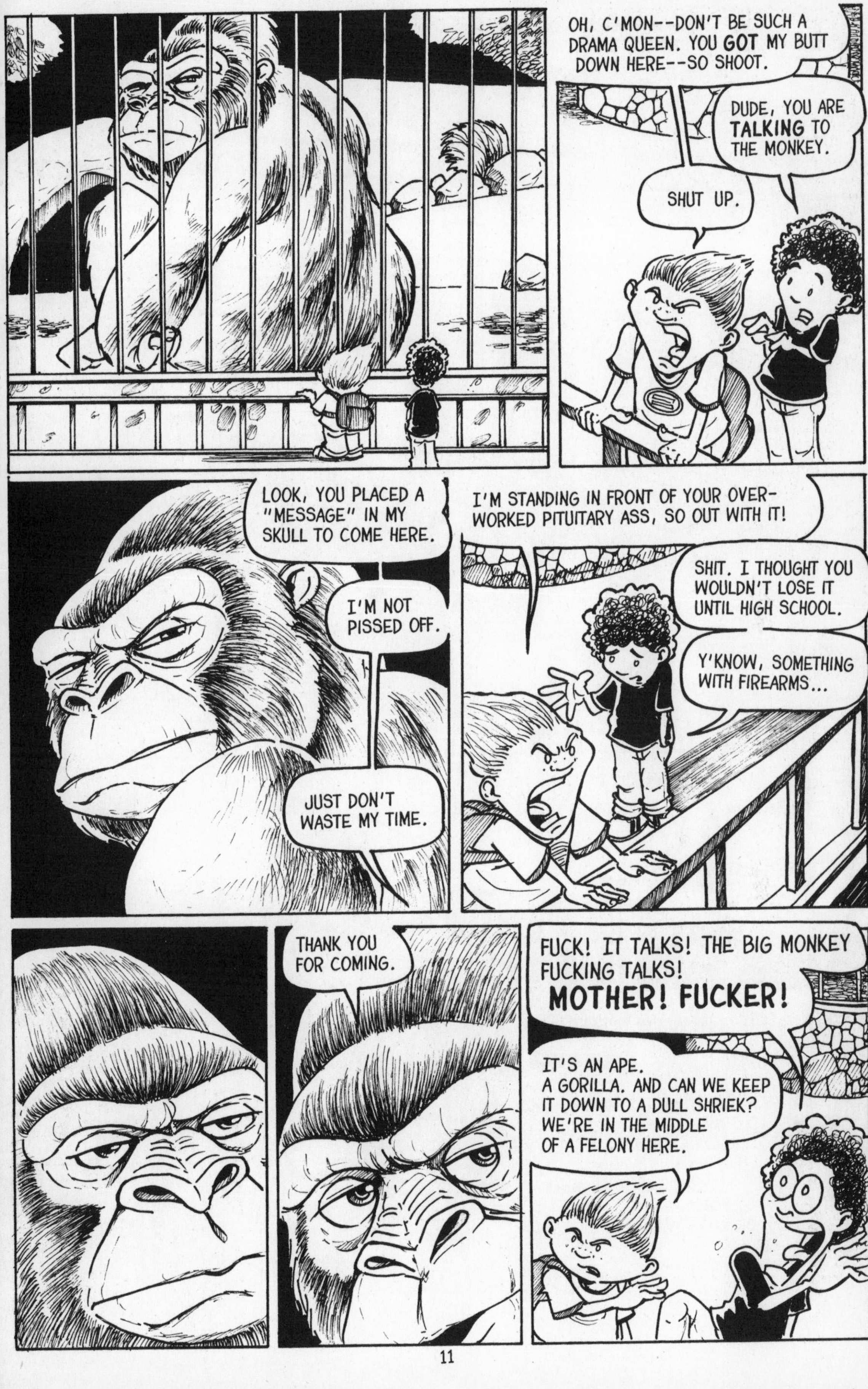
OH, C'MON--DON'T BE SUCH A DRAMA QUEEN. YOU GOT MY BUTT DOWN HERE--SO SHOOT.
DUDE, YOU ARE TALKING TO THE MONKEY.
SHUT UP.
LOOK, YOU PLACED A "MESSAGE" IN MY SKULL TO COME HERE.
I'M NOT PISSED OFF.
JUST DON'T WASTE MY TIME.
I'M STANDING IN FRONT OF YOUR OVER-WORKED PITUITARY ASS, SO OUT WITH IT!
SHIT. I THOUGHT YOU WOULDN'T LOSE IT UNTIL HIGH SCHOOL.
Y'KNOW, SOMETHING WITH FIREARMS...
THANK YOU FOR COMING.
FUCK! IT TALKS! THE BIG MONKEY FUCKING TALKS!
MOTHER! FUCKER!
IT'S AN APE. A GORILLA. AND CAN WE KEEP IT DOWN TO A DULL SHRIEK? WE'RE IN THE MIDDLE OF A FELONY HERE.

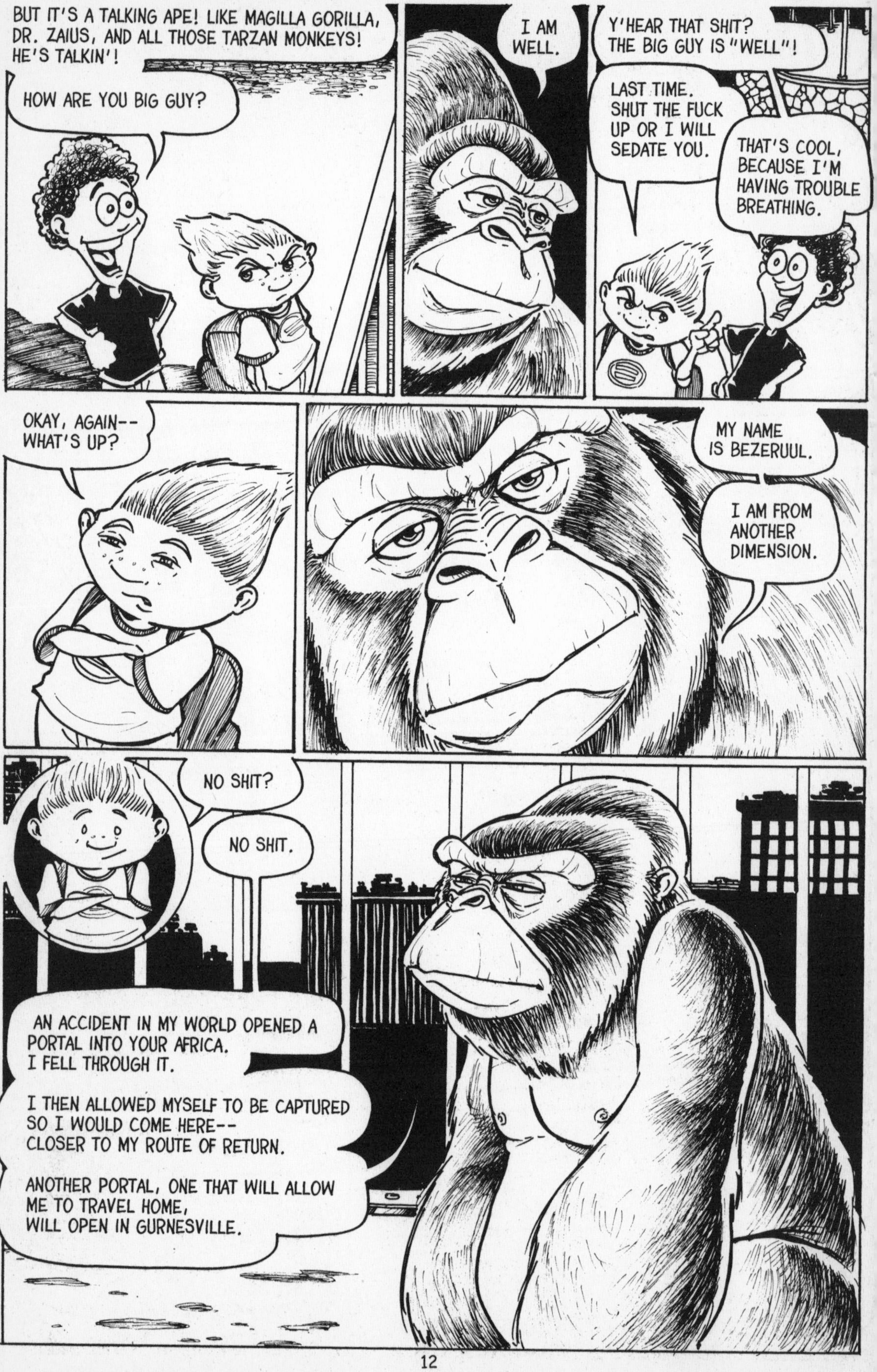
BUT IT'S A TALKING APE! LIKE MAGILLA GORILLA, DR. ZAIUS, AND ALL THOSE TARZAN MONKEYS! HE'S TALKIN'!
HOW ARE YOU BIG GUY?
I AM WELL.
Y'HEAR THAT SHIT? THE BIG GUY IS "WELL"!
LAST TIME. SHUT THE FUCK UP OR I WILL SEDATE YOU.
THAT'S COOL, BECAUSE I'M HAVING TROUBLE BREATHING.
OKAY, AGAIN-- WHAT'S UP?
MY NAME IS BEZERUUL.
I AM FROM ANOTHER DIMENSION.
NO SHIT?
NO SHIT.
AN ACCIDENT IN MY WORLD OPENED A PORTAL INTO YOUR AFRICA. I FELL THROUGH IT.
I THEN ALLOWED MYSELF TO BE CAPTURED SO I WOULD COME HERE-- CLOSER TO MY ROUTE OF RETURN.
ANOTHER PORTAL, ONE THAT WILL ALLOW ME TO TRAVEL HOME, WILL OPEN IN GURNESVILLE.

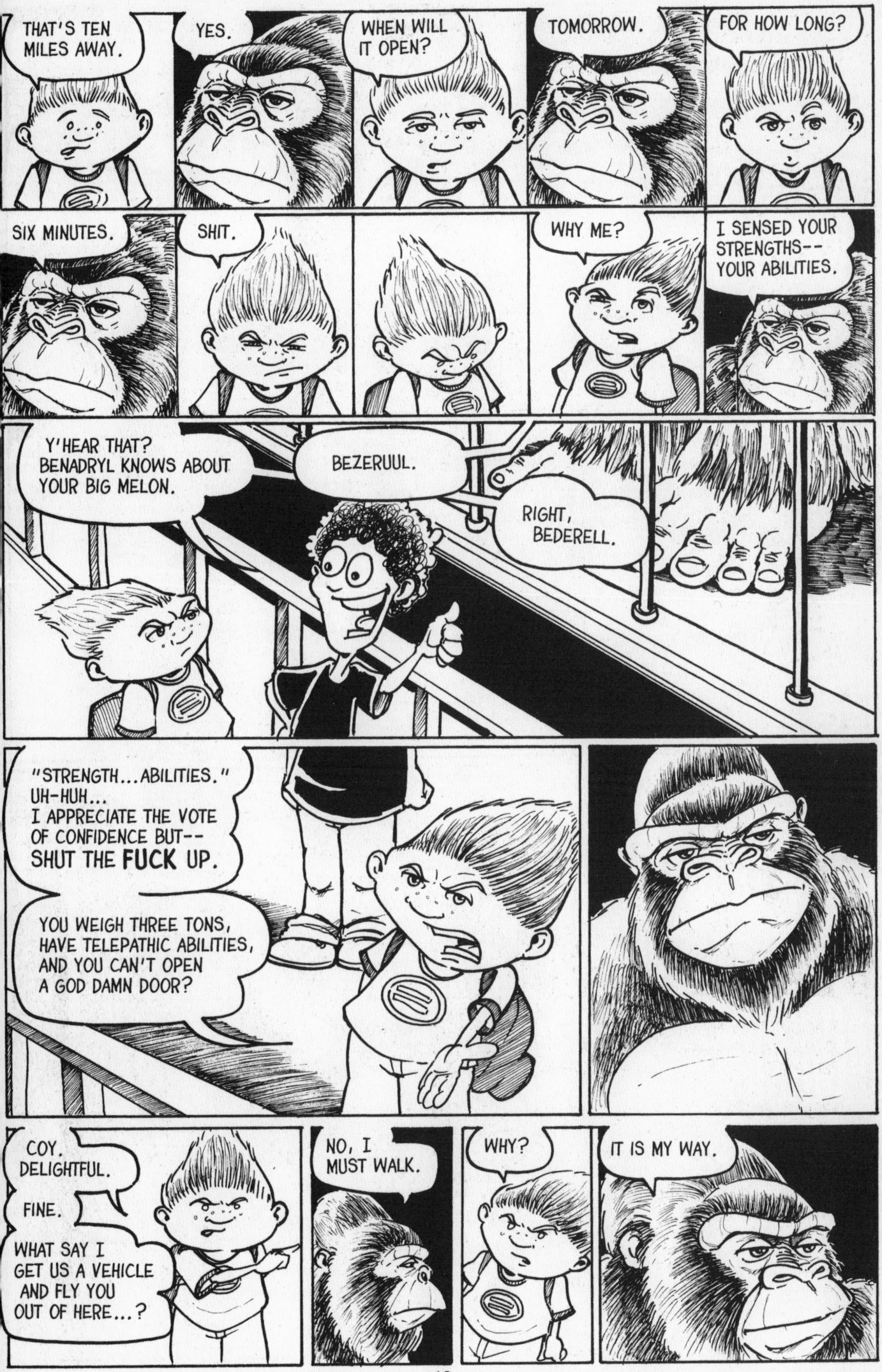
THAT'S TEN MILES AWAY.
YES.
WHEN WILL IT OPEN?
TOMORROW.
FOR HOW LONG?
SIX MINUTES.
SHIT.
WHY ME?
I SENSED YOUR STRENGTHS-- YOUR ABILITIES.
Y'HEAR THAT? BENADRYL KNOWS ABOUT YOUR BIG MELON.
BEZERUUL.
RIGHT, BEDERELL.
"STRENGTH... ABILITIES." UH-HUH... I APPRECIATE THE VOTE OF CONFIDENCE BUT-- SHUT THE FUCK UP.
YOU WEIGH THREE TONS, HAVE TELEPATHIC ABILITIES, AND YOU CAN'T OPEN A GOD DAMN DOOR?
COY. DELIGHTFUL.
FINE.
WHAT SAY I GET US A VEHICLE AND FLY YOU OUT OF HERE...?
NO, I MUST WALK.
WHY?
IT IS MY WAY.

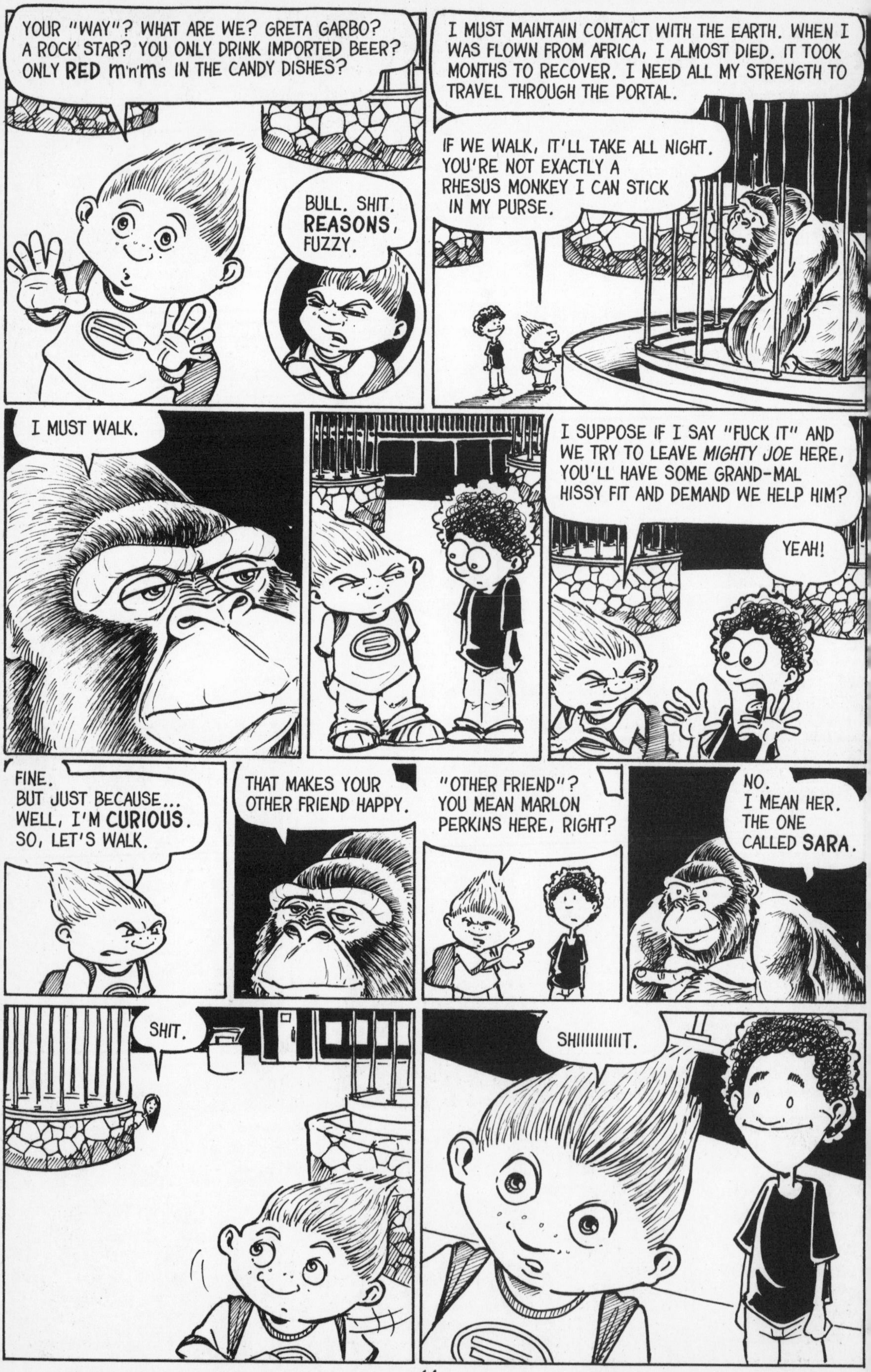
YOUR "WAY"? WHAT ARE WE? GRETA GARBO? A ROCK STAR? YOU ONLY DRINK IMPORTED BEER? ONLY RED m'n'ms IN THE CANDY DISHES?
BULL. SHIT. REASONS, FUZZY.
I MUST MAINTAIN CONTACT WITH THE EARTH. WHEN I WAS FLOWN FROM AFRICA, I ALMOST DIED. IT TOOK MONTHS TO RECOVER. I NEED ALL MY STRENGTH TO TRAVEL THROUGH THE PORTAL.
IF WE WALK, IT'LL TAKE ALL NIGHT. YOU'RE NOT EXACTLY A RHESUS MONKEY I CAN STICK IN MY PURSE.
I MUST WALK.
I SUPPOSE IF I SAY "FUCK IT" AND WE TRY TO LEAVE MIGHTY JOE HERE, YOU'LL HAVE SOME GRAND-MAL HISSY FIT AND DEMAND WE HELP HIM?
YEAH!
FINE. BUT JUST BECAUSE... WELL, I'M CURIOUS. SO, LET'S WALK.
THAT MAKES YOUR OTHER FRIEND HAPPY.
"OTHER FRIEND"? YOU MEAN MARLON PERKINS HERE, RIGHT?
NO. I MEAN HER. THE ONE CALLED SARA.
SHIT.
SHIIIIIIIIIT.

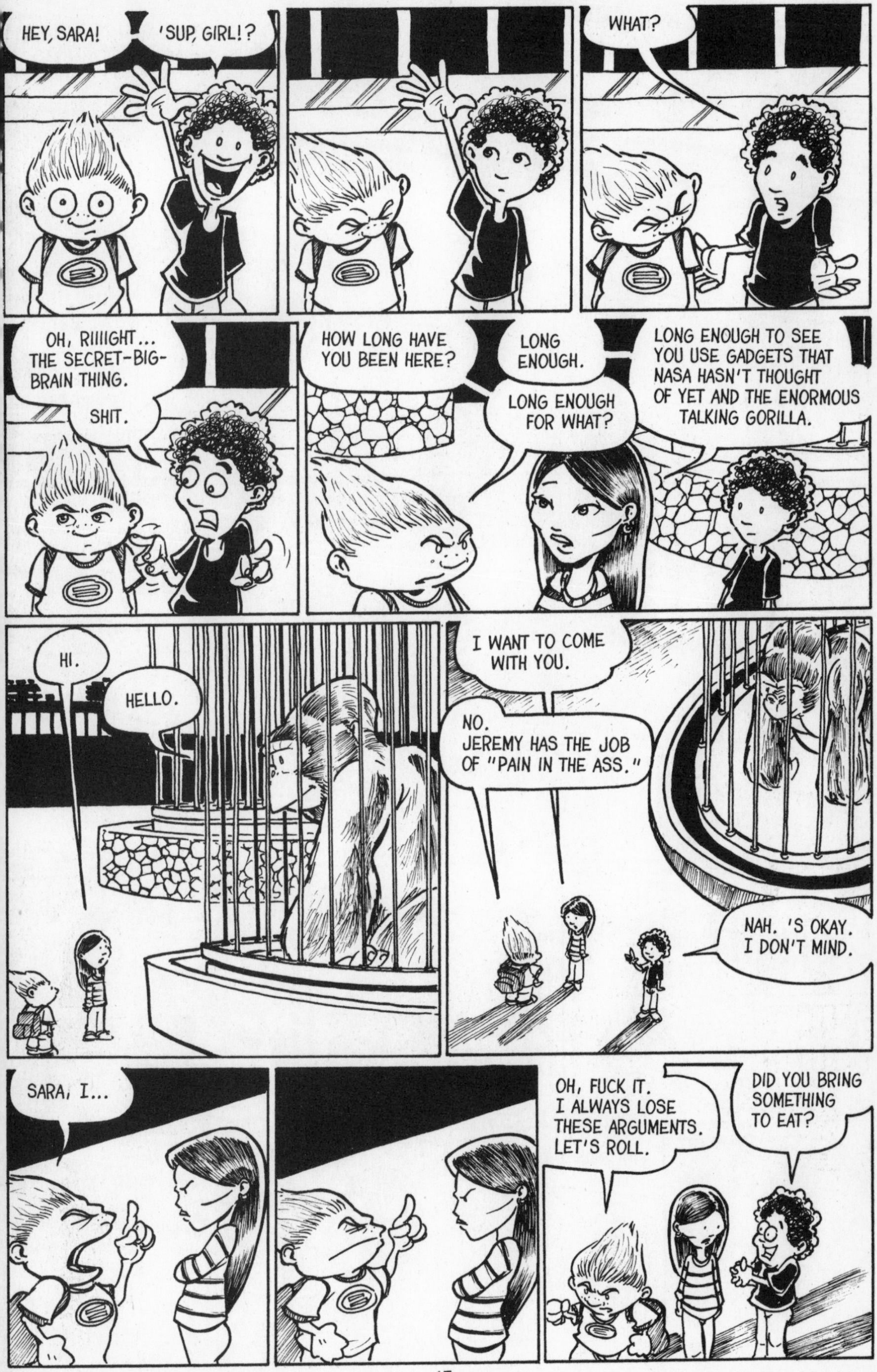
HEY, SARA!
'SUP, GIRL!?
WHAT?
OH, RIIIGHT... THE SECRET-BIG-BRAIN THING.
SHIT.
HOW LONG HAVE YOU BEEN HERE?
LONG ENOUGH.
LONG ENOUGH FOR WHAT?
LONG ENOUGH TO SEE YOU USE GADGETS THAT NASA HASN'T THOUGHT OF YET AND THE ENORMOUS TALKING GORILLA.
HI.
HELLO.
I WANT TO COME WITH YOU.
NO. JEREMY HAS THE JOB OF "PAIN IN THE ASS."
NAH. 'S OKAY. I DON'T MIND.
SARA, I...
OH, FUCK IT. I ALWAYS LOSE THESE ARGUMENTS. LET'S ROLL.
DID YOU BRING SOMETHING TO EAT?

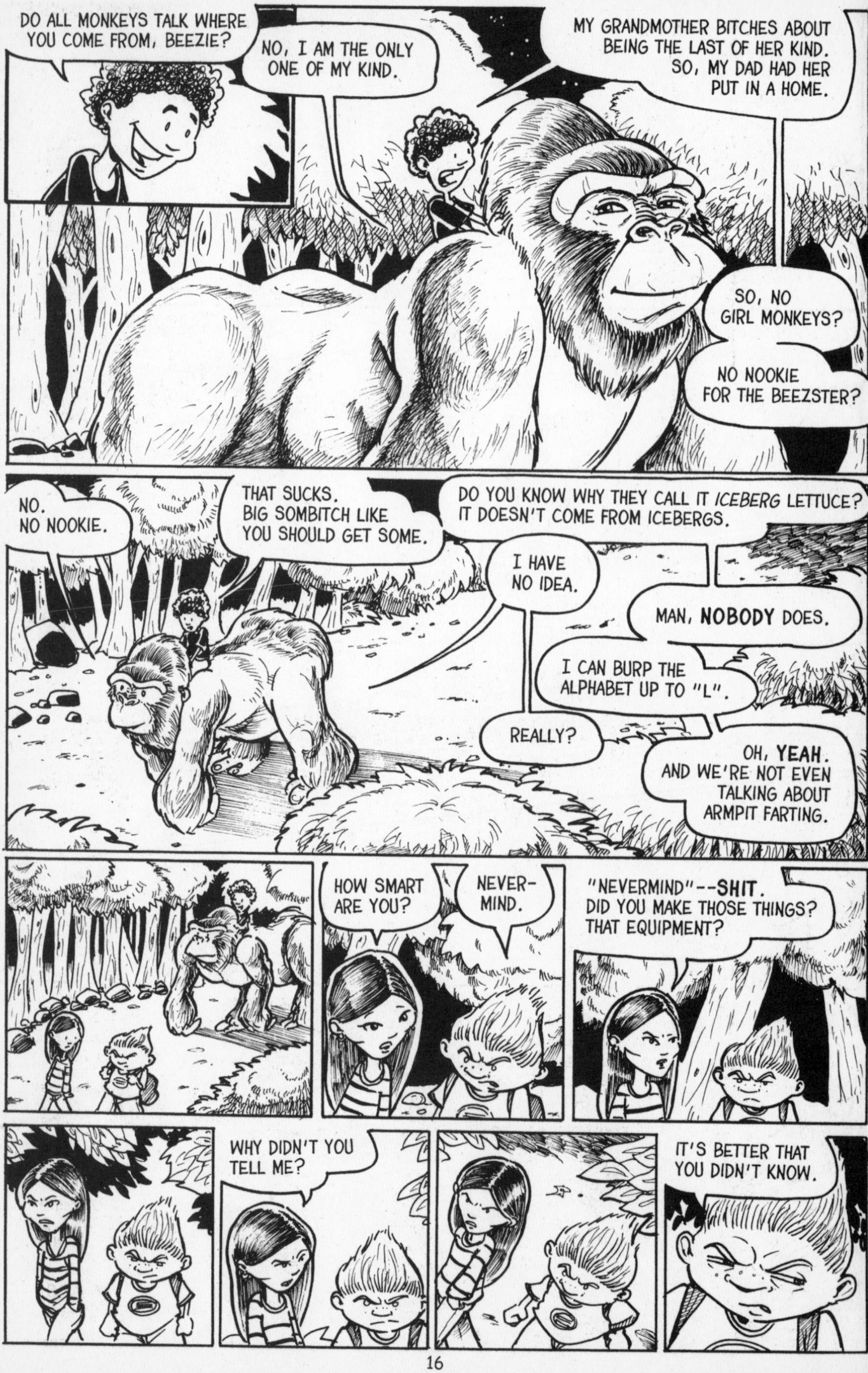
DO ALL MONKEYS TALK WHERE YOU COME FROM, BEEZIE?
NO, I AM THE ONLY ONE OF MY KIND.
MY GRANDMOTHER BITCHES ABOUT BEING THE LAST OF HER KIND. SO, MY DAD HAD HER PUT IN A HOME.
SO, NO GIRL MONKEYS?
NO NOOKIE FOR THE BEEZSTER?
NO. NO NOOKIE.
THAT SUCKS. BIG SOMBITCH LIKE YOU SHOULD GET SOME.
DO YOU KNOW WHY THEY CALL IT *ICEBERG* LETTUCE? IT DOESN'T COME FROM ICEBERGS.
I HAVE NO IDEA.
MAN, **NOBODY** DOES.
I CAN BURP THE ALPHABET UP TO "L".
REALLY?
OH, **YEAH**. AND WE'RE NOT EVEN TALKING ABOUT ARMPIT FARTING.
HOW SMART ARE YOU?
NEVER-MIND.
"NEVERMIND"--**SHIT**. DID YOU MAKE THOSE THINGS? THAT EQUIPMENT?
WHY DIDN'T YOU TELL ME?
IT'S BETTER THAT YOU DIDN'T KNOW.

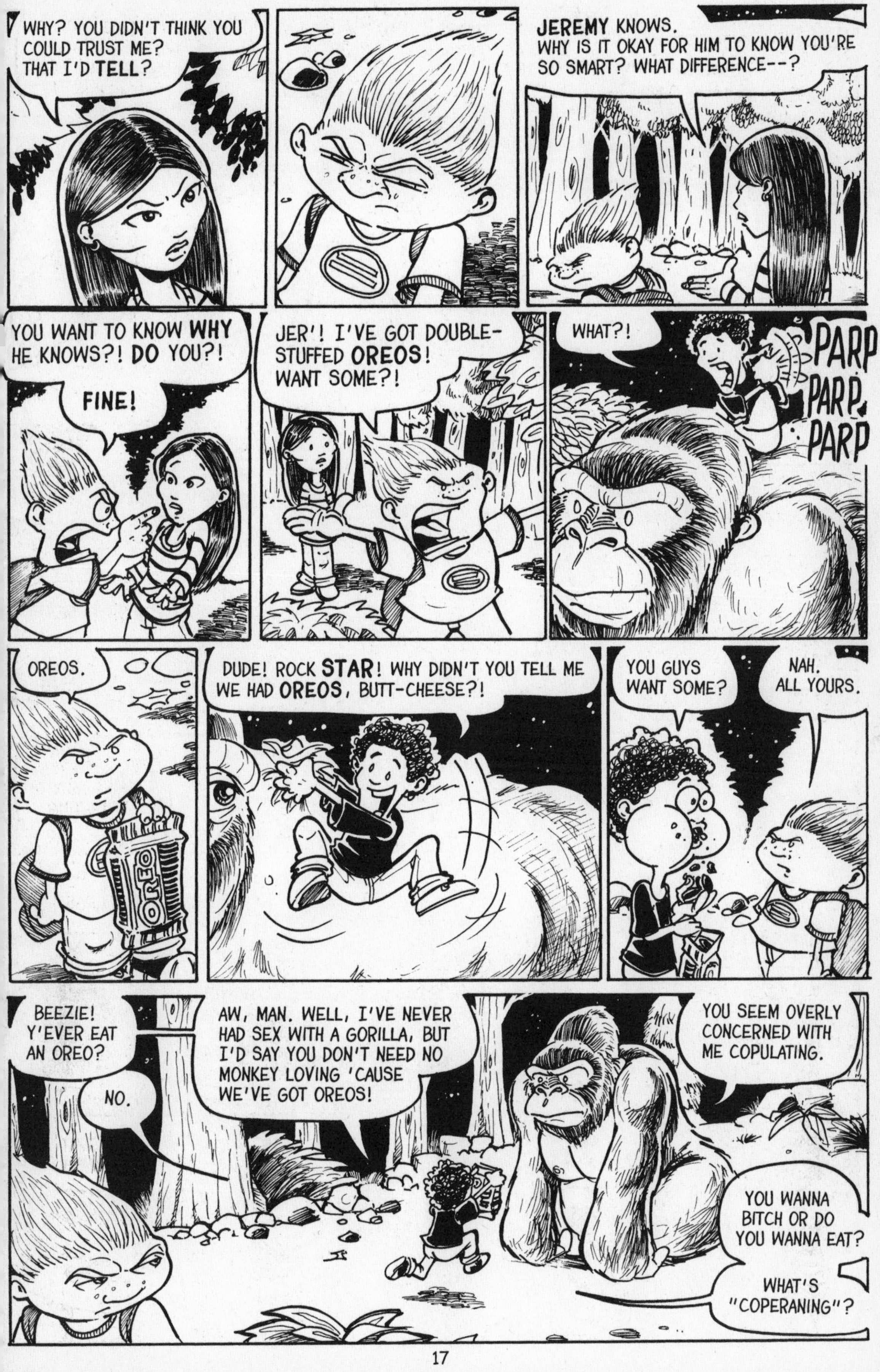
WHY? YOU DIDN'T THINK YOU COULD TRUST ME? THAT I'D TELL?
JEREMY KNOWS. WHY IS IT OKAY FOR HIM TO KNOW YOU'RE SO SMART? WHAT DIFFERENCE--?
YOU WANT TO KNOW WHY HE KNOWS?! DO YOU?!
FINE!
JER'! I'VE GOT DOUBLE-STUFFED OREOS! WANT SOME?!
WHAT?!
PARP PARP PARP
OREOS.
OREO
DUDE! ROCK STAR! WHY DIDN'T YOU TELL ME WE HAD OREOS, BUTT-CHEESE?!
YOU GUYS WANT SOME?
NAH. ALL YOURS.
BEEZIE! Y'EVER EAT AN OREO?
NO.
AW, MAN. WELL, I'VE NEVER HAD SEX WITH A GORILLA, BUT I'D SAY YOU DON'T NEED NO MONKEY LOVING 'CAUSE WE'VE GOT OREOS!
YOU SEEM OVERLY CONCERNED WITH ME COPULATING.
YOU WANNA BITCH OR DO YOU WANNA EAT?
WHAT'S "COPERANING"?

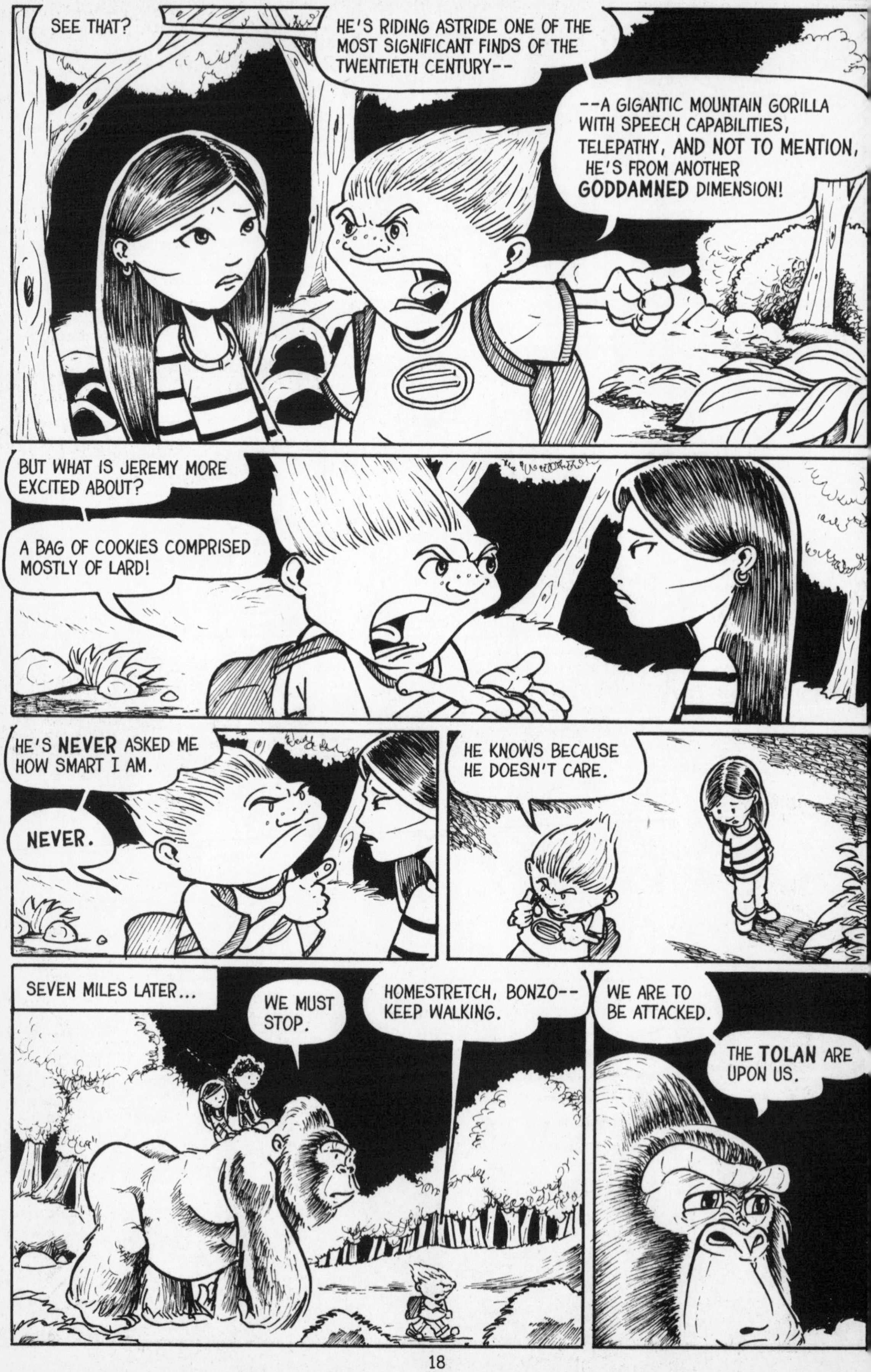
SEE THAT?
HE'S RIDING ASTRIDE ONE OF THE MOST SIGNIFICANT FINDS OF THE TWENTIETH CENTURY--
--A GIGANTIC MOUNTAIN GORILLA WITH SPEECH CAPABILITIES, TELEPATHY, AND NOT TO MENTION, HE'S FROM ANOTHER GODDAMNED DIMENSION!
BUT WHAT IS JEREMY MORE EXCITED ABOUT?
A BAG OF COOKIES COMPRISED MOSTLY OF LARD!
HE'S NEVER ASKED ME HOW SMART I AM.
NEVER.
HE KNOWS BECAUSE HE DOESN'T CARE.
SEVEN MILES LATER...
WE MUST STOP.
HOMESTRETCH, BONZO-- KEEP WALKING.
WE ARE TO BE ATTACKED.
THE TOLAN ARE UPON US.

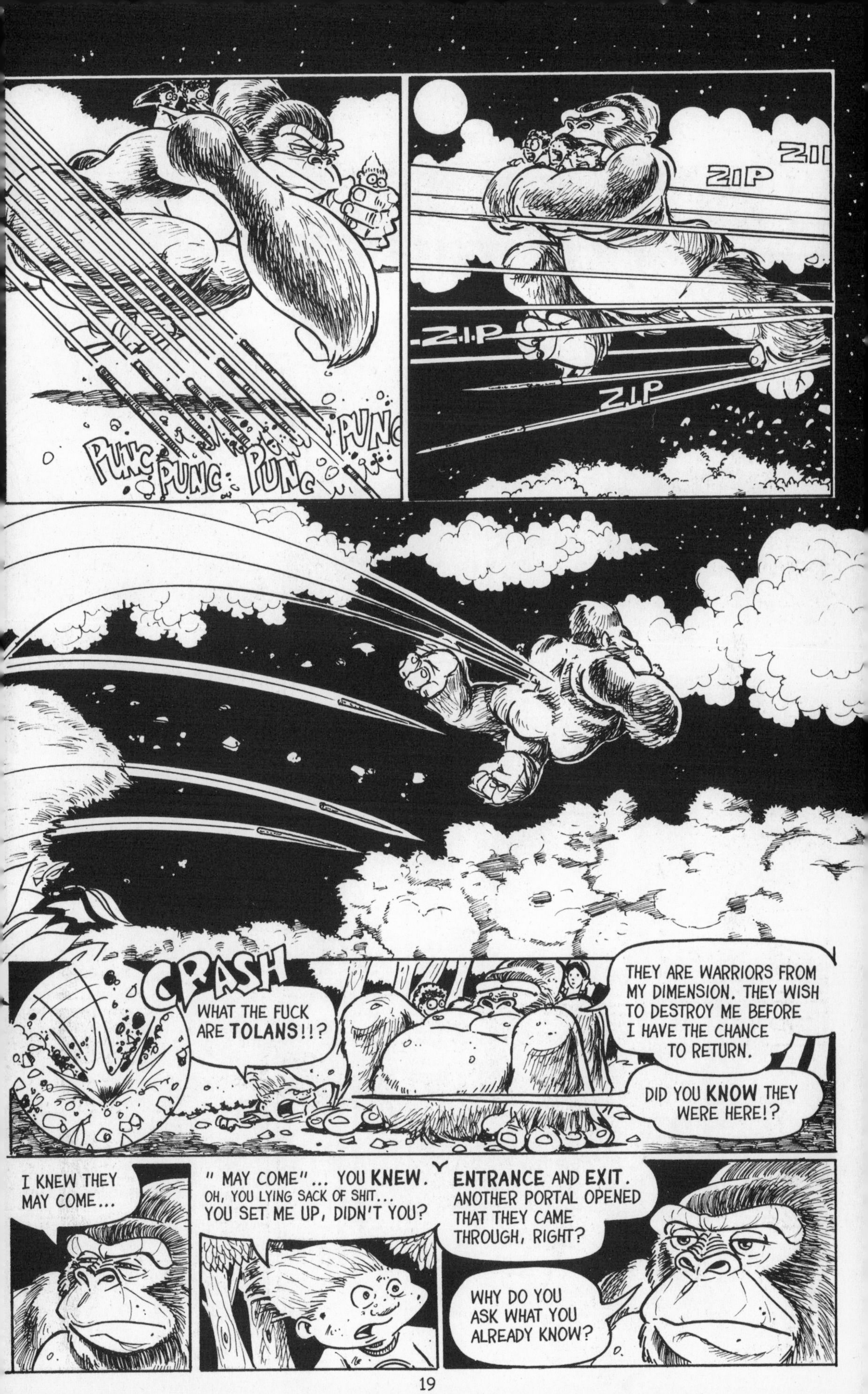
PUNC PUNC PUNC PUNC
ZIP
ZII
-ZIP
ZIP
CRASH
WHAT THE FUCK ARE **TOLANS**!!?
THEY ARE WARRIORS FROM MY DIMENSION. THEY WISH TO DESTROY ME BEFORE I HAVE THE CHANCE TO RETURN.
DID YOU **KNOW** THEY WERE HERE!?
I KNEW THEY MAY COME...
" MAY COME"... YOU **KNEW**.
OH, YOU LYING SACK OF SHIT...
YOU SET ME UP, DIDN'T YOU?
ENTRANCE AND **EXIT**.
ANOTHER PORTAL OPENED THAT THEY CAME THROUGH, RIGHT?
WHY DO YOU ASK WHAT YOU ALREADY KNOW?

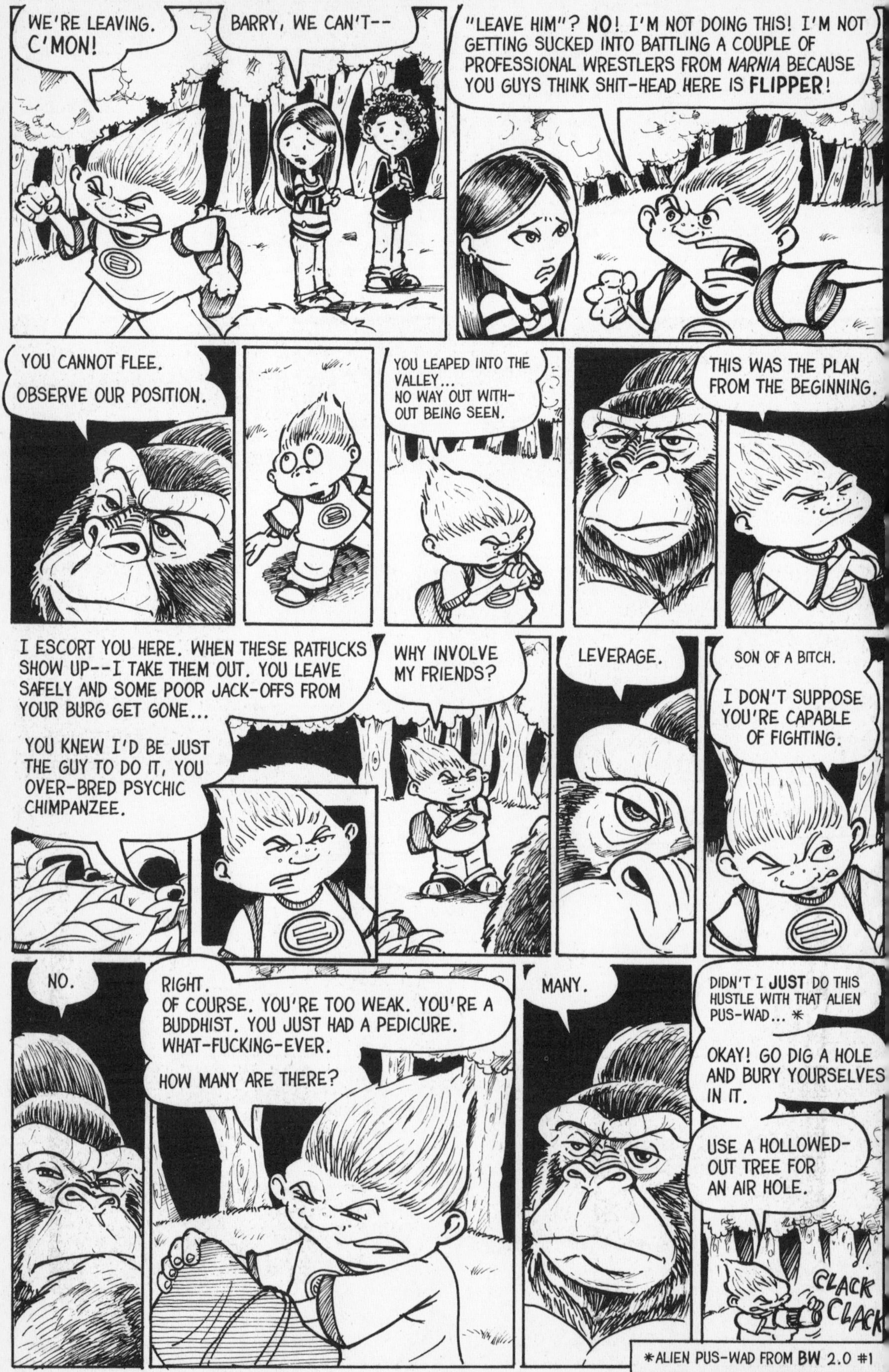
WE'RE LEAVING. C'MON!
BARRY, WE CAN'T--
"LEAVE HIM"? NO! I'M NOT DOING THIS! I'M NOT GETTING SUCKED INTO BATTLING A COUPLE OF PROFESSIONAL WRESTLERS FROM NARNIA BECAUSE YOU GUYS THINK SHIT-HEAD HERE IS FLIPPER!
YOU CANNOT FLEE.
OBSERVE OUR POSITION.
YOU LEAPED INTO THE VALLEY... NO WAY OUT WITHOUT BEING SEEN.
THIS WAS THE PLAN FROM THE BEGINNING.
I ESCORT YOU HERE. WHEN THESE RATFUCKS SHOW UP--I TAKE THEM OUT. YOU LEAVE SAFELY AND SOME POOR JACK-OFFS FROM YOUR BURG GET GONE...
YOU KNEW I'D BE JUST THE GUY TO DO IT, YOU OVER-BRED PSYCHIC CHIMPANZEE.
WHY INVOLVE MY FRIENDS?
LEVERAGE.
SON OF A BITCH.
I DON'T SUPPOSE YOU'RE CAPABLE OF FIGHTING.
NO.
RIGHT.
OF COURSE. YOU'RE TOO WEAK. YOU'RE A BUDDHIST. YOU JUST HAD A PEDICURE. WHAT-FUCKING-EVER.
HOW MANY ARE THERE?
MANY.
DIDN'T I JUST DO THIS HUSTLE WITH THAT ALIEN PUS-WAD... *
OKAY! GO DIG A HOLE AND BURY YOURSELVES IN IT.
USE A HOLLOWED-OUT TREE FOR AN AIR HOLE.
CLACK CLACK
*ALIEN PUS-WAD FROM BW 2.0 #1

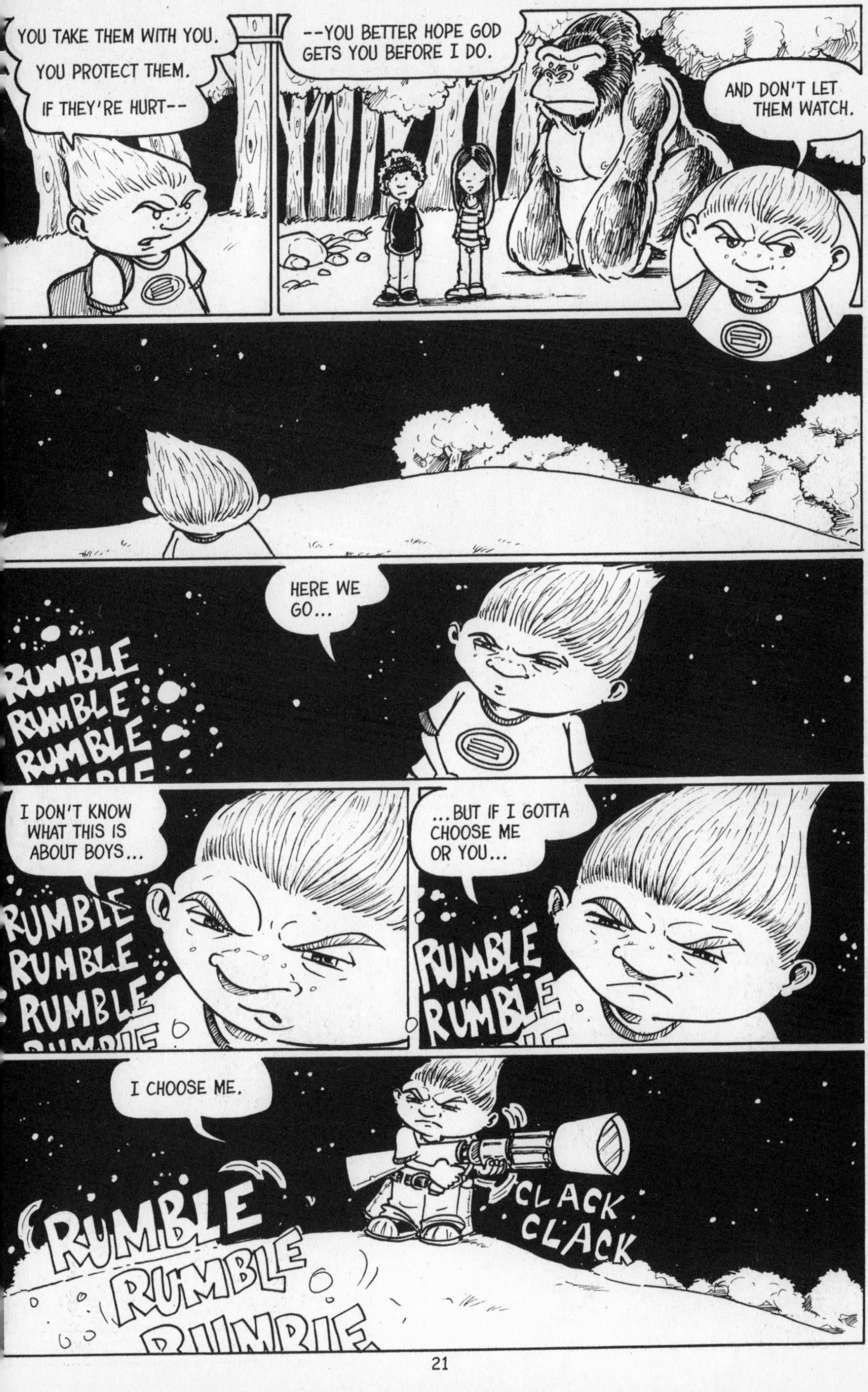
YOU TAKE THEM WITH YOU.
YOU PROTECT THEM.
IF THEY'RE HURT--
--YOU BETTER HOPE GOD GETS YOU BEFORE I DO.
AND DON'T LET THEM WATCH.
HERE WE GO...
RUMBLE
RUMBLE
RUMBLE
I DON'T KNOW WHAT THIS IS ABOUT BOYS...
RUMBLE
RUMBLE
RUMBLE
...BUT IF I GOTTA CHOOSE ME OR YOU...
RUMBLE
RUMBLE
I CHOOSE ME.
RUMBLE
RUMBLE
CLACK
CLACK

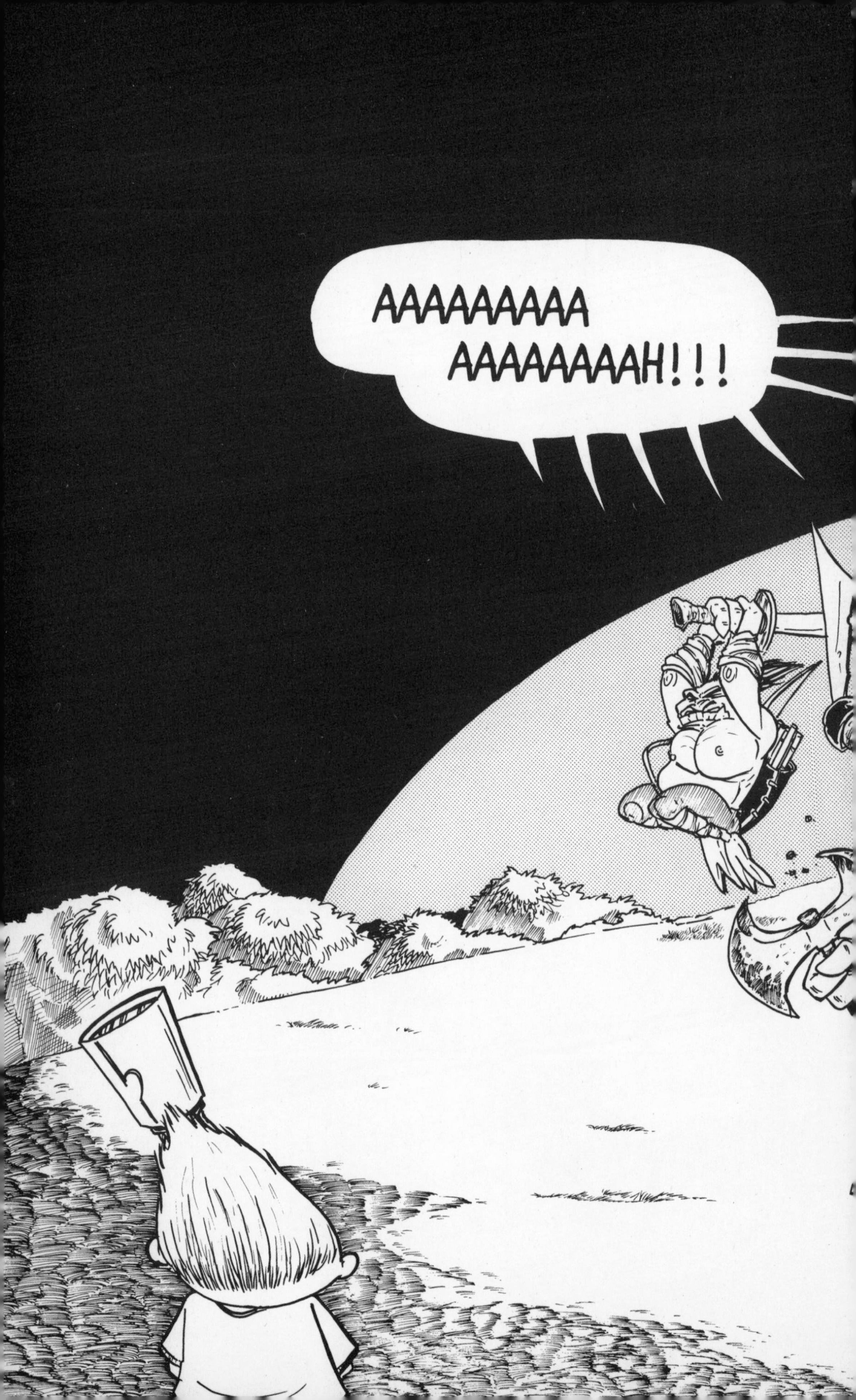
AAAAAAAAA AAAAAAAAAH!!!

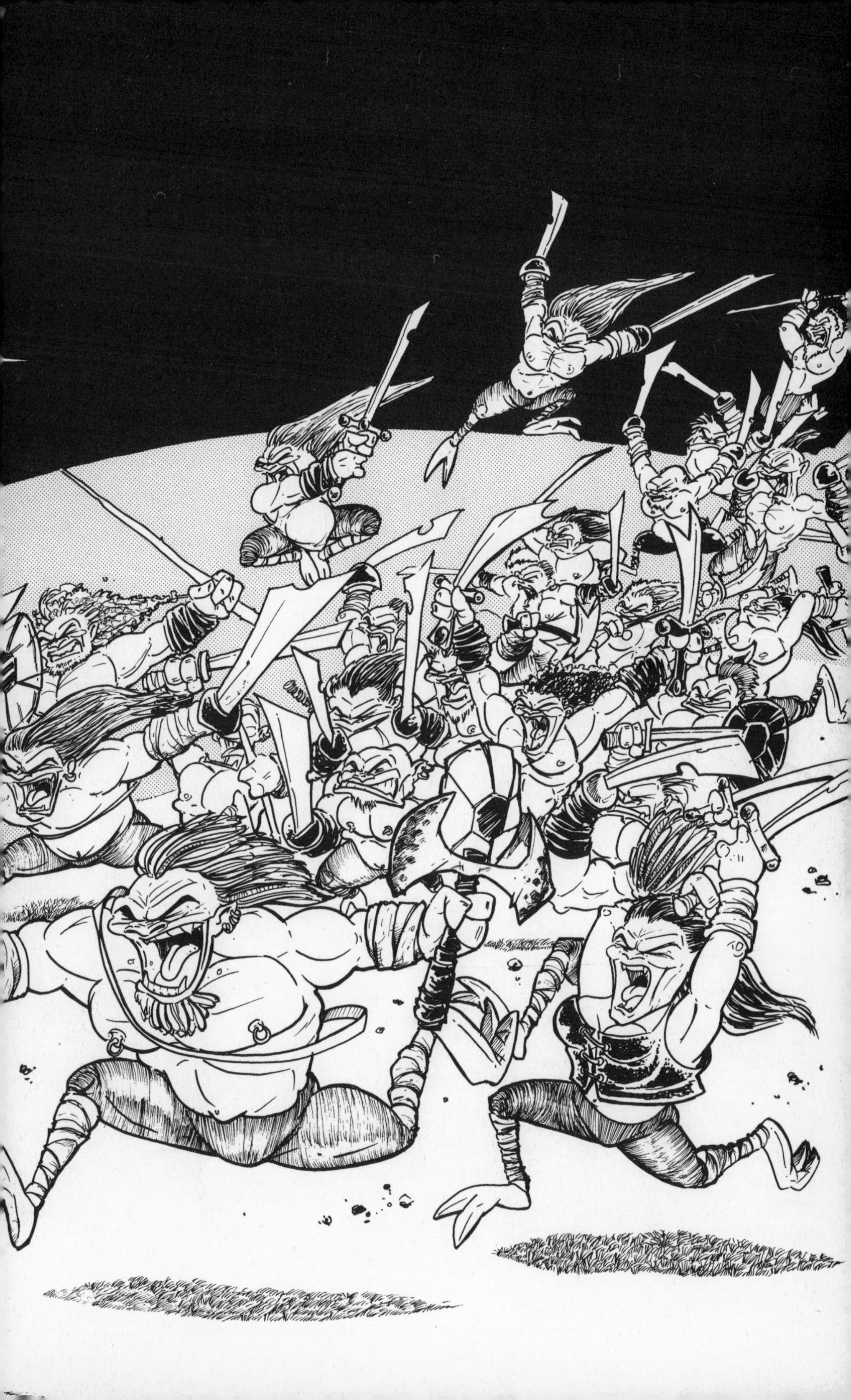

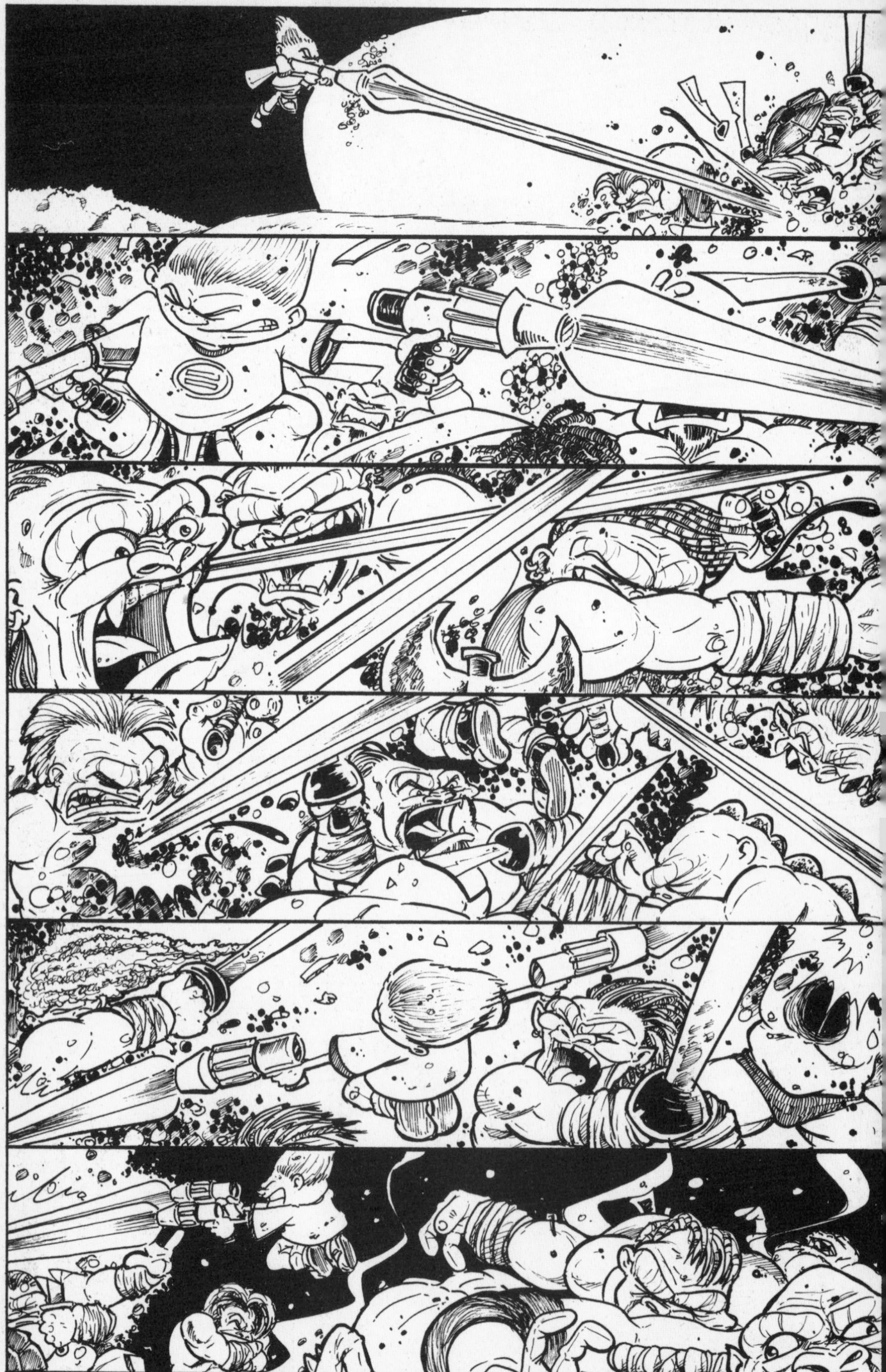

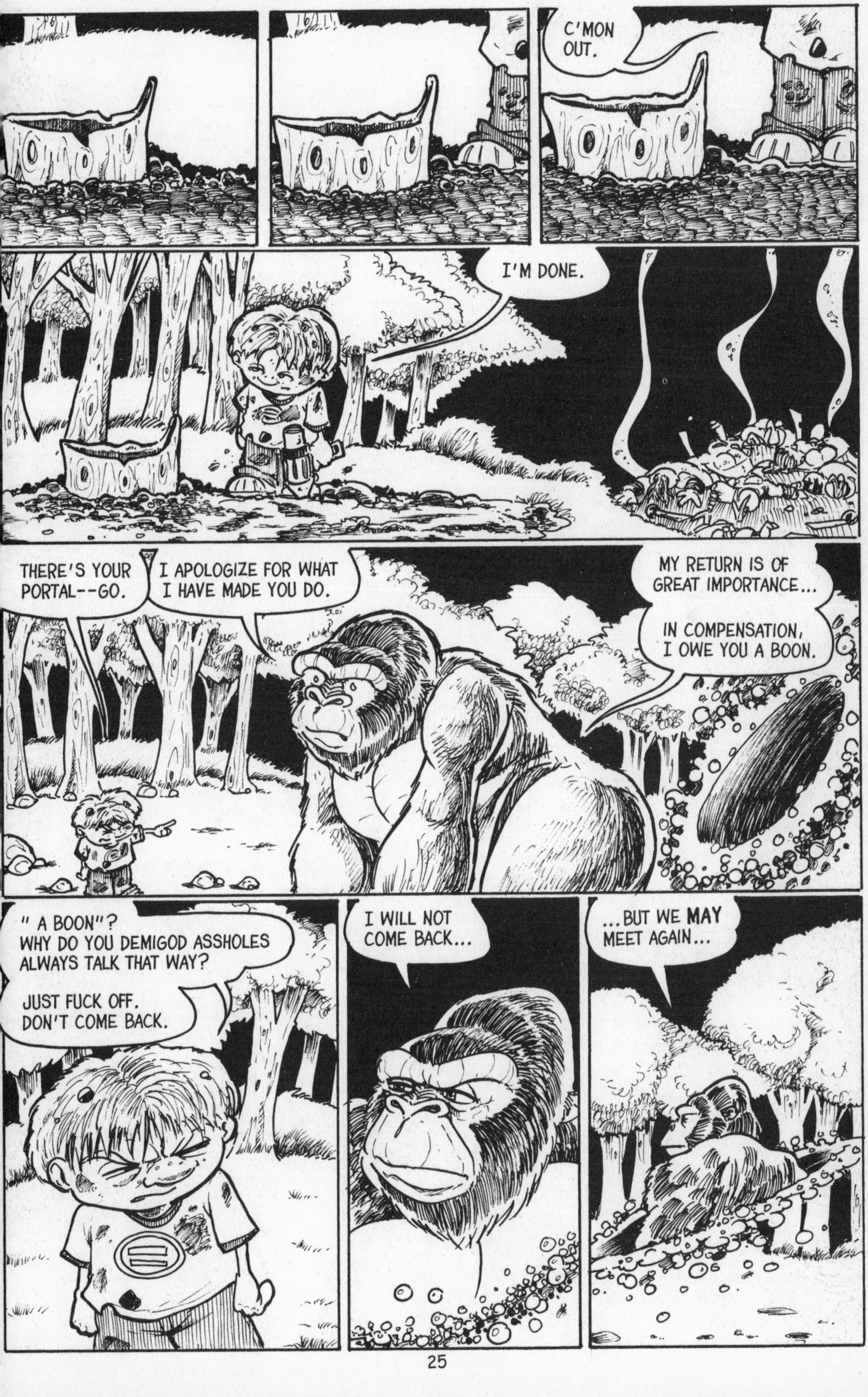
C'MON OUT.
I'M DONE.
THERE'S YOUR PORTAL--GO.
I APOLOGIZE FOR WHAT I HAVE MADE YOU DO.
MY RETURN IS OF GREAT IMPORTANCE...
IN COMPENSATION, I OWE YOU A BOON.
" A BOON"? WHY DO YOU DEMIGOD ASSHOLES ALWAYS TALK THAT WAY?
JUST FUCK OFF. DON'T COME BACK.
I WILL NOT COME BACK...
...BUT WE **MAY** MEET AGAIN...

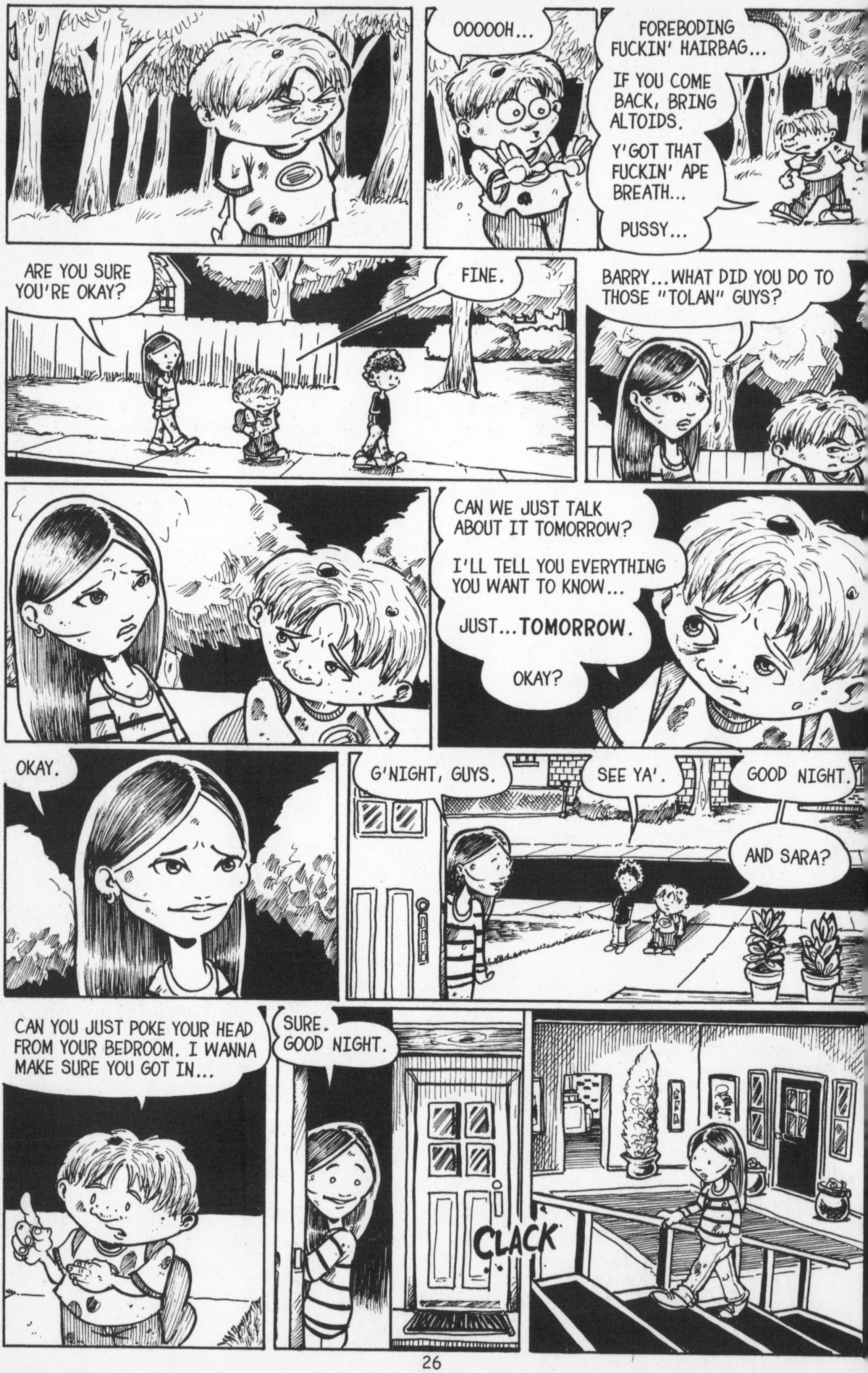
OOOOOH...
FOREBODING FUCKIN' HAIRBAG...
IF YOU COME BACK, BRING ALTOIDS.
Y'GOT THAT FUCKIN' APE BREATH...
PUSSY...
ARE YOU SURE YOU'RE OKAY?
FINE.
BARRY...WHAT DID YOU DO TO THOSE "TOLAN" GUYS?
CAN WE JUST TALK ABOUT IT TOMORROW?
I'LL TELL YOU EVERYTHING YOU WANT TO KNOW...
JUST...TOMORROW.
OKAY?
OKAY.
G'NIGHT, GUYS.
SEE YA'.
GOOD NIGHT.
AND SARA?
CAN YOU JUST POKE YOUR HEAD FROM YOUR BEDROOM. I WANNA MAKE SURE YOU GOT IN...
SURE. GOOD NIGHT.
CLACK

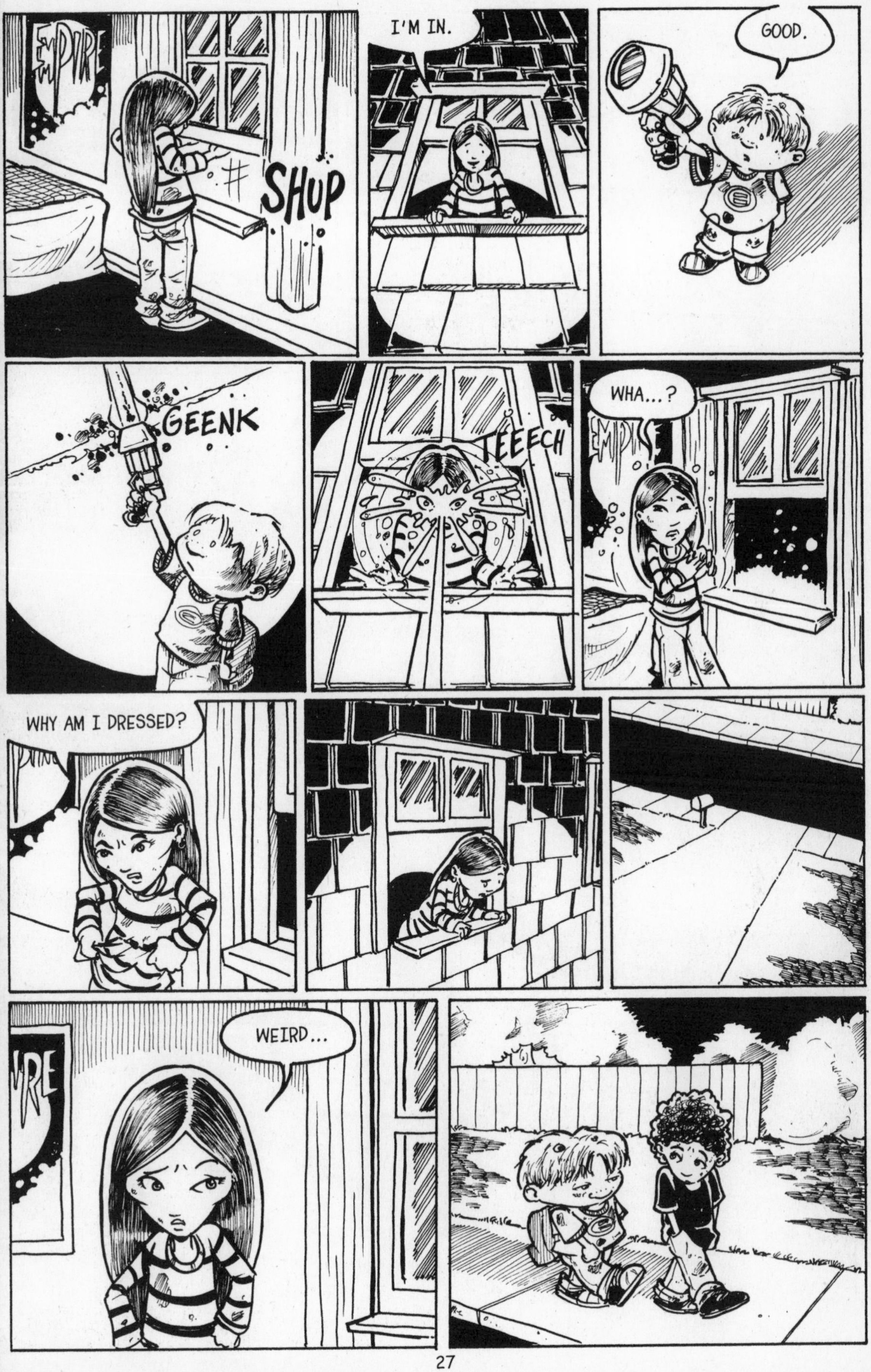
EMPIRE
SHUP
I'M IN.
GOOD.
GEENK
TEEECH
WHA...?
WHY AM I DRESSED?
WEIRD...

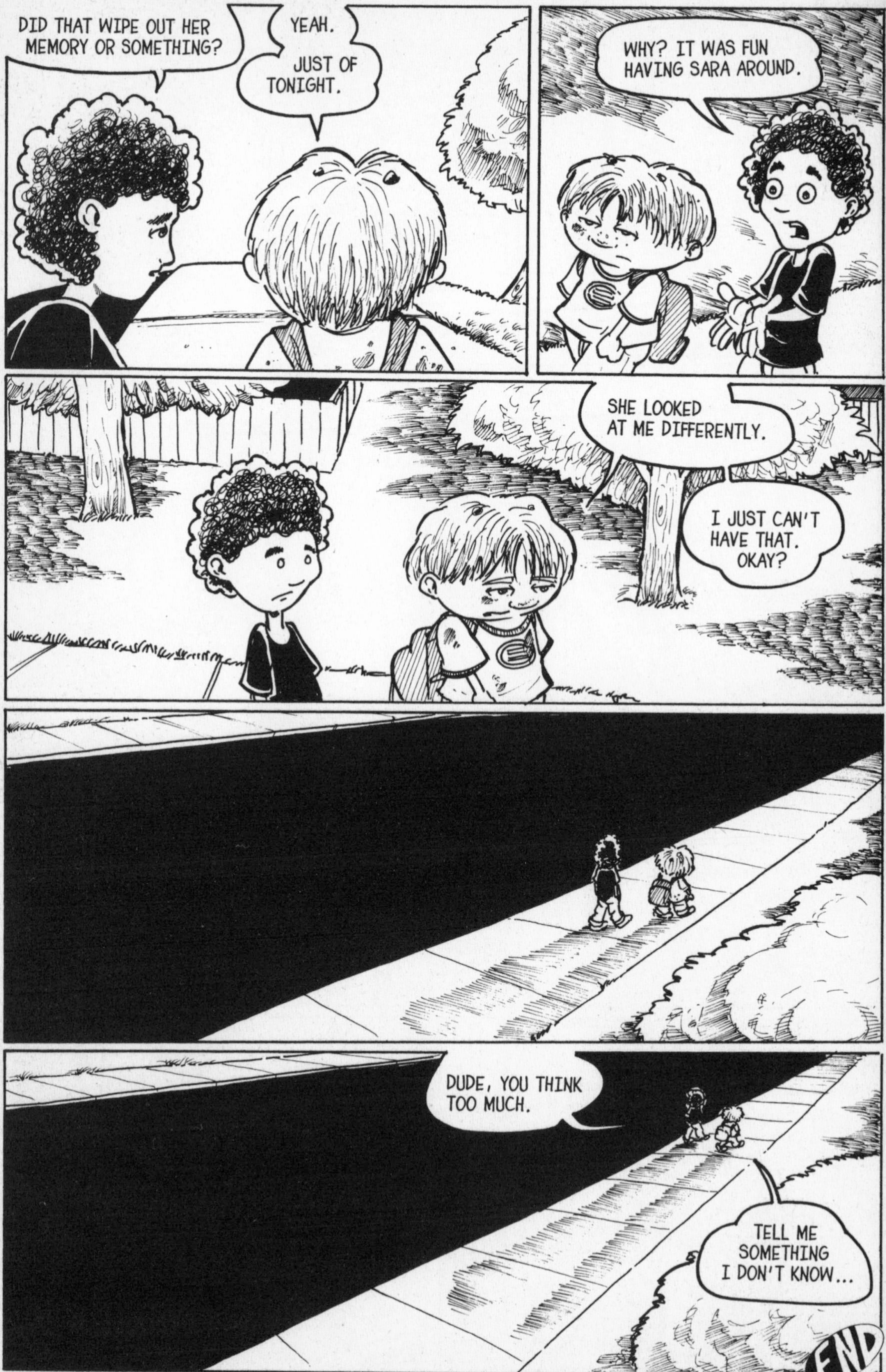
DID THAT WIPE OUT HER MEMORY OR SOMETHING?
YEAH.
JUST OF TONIGHT.
WHY? IT WAS FUN HAVING SARA AROUND.
SHE LOOKED AT ME DIFFERENTLY.
I JUST CAN'T HAVE THAT. OKAY?
DUDE, YOU THINK TOO MUCH.
TELL ME SOMETHING I DON'T KNOW...
END

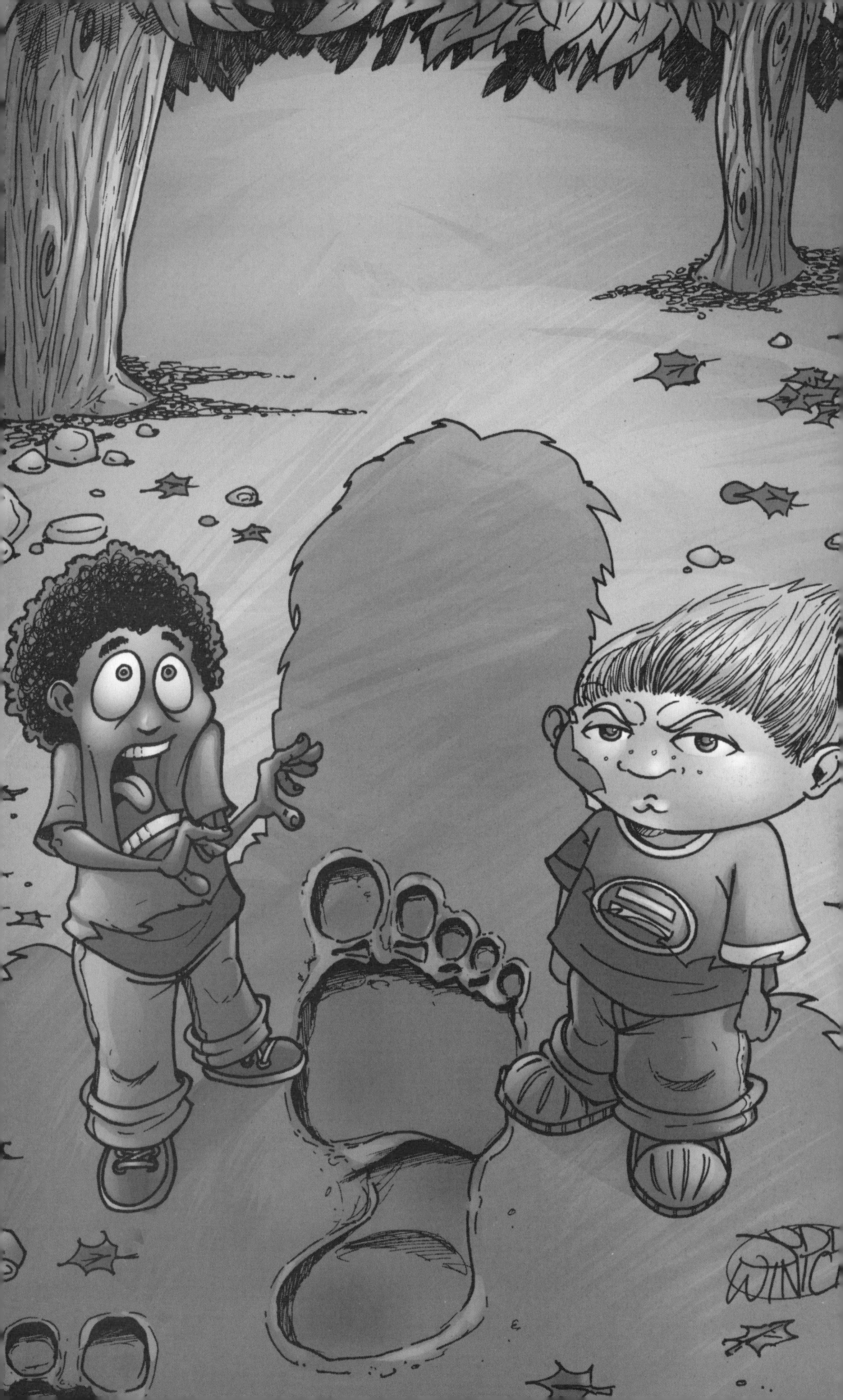

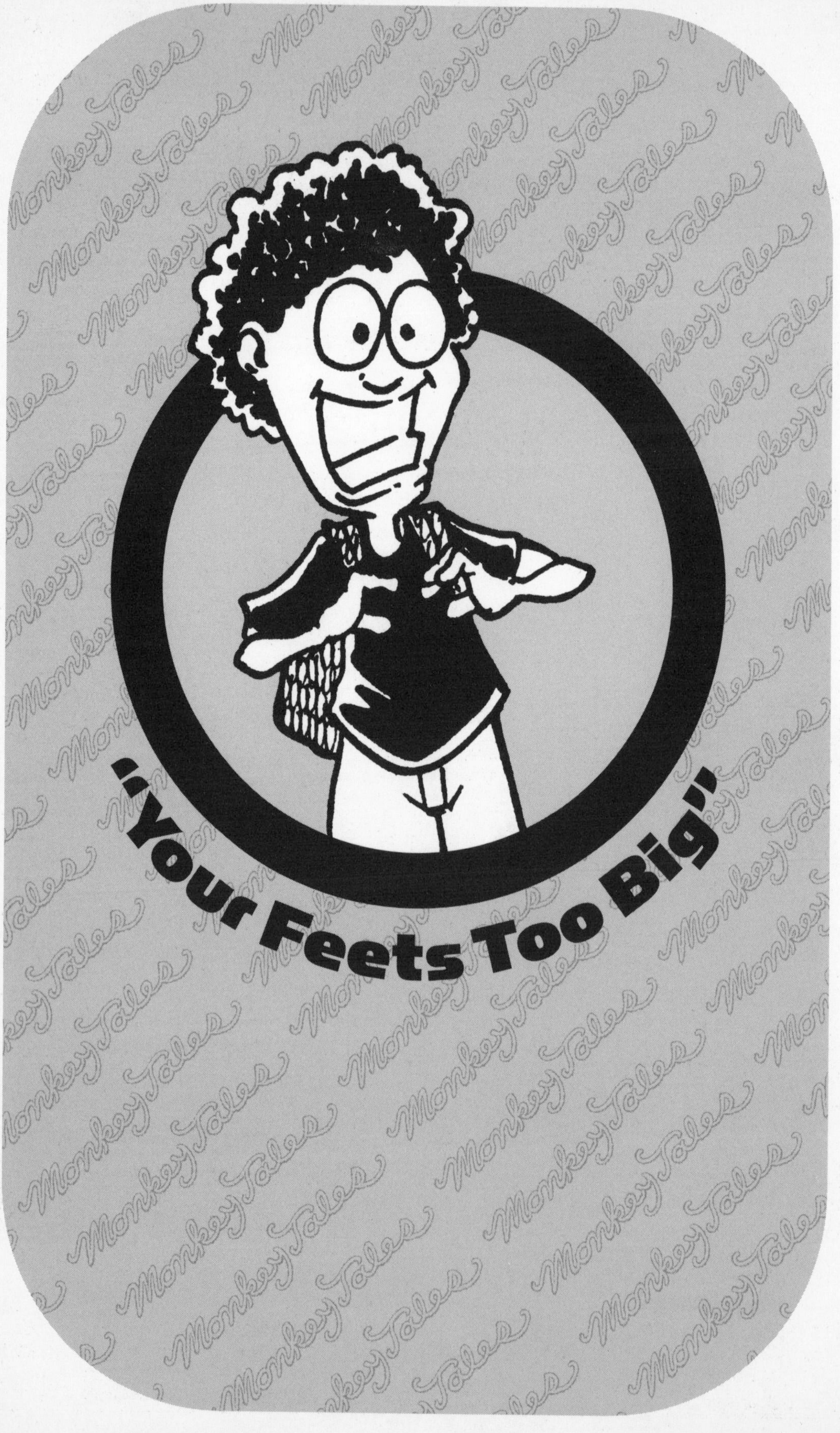
"Your Feets Too Big"

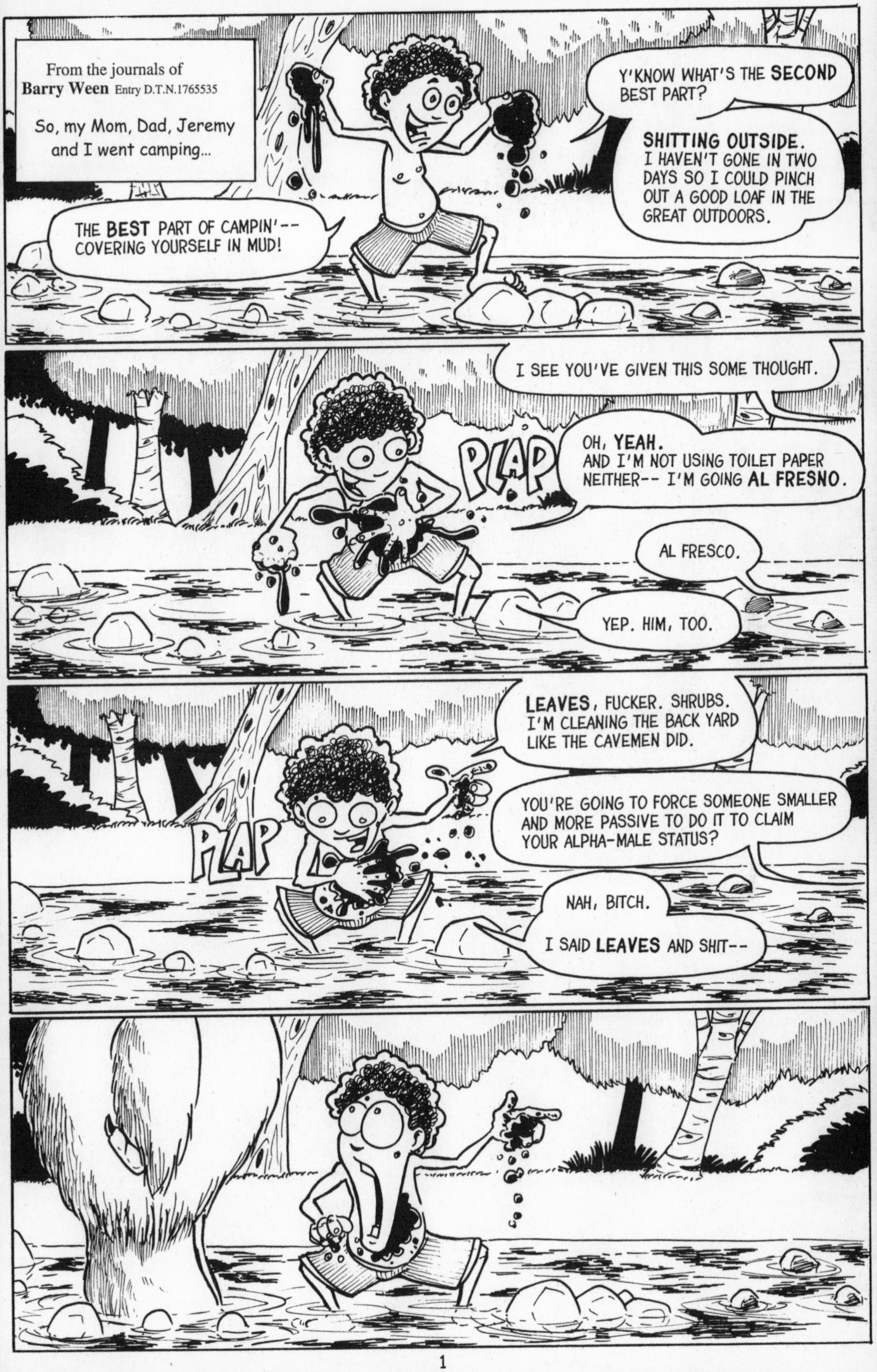
From the journals of
Barry Ween Entry D.T.N.1765535
So, my Mom, Dad, Jeremy and I went camping...
THE BEST PART OF CAMPIN'-- COVERING YOURSELF IN MUD!
Y'KNOW WHAT'S THE SECOND BEST PART?
SHITTING OUTSIDE. I HAVEN'T GONE IN TWO DAYS SO I COULD PINCH OUT A GOOD LOAF IN THE GREAT OUTDOORS.
I SEE YOU'VE GIVEN THIS SOME THOUGHT.
PLAP
OH, YEAH. AND I'M NOT USING TOILET PAPER NEITHER-- I'M GOING AL FRESNO.
AL FRESCO.
YEP. HIM, TOO.
LEAVES, FUCKER. SHRUBS. I'M CLEANING THE BACK YARD LIKE THE CAVEMEN DID.
PLAP
YOU'RE GOING TO FORCE SOMEONE SMALLER AND MORE PASSIVE TO DO IT TO CLAIM YOUR ALPHA-MALE STATUS?
NAH, BITCH.
I SAID LEAVES AND SHIT--

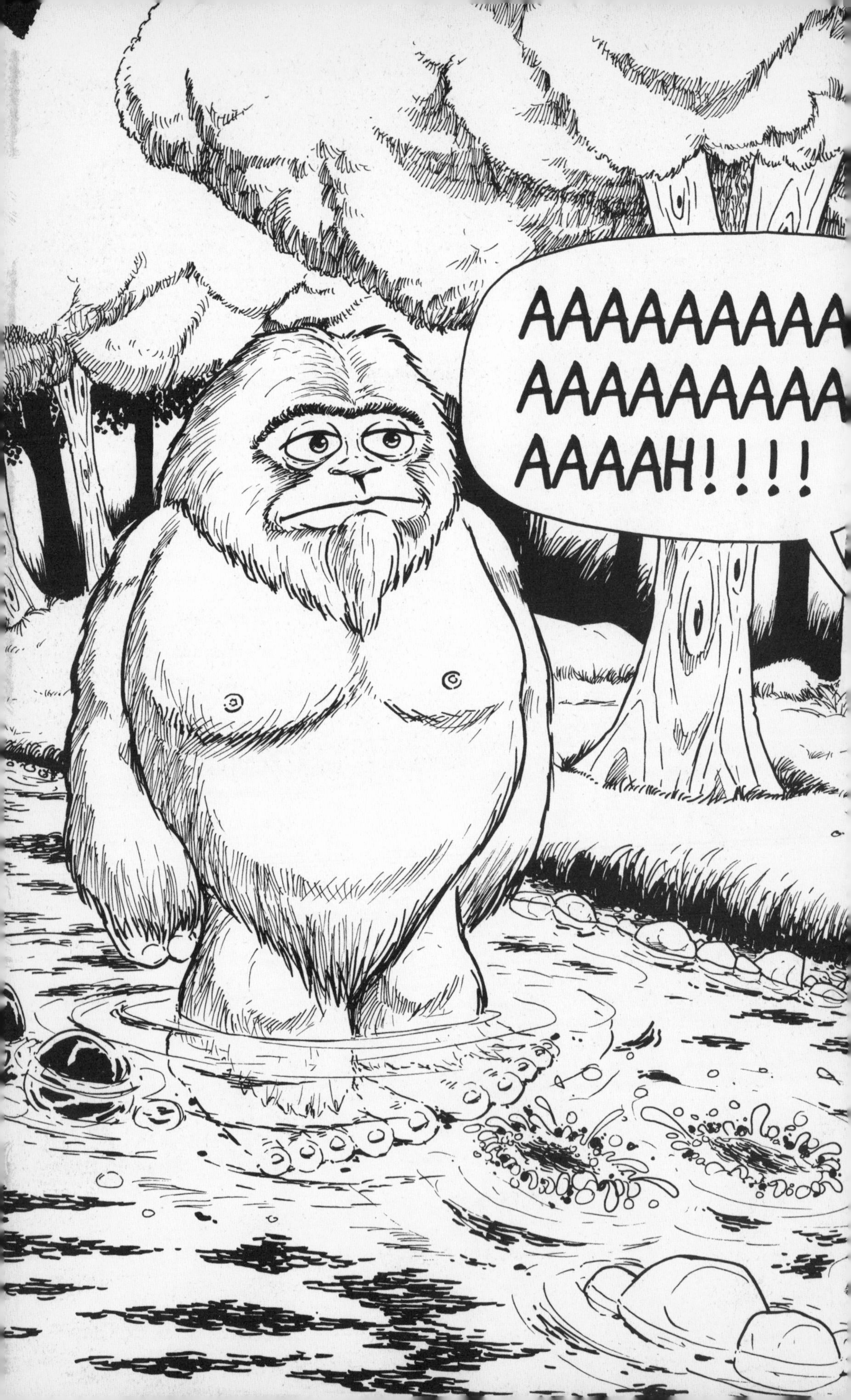
AAAAAAAAAA AAAAAAAAAA AAAAH!!!!

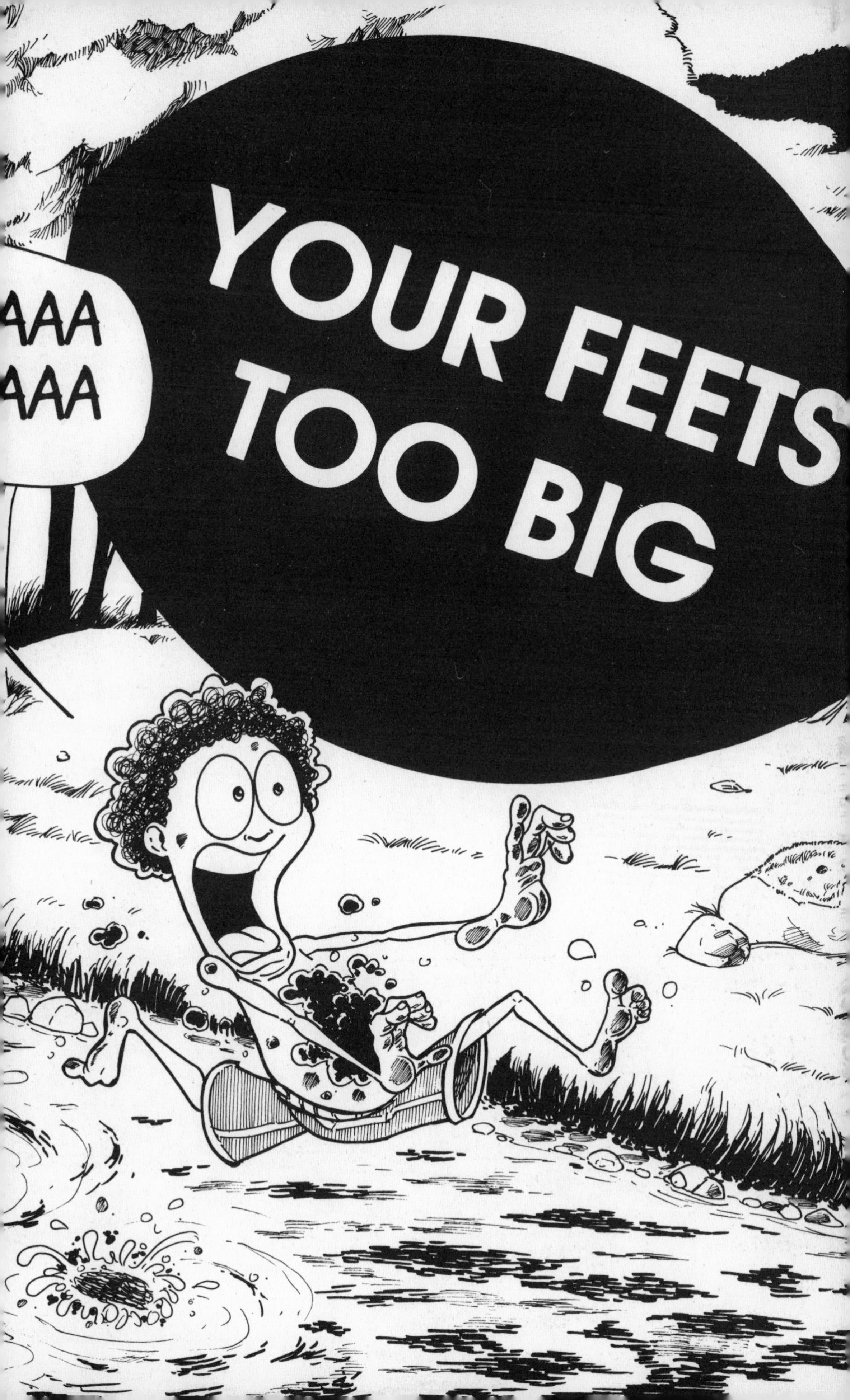
AAA
AAA
YOUR FEETS TOO BIG

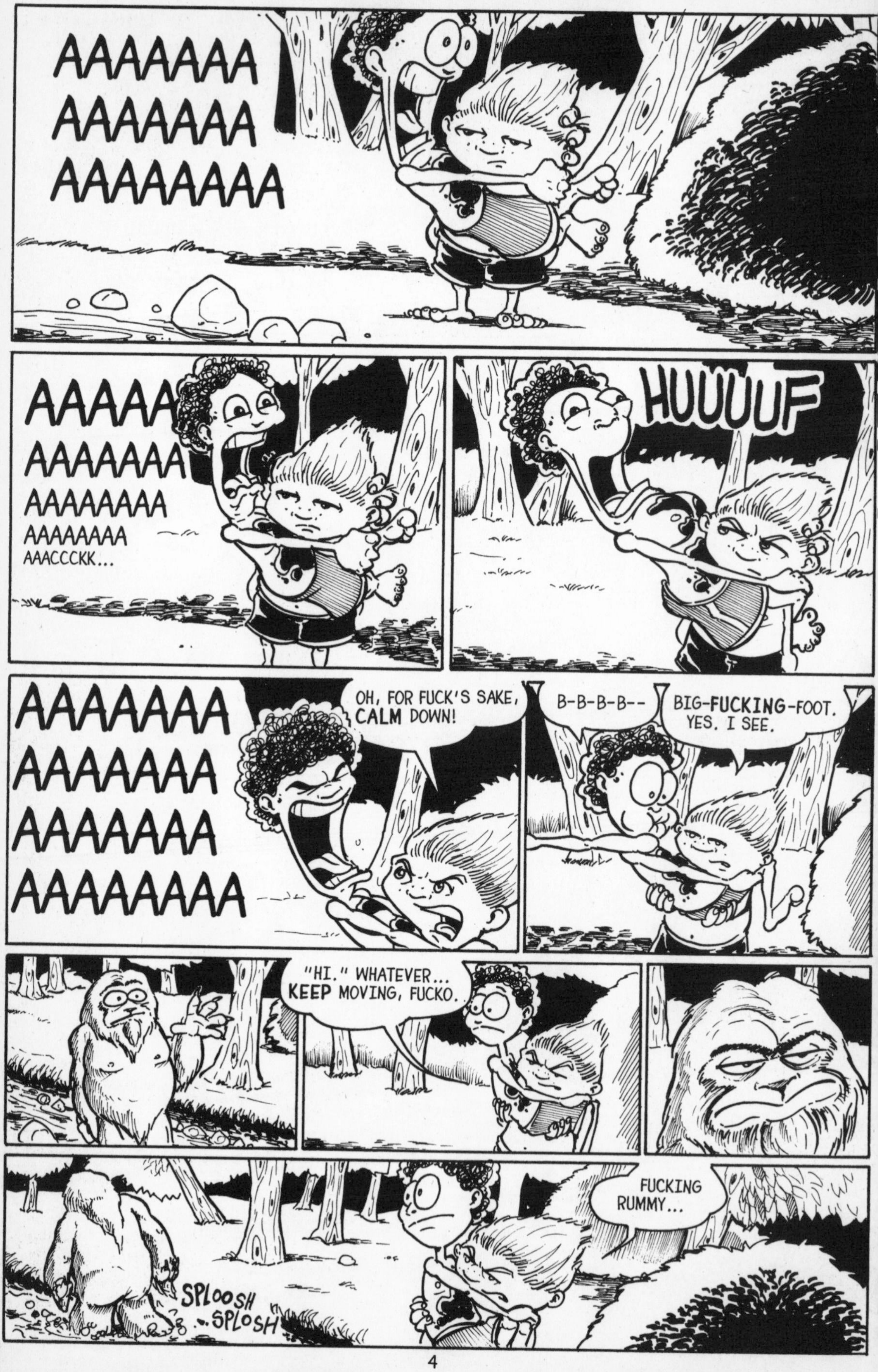
AAAAAAA
AAAAAAA
AAAAAAAA
AAAAA
AAAAAAA
AAAAAAAA
AAAAAAAA
AAACCCKK...
HUUUUF
AAAAAAA
AAAAAAA
AAAAAAA
AAAAAAAA
OH, FOR FUCK'S SAKE, CALM DOWN!
B-B-B-B--
BIG-FUCKING-FOOT. YES. I SEE.
"HI." WHATEVER... KEEP MOVING, FUCKO.
FUCKING RUMMY...
SPLOOSH
SPLOSH

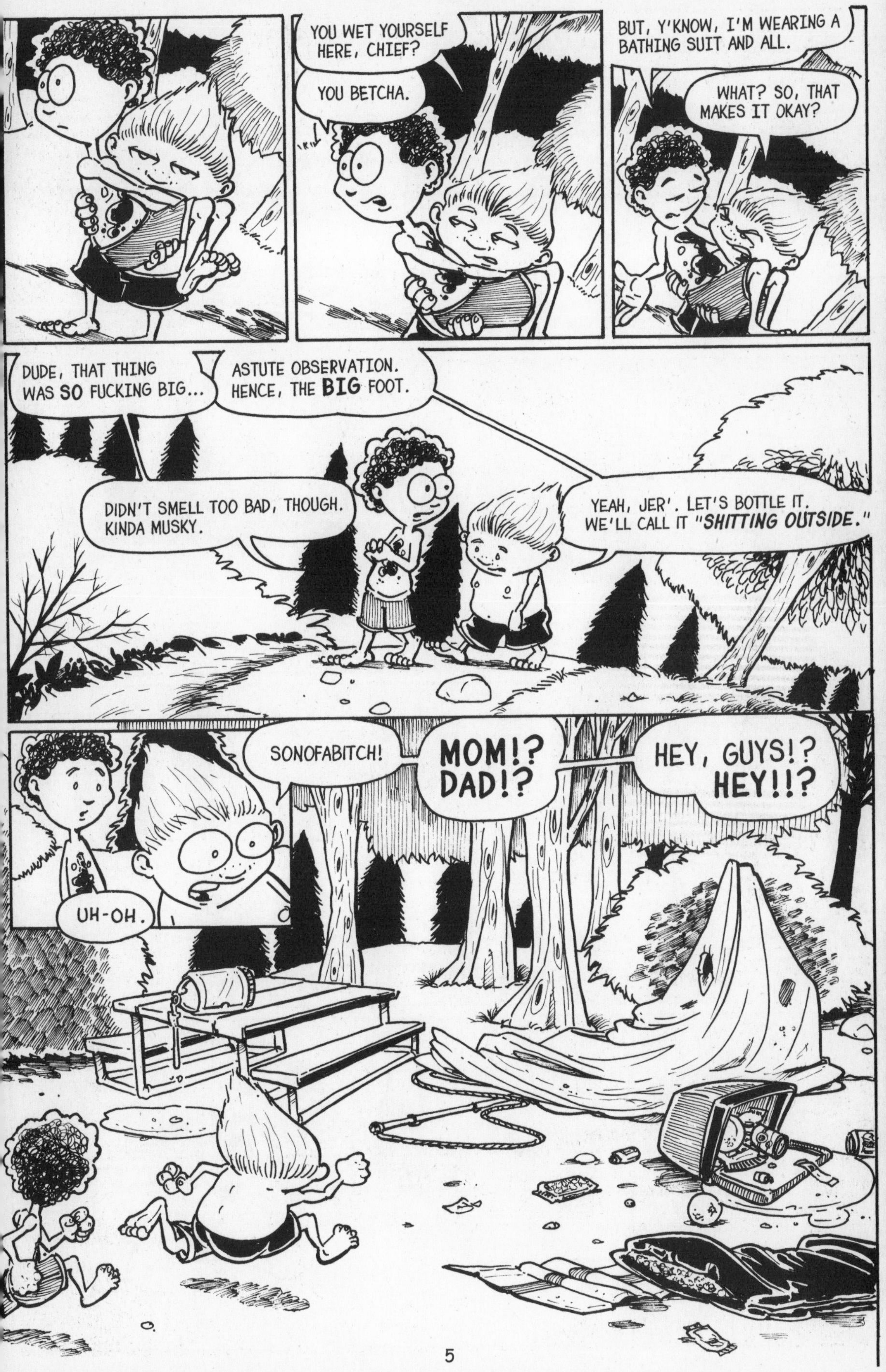
YOU WET YOURSELF HERE, CHIEF?
YOU BETCHA.
BUT, Y'KNOW, I'M WEARING A BATHING SUIT AND ALL.
WHAT? SO, THAT MAKES IT OKAY?
DUDE, THAT THING WAS SO FUCKING BIG...
ASTUTE OBSERVATION. HENCE, THE BIG FOOT.
DIDN'T SMELL TOO BAD, THOUGH. KINDA MUSKY.
YEAH, JER'. LET'S BOTTLE IT. WE'LL CALL IT "SHITTING OUTSIDE."
UH-OH.
SONOFABITCH!
MOM!? DAD!?
HEY, GUYS!? HEY!!?

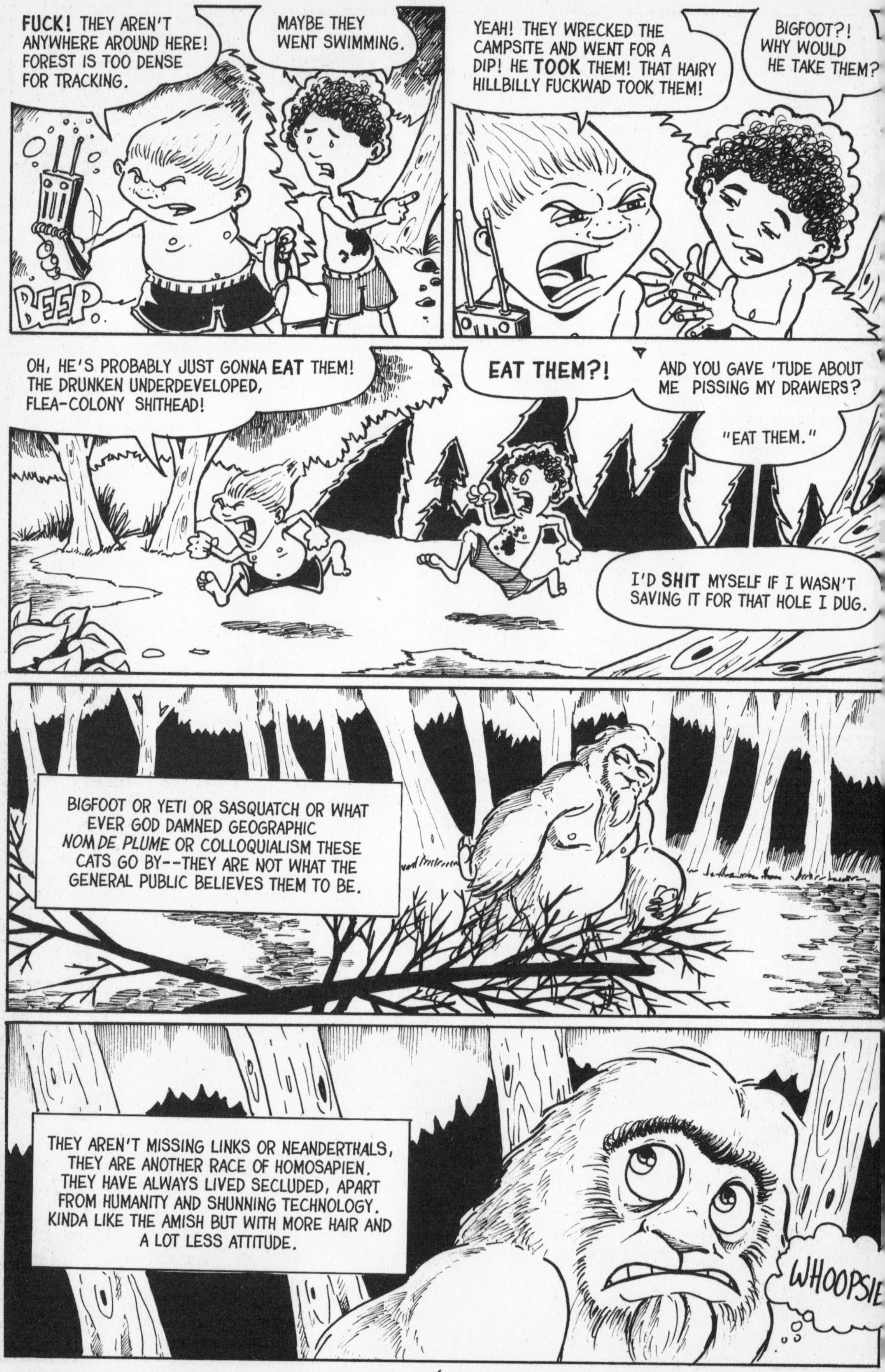
FUCK! THEY AREN'T ANYWHERE AROUND HERE! FOREST IS TOO DENSE FOR TRACKING.
MAYBE THEY WENT SWIMMING.
BEEP
YEAH! THEY WRECKED THE CAMPSITE AND WENT FOR A DIP! HE TOOK THEM! THAT HAIRY HILLBILLY FUCKWAD TOOK THEM!
BIGFOOT?! WHY WOULD HE TAKE THEM?
OH, HE'S PROBABLY JUST GONNA EAT THEM! THE DRUNKEN UNDERDEVELOPED, FLEA-COLONY SHITHEAD!
EAT THEM?!
AND YOU GAVE 'TUDE ABOUT ME PISSING MY DRAWERS?
"EAT THEM."
I'D SHIT MYSELF IF I WASN'T SAVING IT FOR THAT HOLE I DUG.
BIGFOOT OR YETI OR SASQUATCH OR WHAT EVER GOD DAMNED GEOGRAPHIC *NOM DE PLUME* OR COLLOQUIALISM THESE CATS GO BY--THEY ARE NOT WHAT THE GENERAL PUBLIC BELIEVES THEM TO BE.
THEY AREN'T MISSING LINKS OR NEANDERTHALS, THEY ARE ANOTHER RACE OF HOMOSAPIEN. THEY HAVE ALWAYS LIVED SECLUDED, APART FROM HUMANITY AND SHUNNING TECHNOLOGY. KINDA LIKE THE AMISH BUT WITH MORE HAIR AND A LOT LESS ATTITUDE.
WHOOPSIE

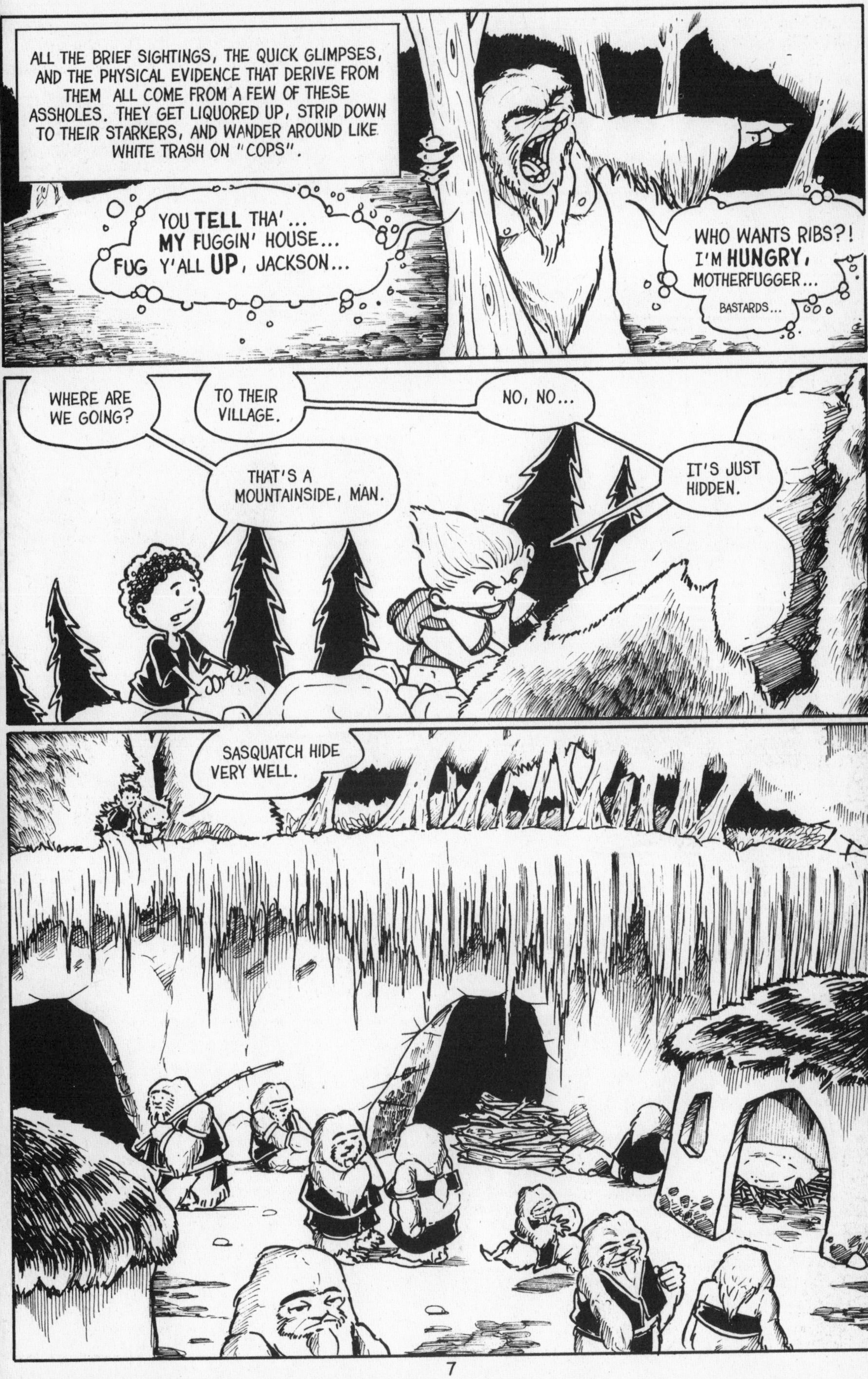
ALL THE BRIEF SIGHTINGS, THE QUICK GLIMPSES, AND THE PHYSICAL EVIDENCE THAT DERIVE FROM THEM ALL COME FROM A FEW OF THESE ASSHOLES. THEY GET LIQUORED UP, STRIP DOWN TO THEIR STARKERS, AND WANDER AROUND LIKE WHITE TRASH ON "COPS".
YOU TELL THA'... MY FUGGIN' HOUSE... FUG Y'ALL UP, JACKSON...
WHO WANTS RIBS?! I'M HUNGRY, MOTHERFUGGER...
BASTARDS...
WHERE ARE WE GOING?
TO THEIR VILLAGE.
THAT'S A MOUNTAINSIDE, MAN.
NO, NO...
IT'S JUST HIDDEN.
SASQUATCH HIDE VERY WELL.

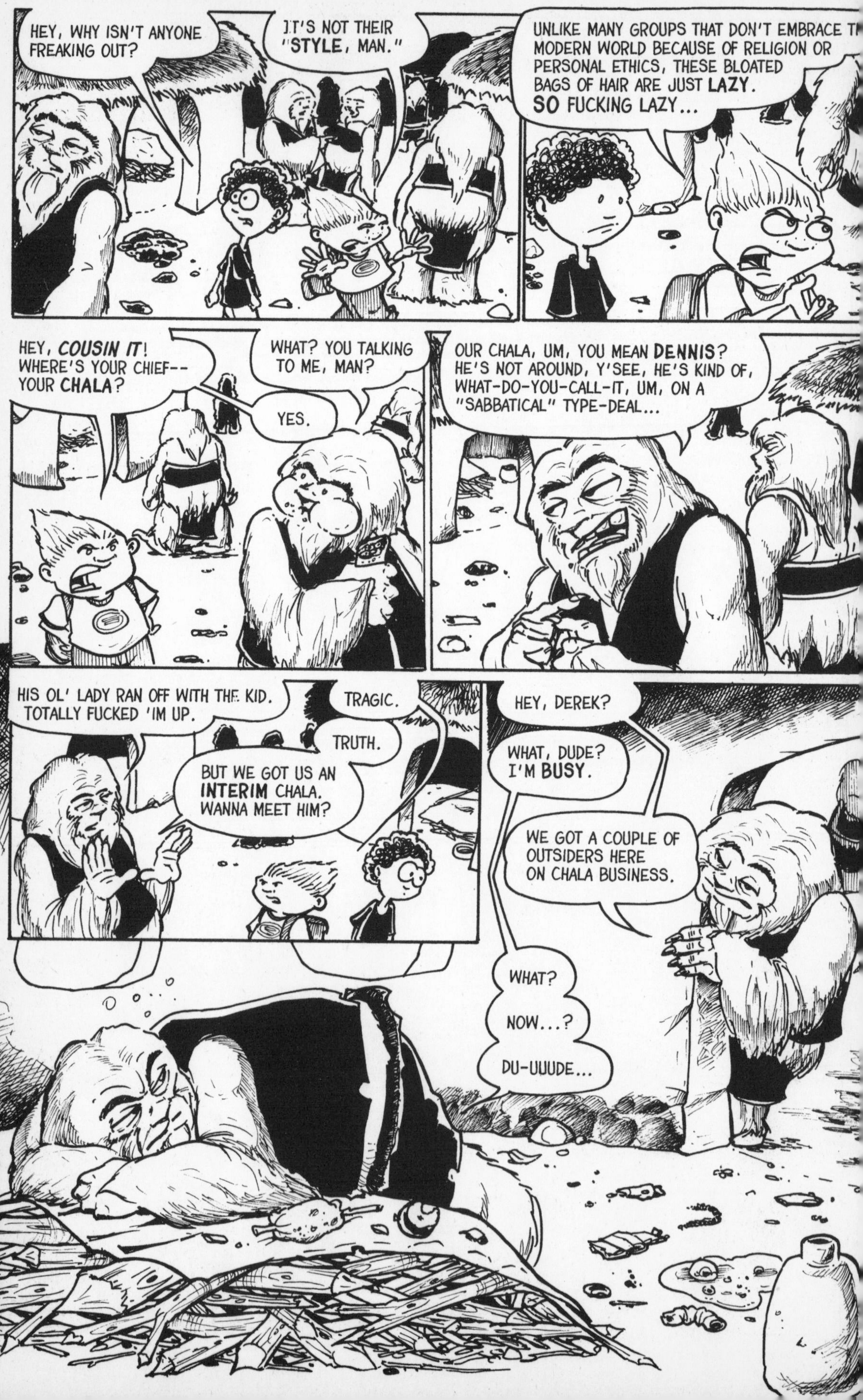
HEY, WHY ISN'T ANYONE FREAKING OUT?
IT'S NOT THEIR "STYLE, MAN."
UNLIKE MANY GROUPS THAT DON'T EMBRACE TH MODERN WORLD BECAUSE OF RELIGION OR PERSONAL ETHICS, THESE BLOATED BAGS OF HAIR ARE JUST LAZY. SO FUCKING LAZY...
HEY, COUSIN IT! WHERE'S YOUR CHIEF-- YOUR CHALA?
WHAT? YOU TALKING TO ME, MAN?
YES.
OUR CHALA, UM, YOU MEAN DENNIS? HE'S NOT AROUND, Y'SEE, HE'S KIND OF, WHAT-DO-YOU-CALL-IT, UM, ON A "SABBATICAL" TYPE-DEAL...
HIS OL' LADY RAN OFF WITH THE KID. TOTALLY FUCKED 'IM UP.
TRAGIC.
TRUTH.
BUT WE GOT US AN INTERIM CHALA. WANNA MEET HIM?
HEY, DEREK?
WHAT, DUDE? I'M BUSY.
WE GOT A COUPLE OF OUTSIDERS HERE ON CHALA BUSINESS.
WHAT?
NOW...?
DU-UUUDE...

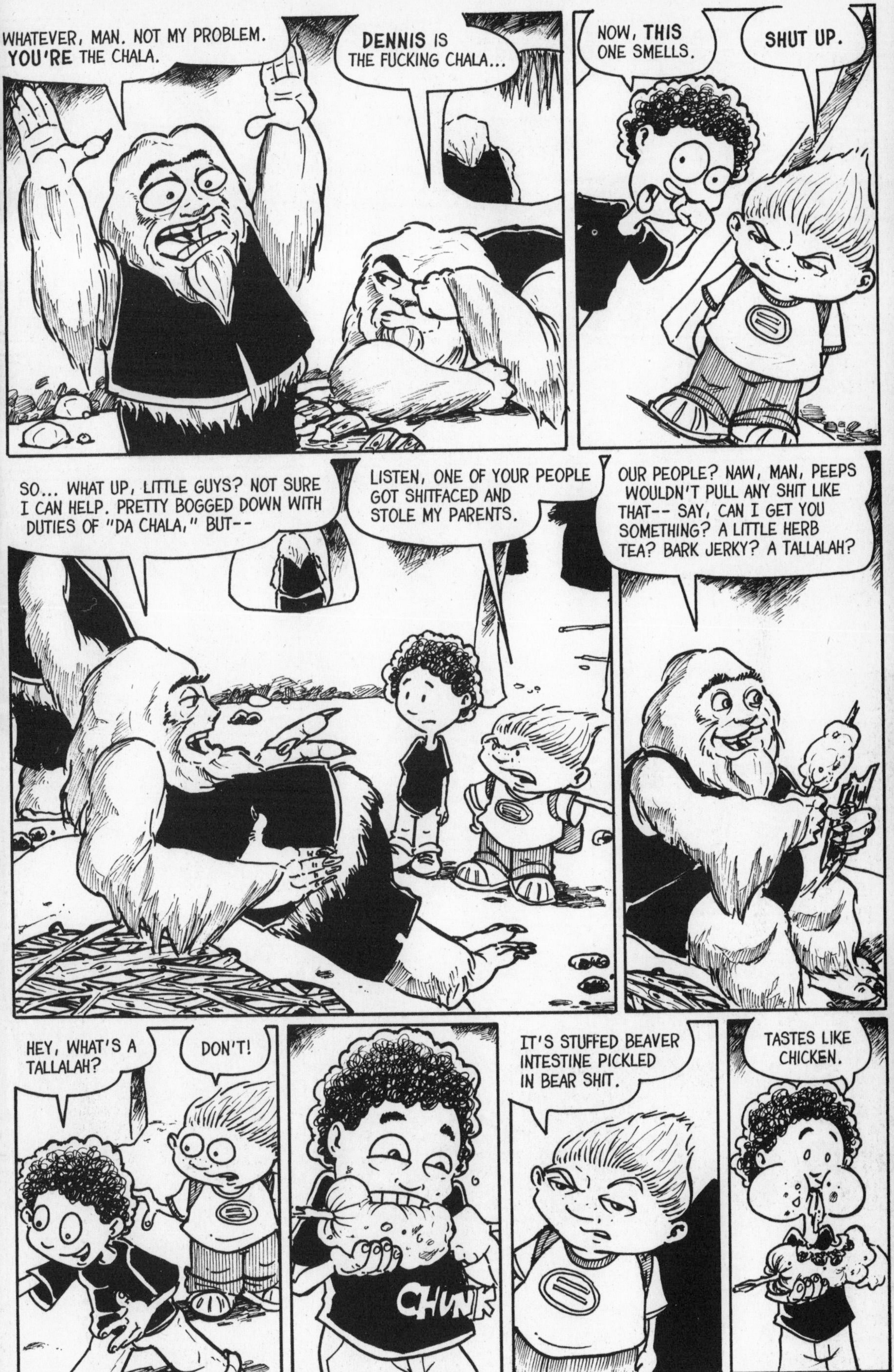
WHATEVER, MAN. NOT MY PROBLEM. YOU'RE THE CHALA.
DENNIS IS THE FUCKING CHALA...
NOW, THIS ONE SMELLS.
SHUT UP.
SO... WHAT UP, LITTLE GUYS? NOT SURE I CAN HELP. PRETTY BOGGED DOWN WITH DUTIES OF "DA CHALA," BUT--
LISTEN, ONE OF YOUR PEOPLE GOT SHITFACED AND STOLE MY PARENTS.
OUR PEOPLE? NAW, MAN, PEEPS WOULDN'T PULL ANY SHIT LIKE THAT-- SAY, CAN I GET YOU SOMETHING? A LITTLE HERB TEA? BARK JERKY? A TALLALAH?
HEY, WHAT'S A TALLALAH?
DON'T!
CHUNK
IT'S STUFFED BEAVER INTESTINE PICKLED IN BEAR SHIT.
TASTES LIKE CHICKEN.

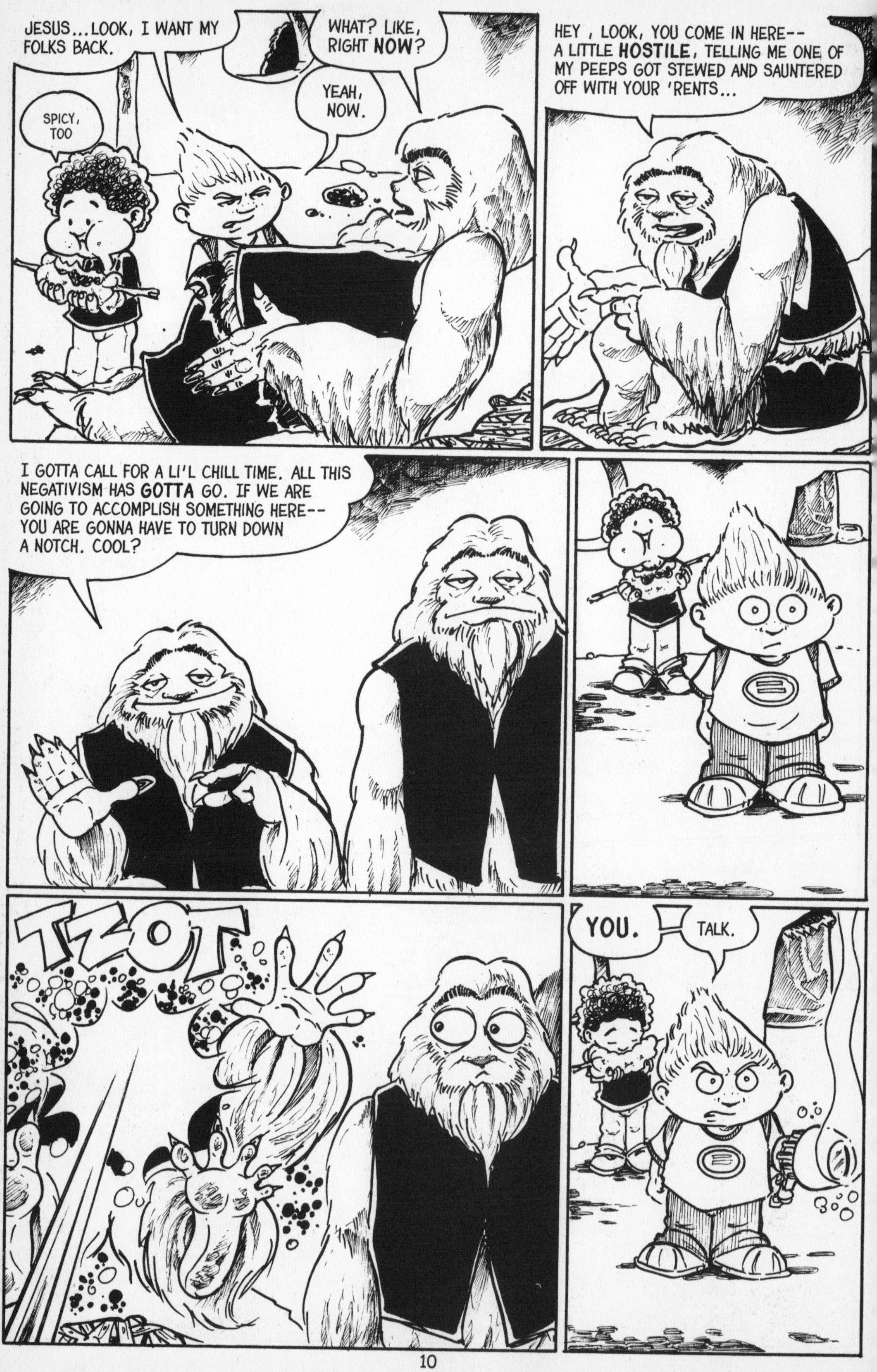
JESUS...LOOK, I WANT MY FOLKS BACK.
SPICY, TOO
WHAT? LIKE, RIGHT NOW?
YEAH, NOW.
HEY , LOOK, YOU COME IN HERE-- A LITTLE HOSTILE, TELLING ME ONE OF MY PEEPS GOT STEWED AND SAUNTERED OFF WITH YOUR 'RENTS...
I GOTTA CALL FOR A LI'L CHILL TIME. ALL THIS NEGATIVISM HAS GOTTA GO. IF WE ARE GOING TO ACCOMPLISH SOMETHING HERE-- YOU ARE GONNA HAVE TO TURN DOWN A NOTCH. COOL?
TZOT
YOU.
TALK.

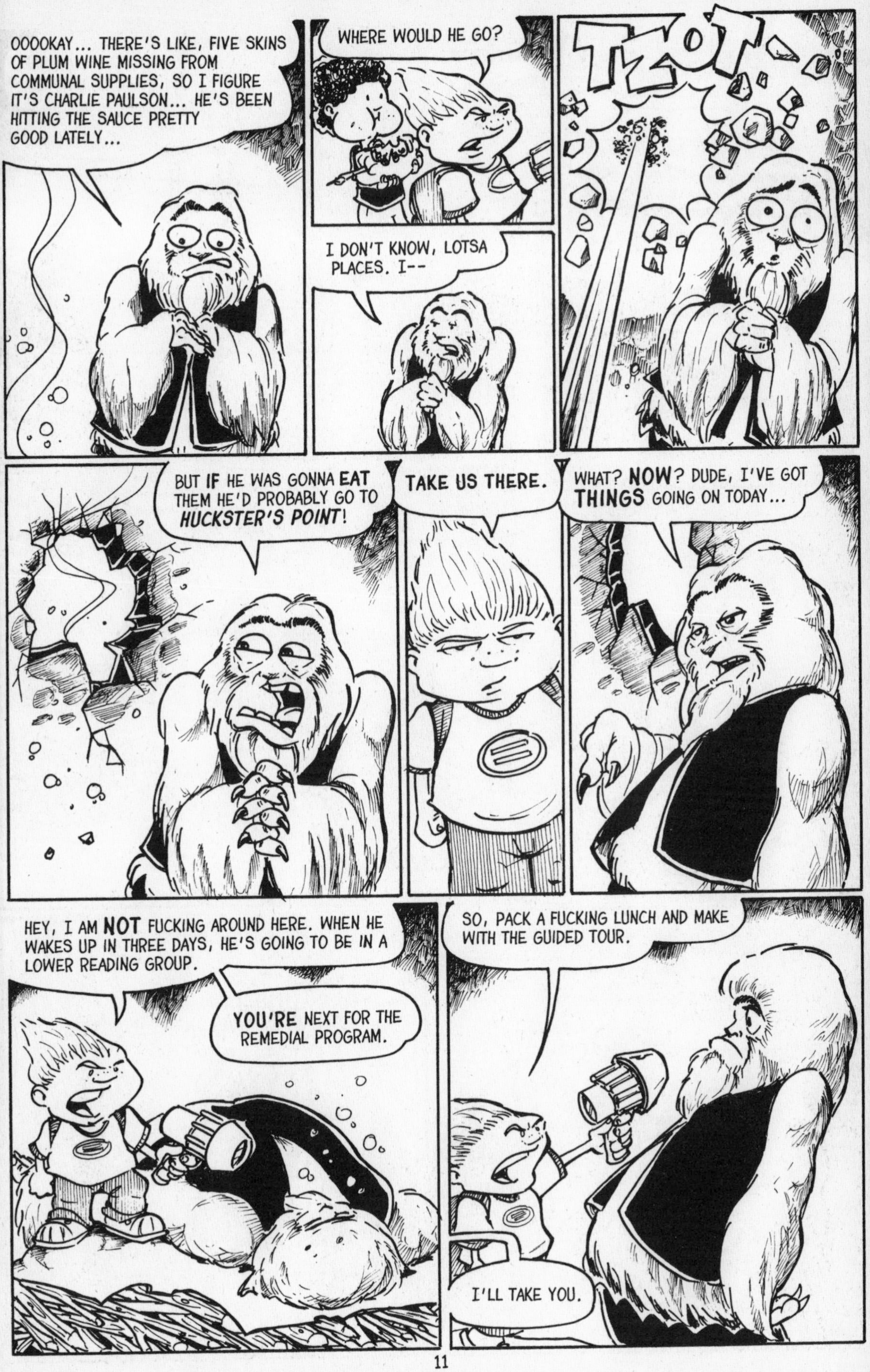
OOOOKAY... THERE'S LIKE, FIVE SKINS OF PLUM WINE MISSING FROM COMMUNAL SUPPLIES, SO I FIGURE IT'S CHARLIE PAULSON... HE'S BEEN HITTING THE SAUCE PRETTY GOOD LATELY...
WHERE WOULD HE GO?
I DON'T KNOW, LOTSA PLACES. I--
TZOT!
BUT IF HE WAS GONNA EAT THEM HE'D PROBABLY GO TO HUCKSTER'S POINT!
TAKE US THERE.
WHAT? NOW? DUDE, I'VE GOT THINGS GOING ON TODAY...
HEY, I AM NOT FUCKING AROUND HERE. WHEN HE WAKES UP IN THREE DAYS, HE'S GOING TO BE IN A LOWER READING GROUP.
YOU'RE NEXT FOR THE REMEDIAL PROGRAM.
SO, PACK A FUCKING LUNCH AND MAKE WITH THE GUIDED TOUR.
I'LL TAKE YOU.

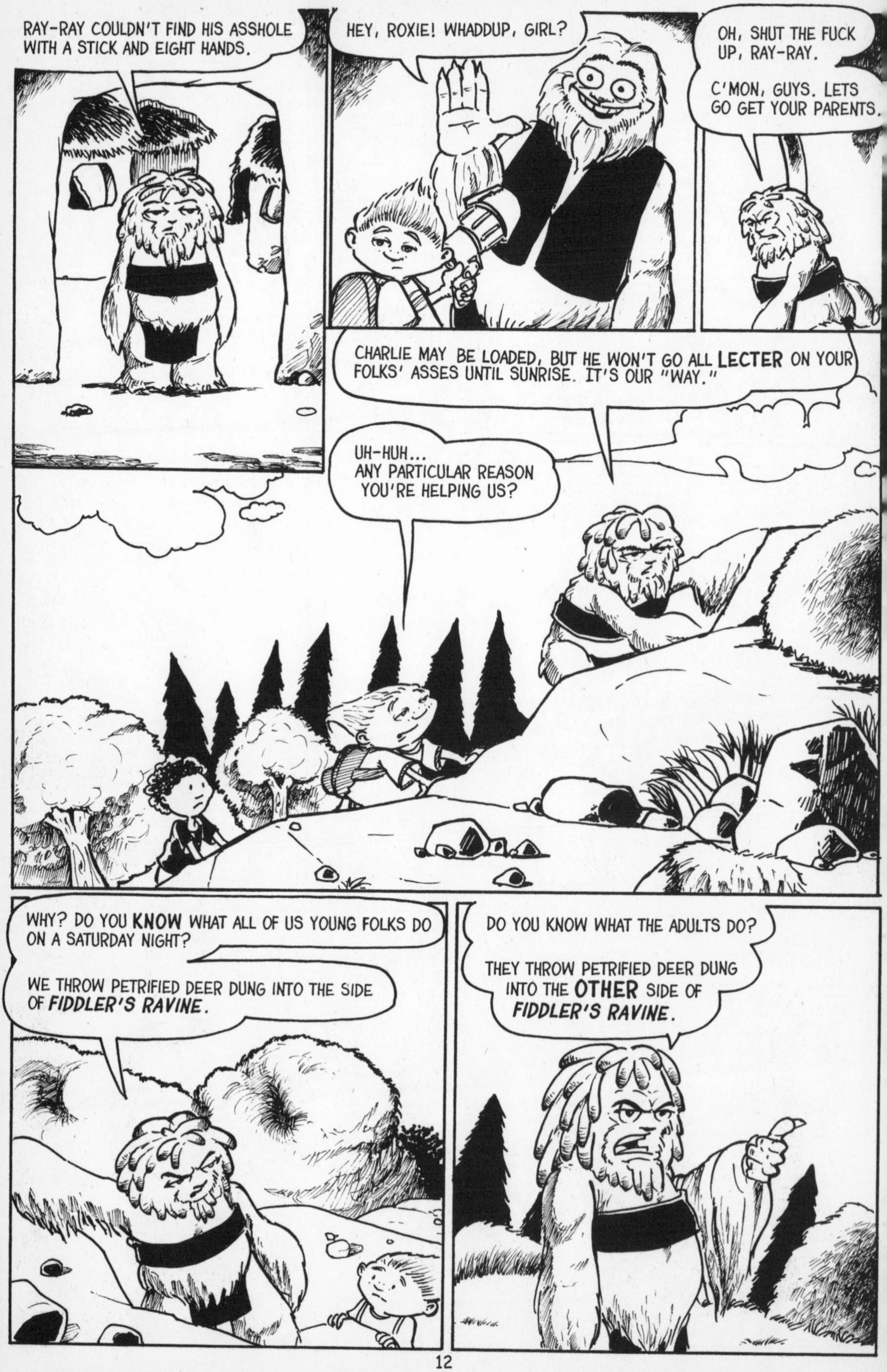
RAY-RAY COULDN'T FIND HIS ASSHOLE WITH A STICK AND EIGHT HANDS.
HEY, ROXIE! WHADDUP, GIRL?
OH, SHUT THE FUCK UP, RAY-RAY.
C'MON, GUYS. LETS GO GET YOUR PARENTS.
CHARLIE MAY BE LOADED, BUT HE WON'T GO ALL LECTER ON YOUR FOLKS' ASSES UNTIL SUNRISE. IT'S OUR "WAY."
UH-HUH... ANY PARTICULAR REASON YOU'RE HELPING US?
WHY? DO YOU KNOW WHAT ALL OF US YOUNG FOLKS DO ON A SATURDAY NIGHT?
WE THROW PETRIFIED DEER DUNG INTO THE SIDE OF FIDDLER'S RAVINE.
DO YOU KNOW WHAT THE ADULTS DO?
THEY THROW PETRIFIED DEER DUNG INTO THE OTHER SIDE OF FIDDLER'S RAVINE.

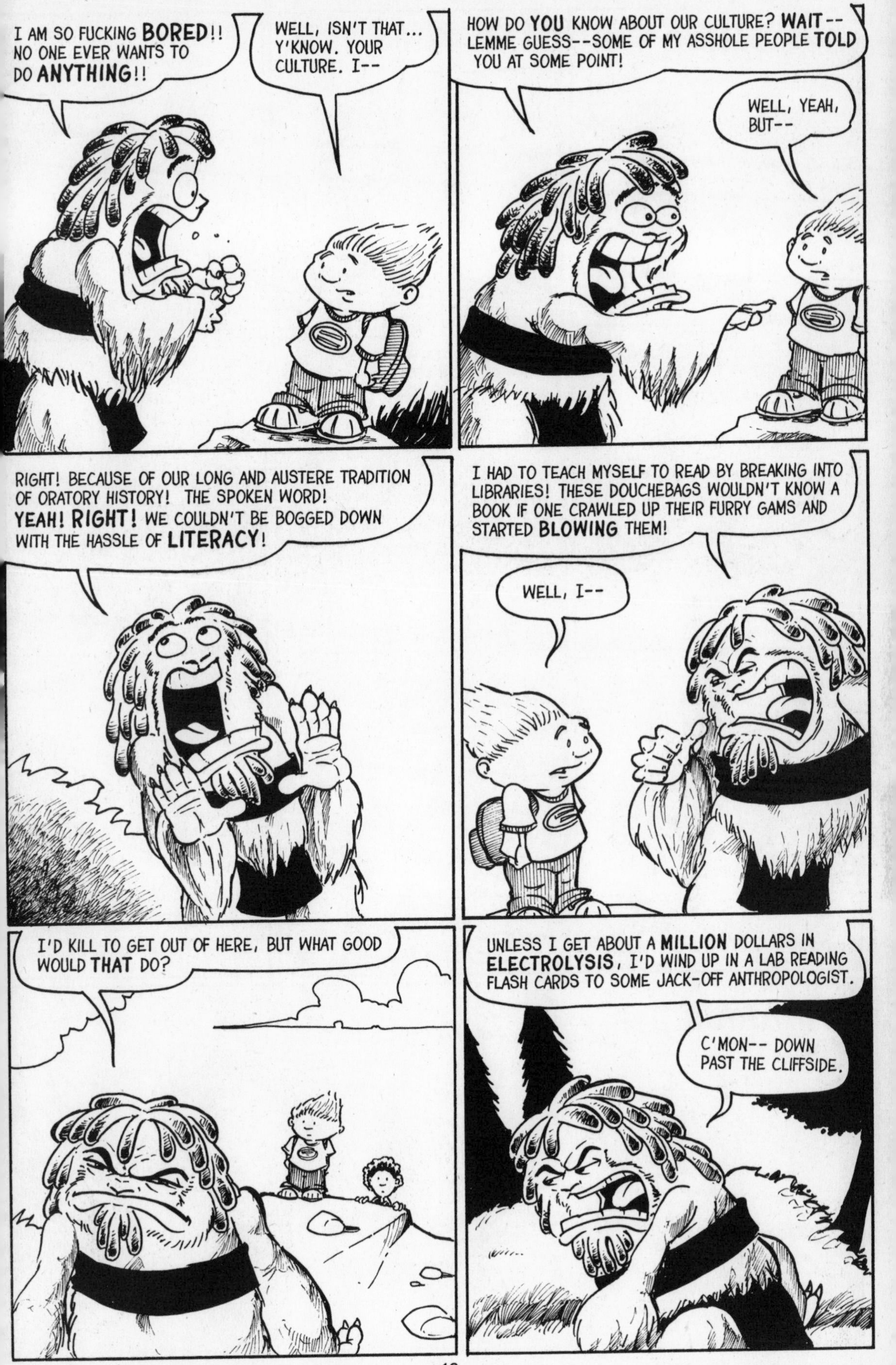
I AM SO FUCKING BORED!! NO ONE EVER WANTS TO DO ANYTHING!!
WELL, ISN'T THAT... Y'KNOW. YOUR CULTURE. I--
HOW DO YOU KNOW ABOUT OUR CULTURE? WAIT-- LEMME GUESS--SOME OF MY ASSHOLE PEOPLE TOLD YOU AT SOME POINT!
WELL, YEAH, BUT--
RIGHT! BECAUSE OF OUR LONG AND AUSTERE TRADITION OF ORATORY HISTORY! THE SPOKEN WORD! YEAH! RIGHT! WE COULDN'T BE BOGGED DOWN WITH THE HASSLE OF LITERACY!
I HAD TO TEACH MYSELF TO READ BY BREAKING INTO LIBRARIES! THESE DOUCHEBAGS WOULDN'T KNOW A BOOK IF ONE CRAWLED UP THEIR FURRY GAMS AND STARTED BLOWING THEM!
WELL, I--
I'D KILL TO GET OUT OF HERE, BUT WHAT GOOD WOULD THAT DO?
UNLESS I GET ABOUT A MILLION DOLLARS IN ELECTROLYSIS, I'D WIND UP IN A LAB READING FLASH CARDS TO SOME JACK-OFF ANTHROPOLOGIST.
C'MON-- DOWN PAST THE CLIFFSIDE.

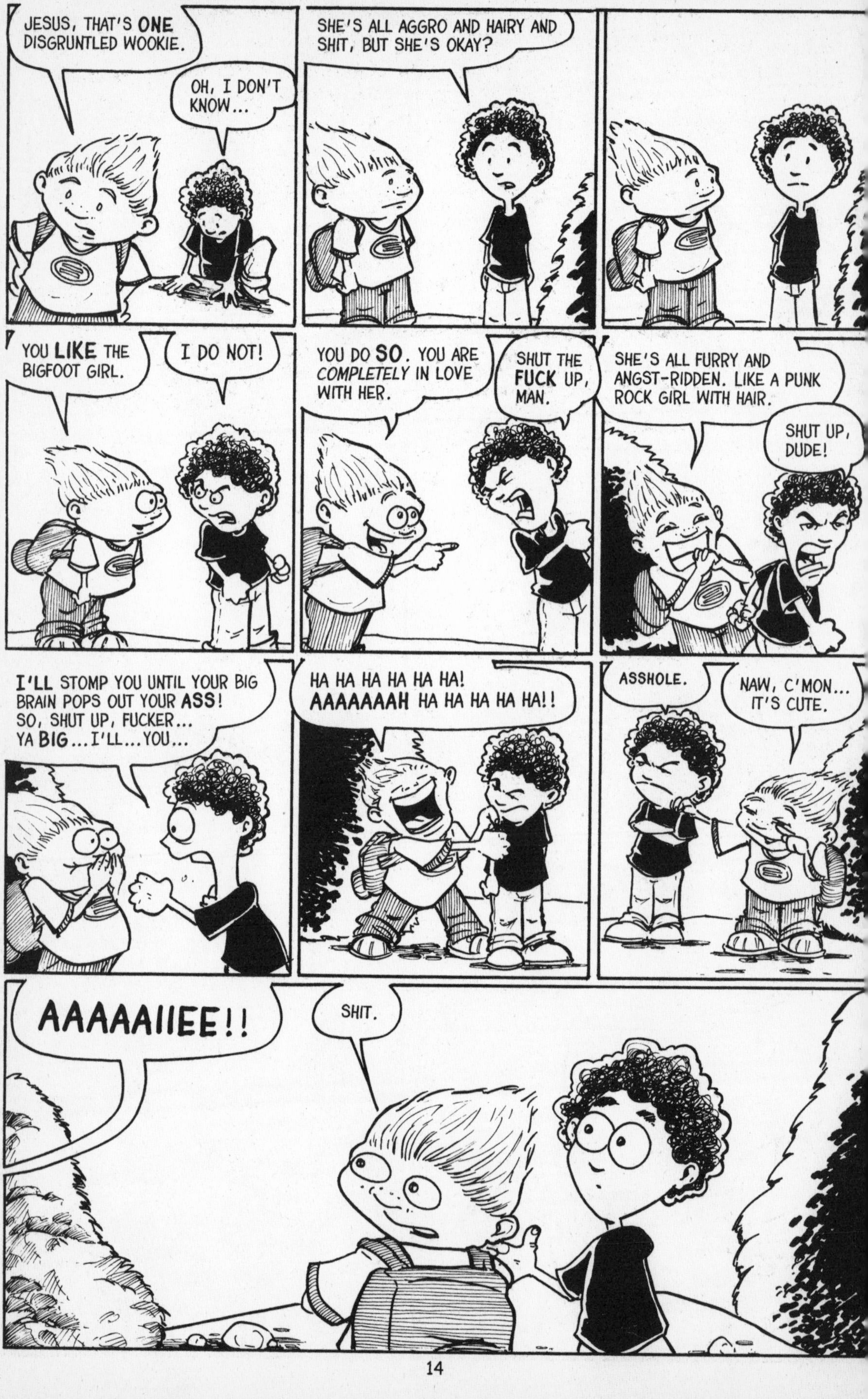
JESUS, THAT'S ONE DISGRUNTLED WOOKIE.
OH, I DON'T KNOW...
SHE'S ALL AGGRO AND HAIRY AND SHIT, BUT SHE'S OKAY?
YOU LIKE THE BIGFOOT GIRL.
I DO NOT!
YOU DO SO. YOU ARE COMPLETELY IN LOVE WITH HER.
SHUT THE FUCK UP, MAN.
SHE'S ALL FURRY AND ANGST-RIDDEN. LIKE A PUNK ROCK GIRL WITH HAIR.
SHUT UP, DUDE!
I'LL STOMP YOU UNTIL YOUR BIG BRAIN POPS OUT YOUR ASS! SO, SHUT UP, FUCKER... YA BIG... I'LL... YOU...
HA HA HA HA HA HA! AAAAAAAH HA HA HA HA HA!!
ASSHOLE.
NAW, C'MON... IT'S CUTE.
AAAAAIIEE!!
SHIT.

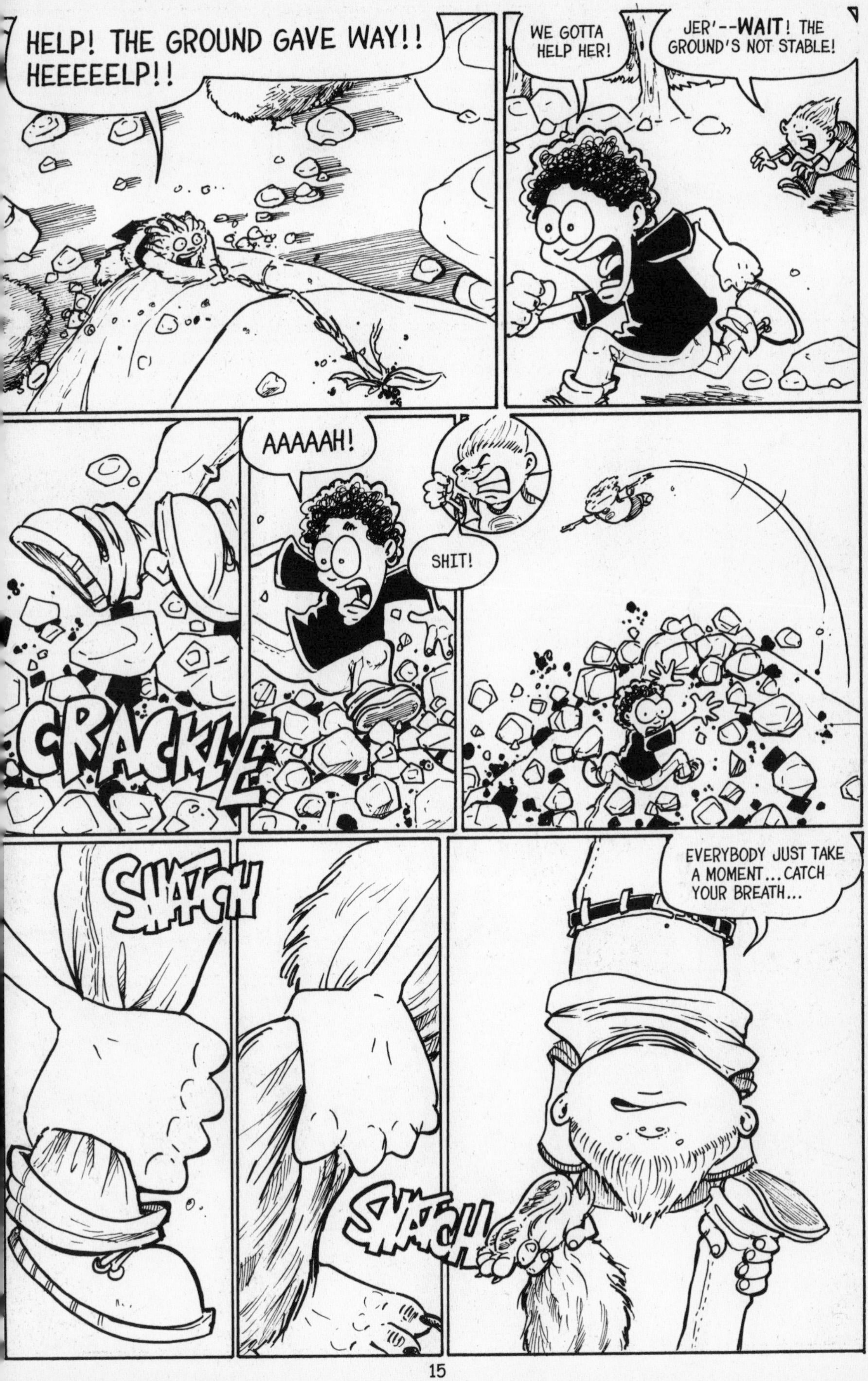
HELP! THE GROUND GAVE WAY!!
HEEEEELP!!
WE GOTTA HELP HER!
JER'--WAIT! THE GROUND'S NOT STABLE!
AAAAAH!
SHIT!
CRACKLE
SNATCH
SNATCH
EVERYBODY JUST TAKE A MOMENT...CATCH YOUR BREATH...

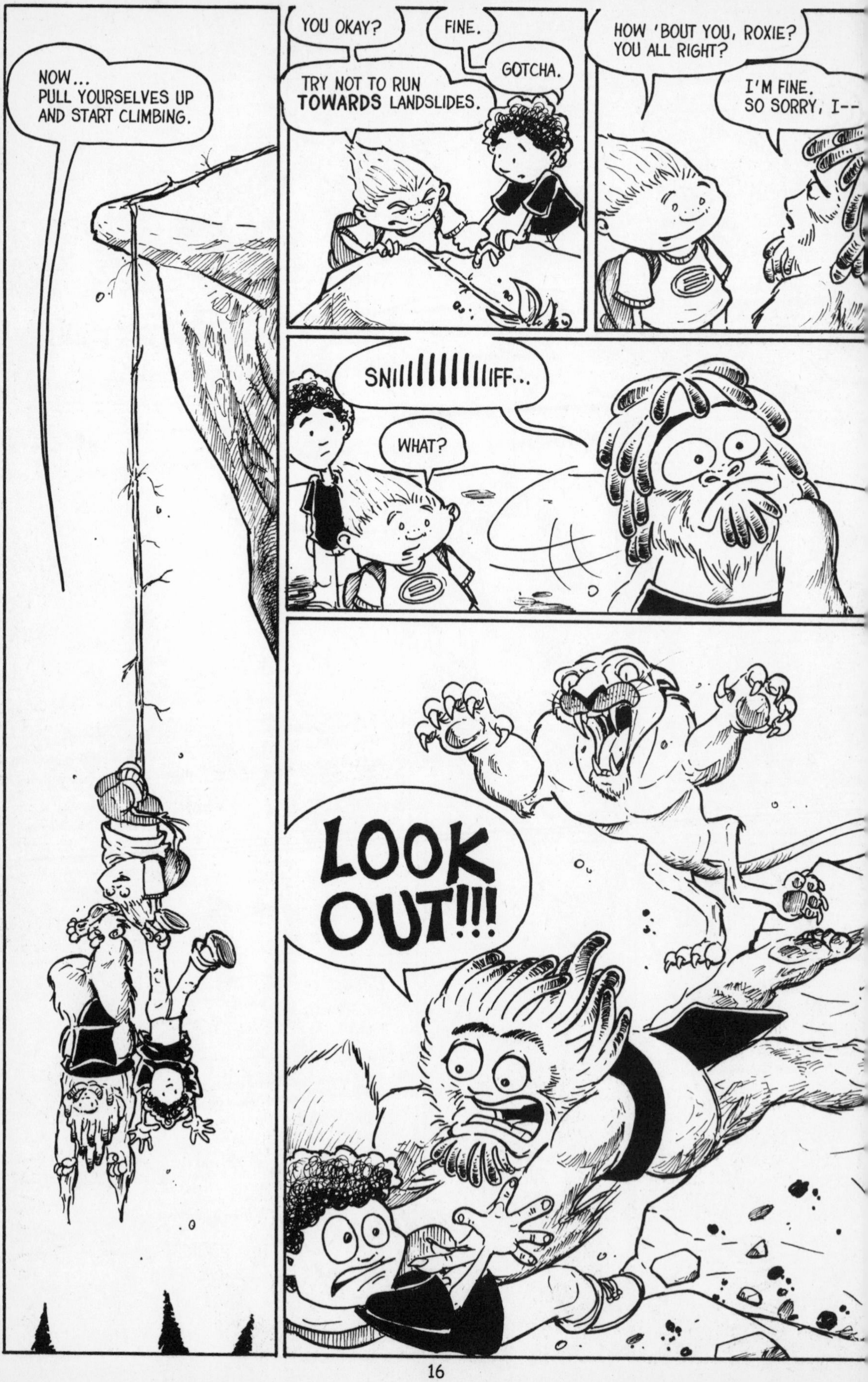
NOW... PULL YOURSELVES UP AND START CLIMBING.
YOU OKAY?
FINE.
TRY NOT TO RUN **TOWARDS** LANDSLIDES.
GOTCHA.
HOW 'BOUT YOU, ROXIE? YOU ALL RIGHT?
I'M FINE. SO SORRY, I--
SNIIIIIIIIIIIFF...
WHAT?
LOOK OUT!!!

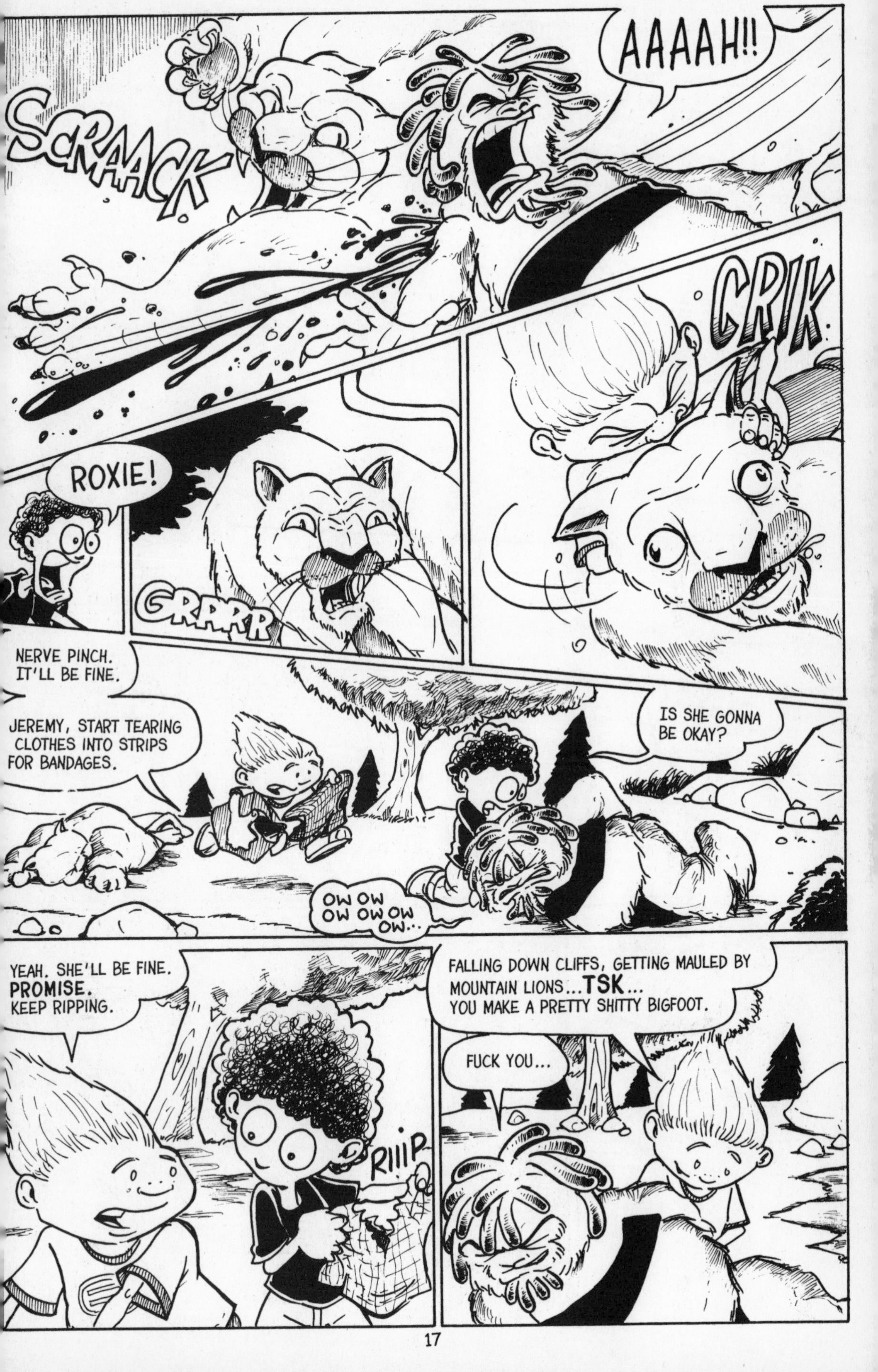
SCRAAACK
AAAAH!!
CRIK
ROXIE!
GRRRR
NERVE PINCH. IT'LL BE FINE.
JEREMY, START TEARING CLOTHES INTO STRIPS FOR BANDAGES.
IS SHE GONNA BE OKAY?
OW OW OW OW OW OW...
YEAH. SHE'LL BE FINE. PROMISE. KEEP RIPPING.
RIIIP
FALLING DOWN CLIFFS, GETTING MAULED BY MOUNTAIN LIONS...TSK... YOU MAKE A PRETTY SHITTY BIGFOOT.
FUCK YOU...

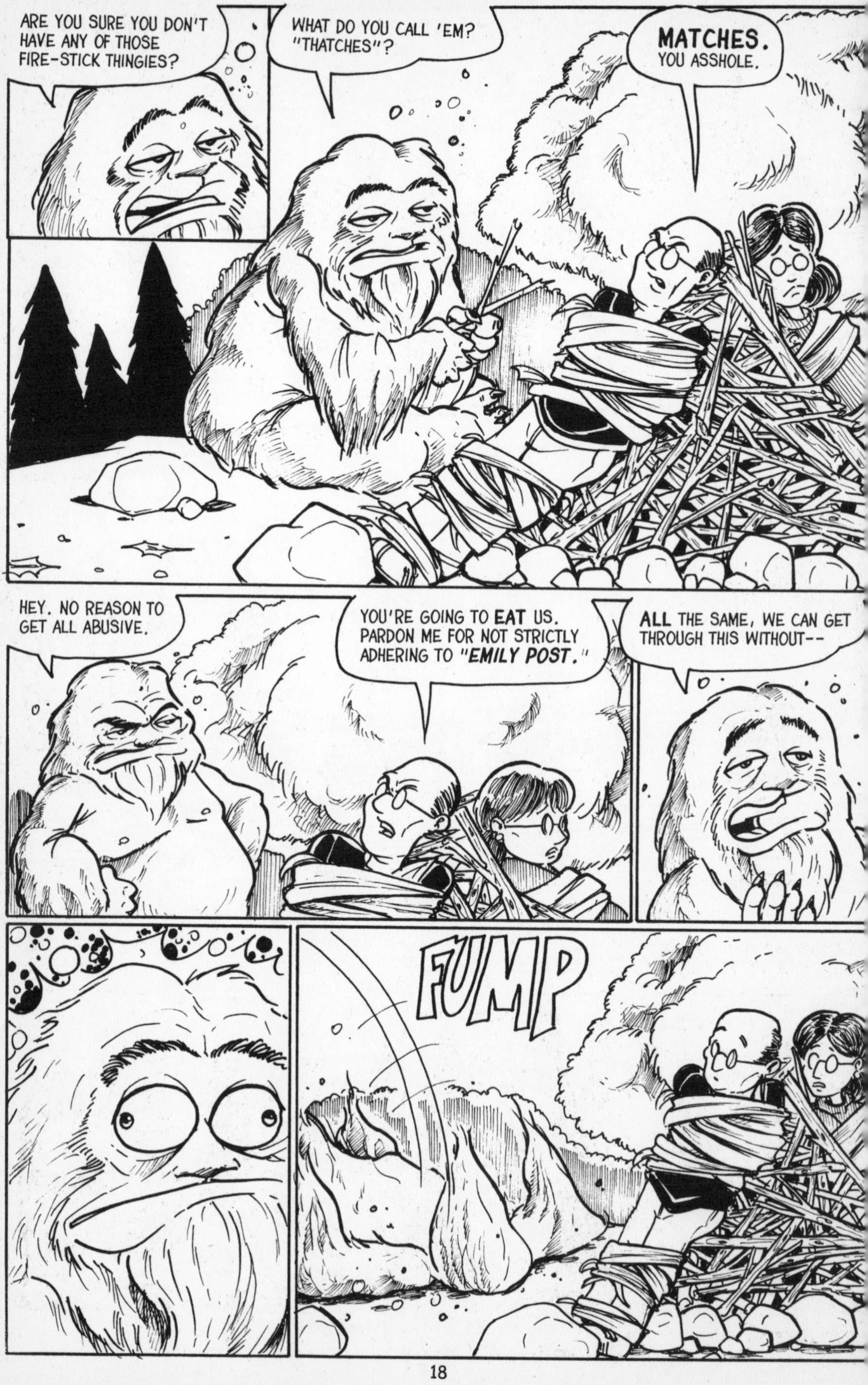
ARE YOU SURE YOU DON'T HAVE ANY OF THOSE FIRE-STICK THINGIES?
WHAT DO YOU CALL 'EM? "THATCHES"?
MATCHES. YOU ASSHOLE.
HEY. NO REASON TO GET ALL ABUSIVE.
YOU'RE GOING TO EAT US. PARDON ME FOR NOT STRICTLY ADHERING TO "EMILY POST."
ALL THE SAME, WE CAN GET THROUGH THIS WITHOUT--
FUMP

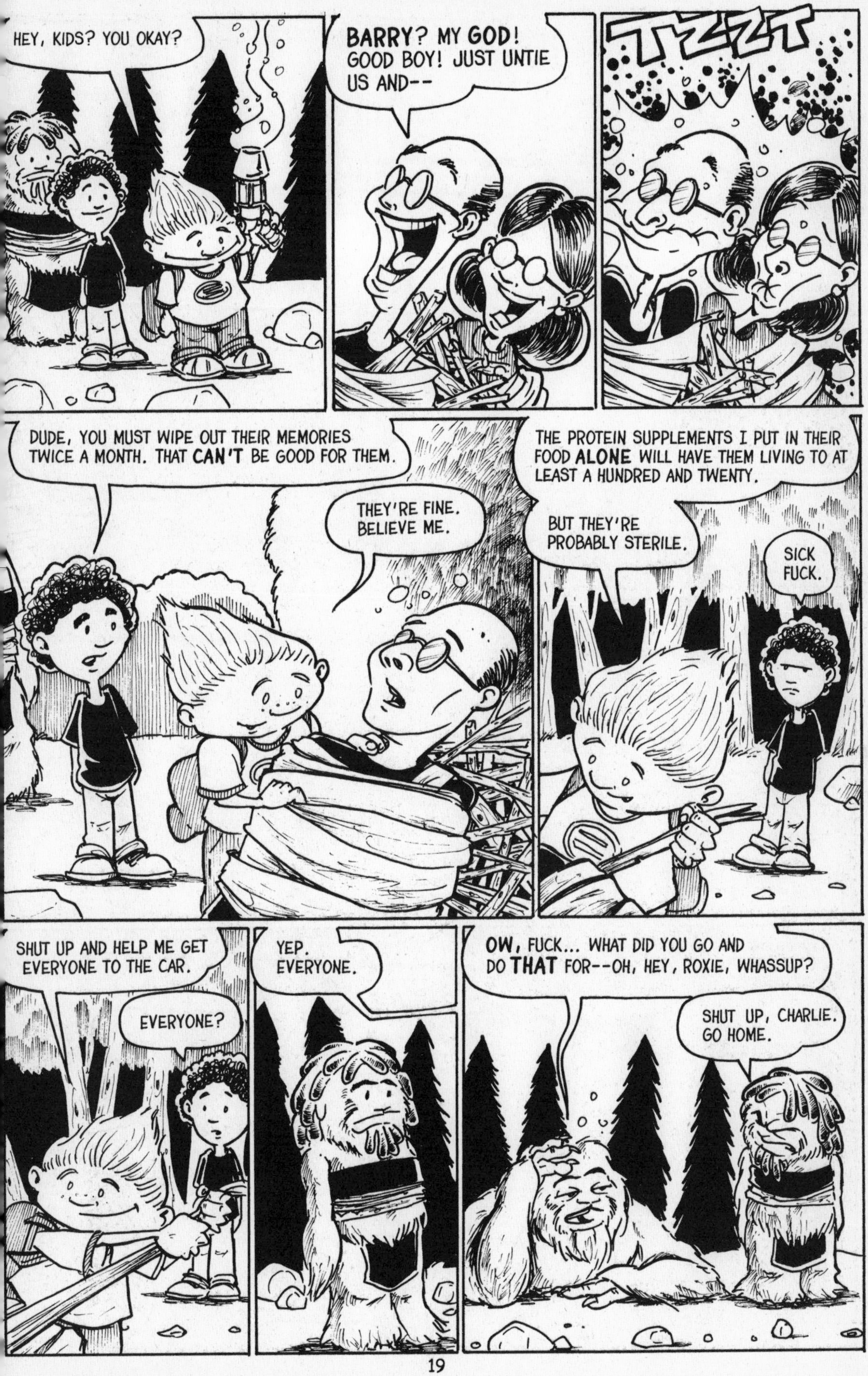
HEY, KIDS? YOU OKAY?
BARRY? MY GOD! GOOD BOY! JUST UNTIE US AND--
TZZZT
DUDE, YOU MUST WIPE OUT THEIR MEMORIES TWICE A MONTH. THAT CAN'T BE GOOD FOR THEM.
THEY'RE FINE. BELIEVE ME.
THE PROTEIN SUPPLEMENTS I PUT IN THEIR FOOD ALONE WILL HAVE THEM LIVING TO AT LEAST A HUNDRED AND TWENTY.
BUT THEY'RE PROBABLY STERILE.
SICK FUCK.
SHUT UP AND HELP ME GET EVERYONE TO THE CAR.
EVERYONE?
YEP. EVERYONE.
OW, FUCK... WHAT DID YOU GO AND DO THAT FOR--OH, HEY, ROXIE, WHASSUP?
SHUT UP, CHARLIE. GO HOME.

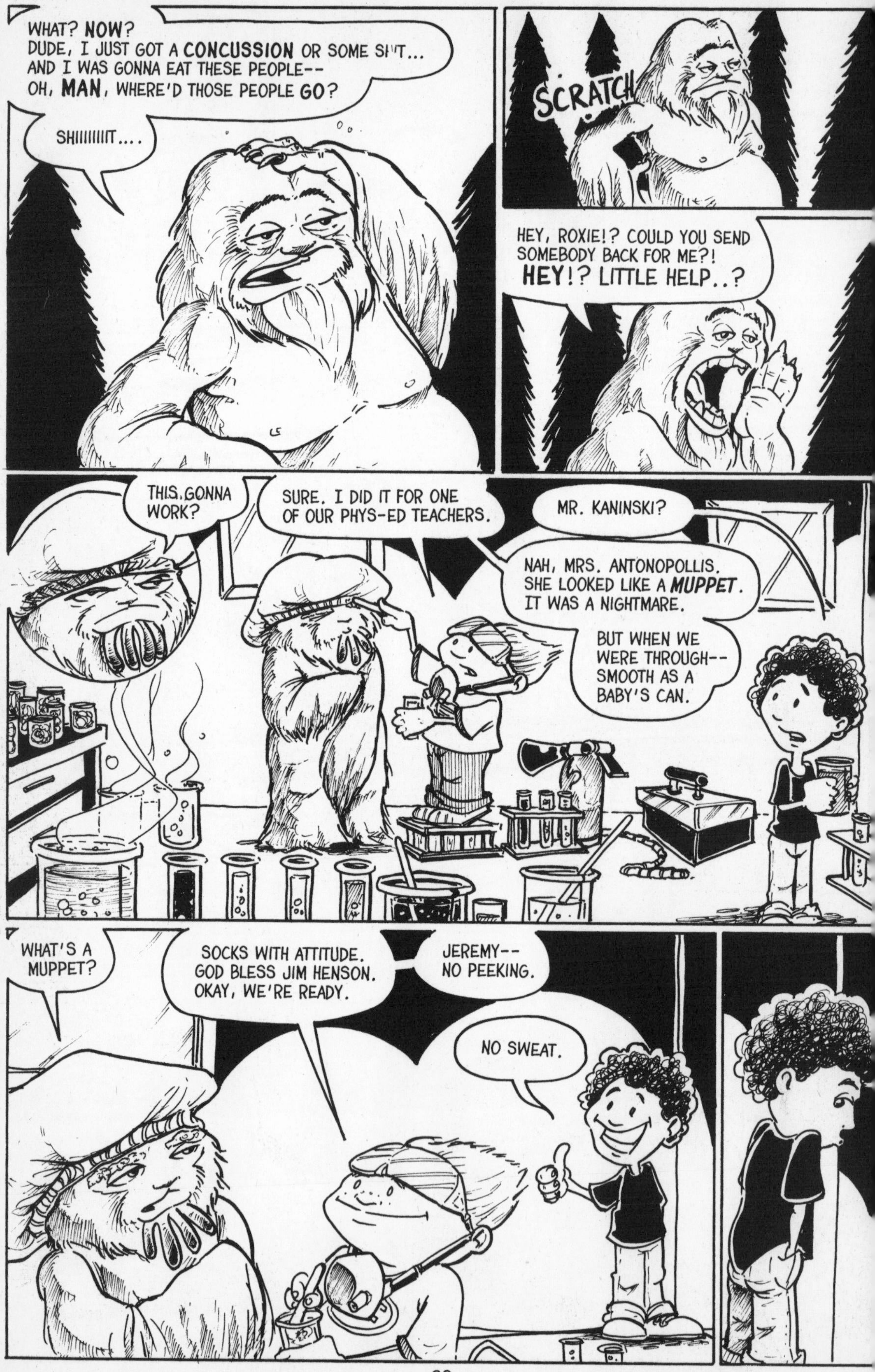
WHAT? NOW?
DUDE, I JUST GOT A CONCUSSION OR SOME SH*T... AND I WAS GONNA EAT THESE PEOPLE-- OH, MAN, WHERE'D THOSE PEOPLE GO?
SHIIIIIIIT....
SCRATCH
HEY, ROXIE!? COULD YOU SEND SOMEBODY BACK FOR ME?! HEY!? LITTLE HELP..?
THIS GONNA WORK?
SURE. I DID IT FOR ONE OF OUR PHYS-ED TEACHERS.
MR. KANINSKI?
NAH, MRS. ANTONOPOLLIS. SHE LOOKED LIKE A MUPPET. IT WAS A NIGHTMARE.
BUT WHEN WE WERE THROUGH-- SMOOTH AS A BABY'S CAN.
WHAT'S A MUPPET?
SOCKS WITH ATTITUDE. GOD BLESS JIM HENSON. OKAY, WE'RE READY.
JEREMY-- NO PEEKING.
NO SWEAT.

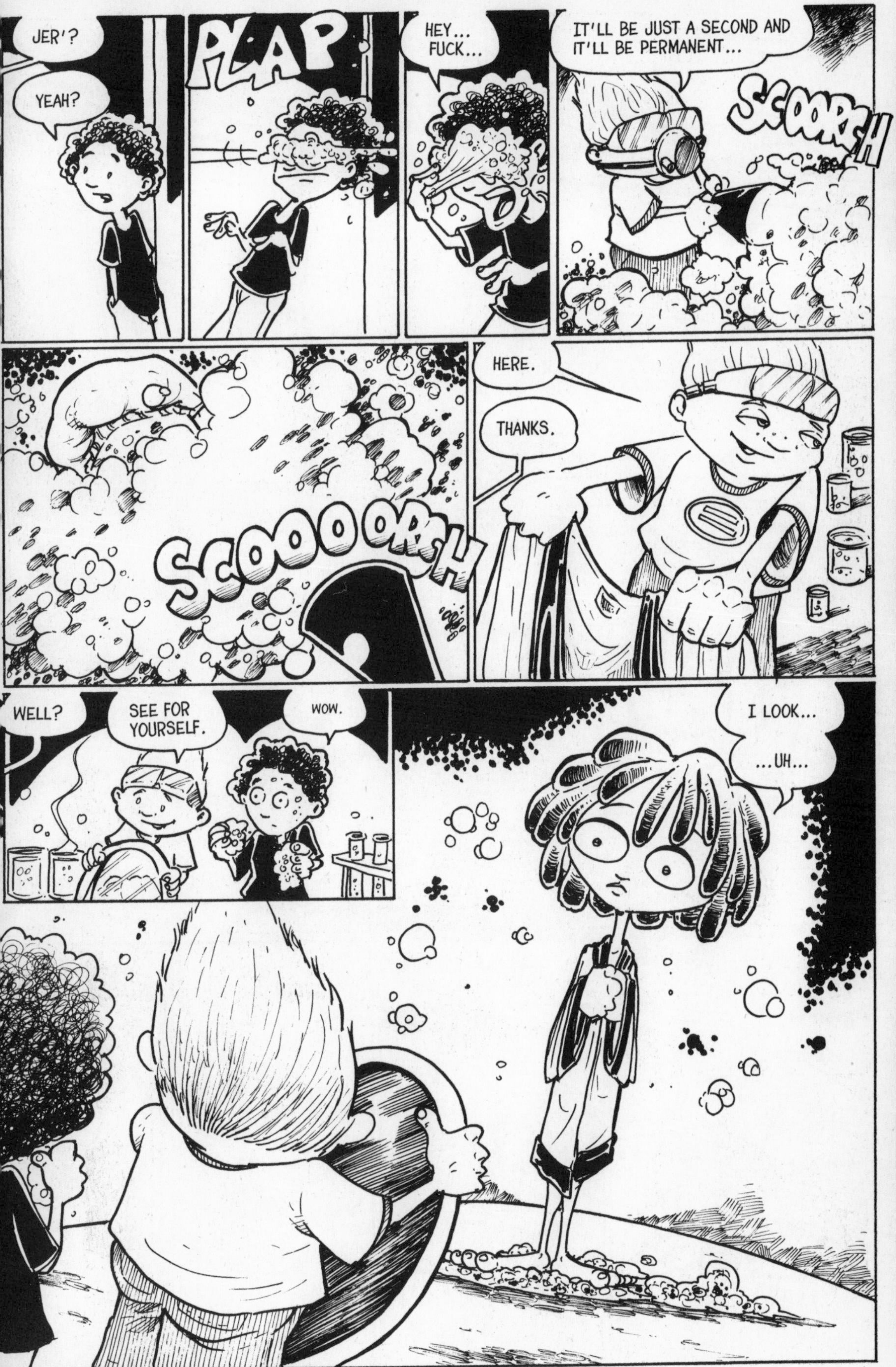
JER'?
YEAH?
PLAP
HEY... FUCK...
IT'LL BE JUST A SECOND AND IT'LL BE PERMANENT...
SCOORCH
SCOOOORSH
HERE.
THANKS.
WELL?
SEE FOR YOURSELF.
WOW.
I LOOK...
...UH...

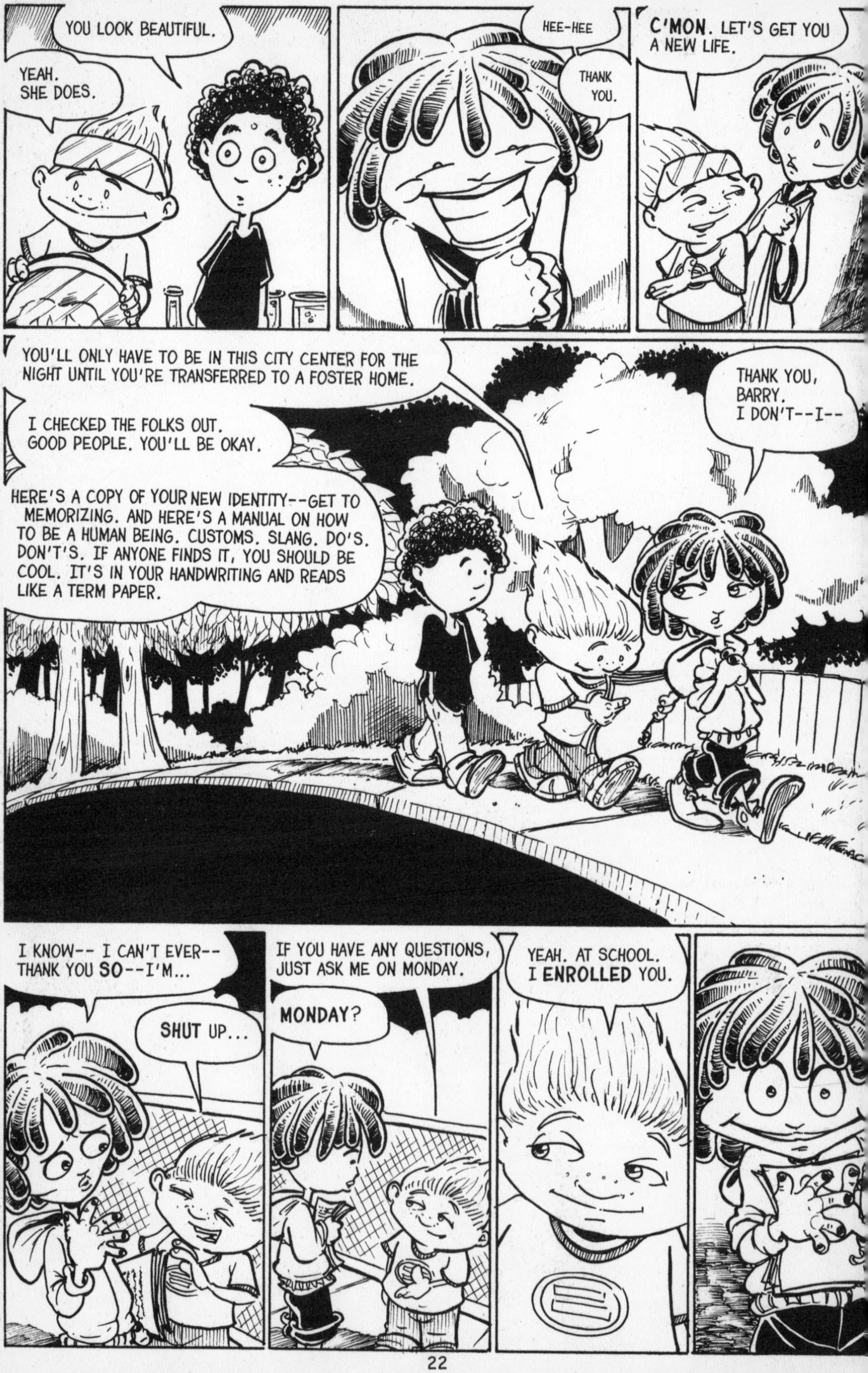
YOU LOOK BEAUTIFUL.
YEAH. SHE DOES.
HEE-HEE
THANK YOU.
C'MON. LET'S GET YOU A NEW LIFE.
YOU'LL ONLY HAVE TO BE IN THIS CITY CENTER FOR THE NIGHT UNTIL YOU'RE TRANSFERRED TO A FOSTER HOME.
I CHECKED THE FOLKS OUT. GOOD PEOPLE. YOU'LL BE OKAY.
HERE'S A COPY OF YOUR NEW IDENTITY--GET TO MEMORIZING. AND HERE'S A MANUAL ON HOW TO BE A HUMAN BEING. CUSTOMS. SLANG. DO'S. DON'T'S. IF ANYONE FINDS IT, YOU SHOULD BE COOL. IT'S IN YOUR HANDWRITING AND READS LIKE A TERM PAPER.
THANK YOU, BARRY. I DON'T--I--
I KNOW-- I CAN'T EVER-- THANK YOU SO--I'M...
SHUT UP...
IF YOU HAVE ANY QUESTIONS, JUST ASK ME ON MONDAY.
MONDAY?
YEAH. AT SCHOOL. I ENROLLED YOU.

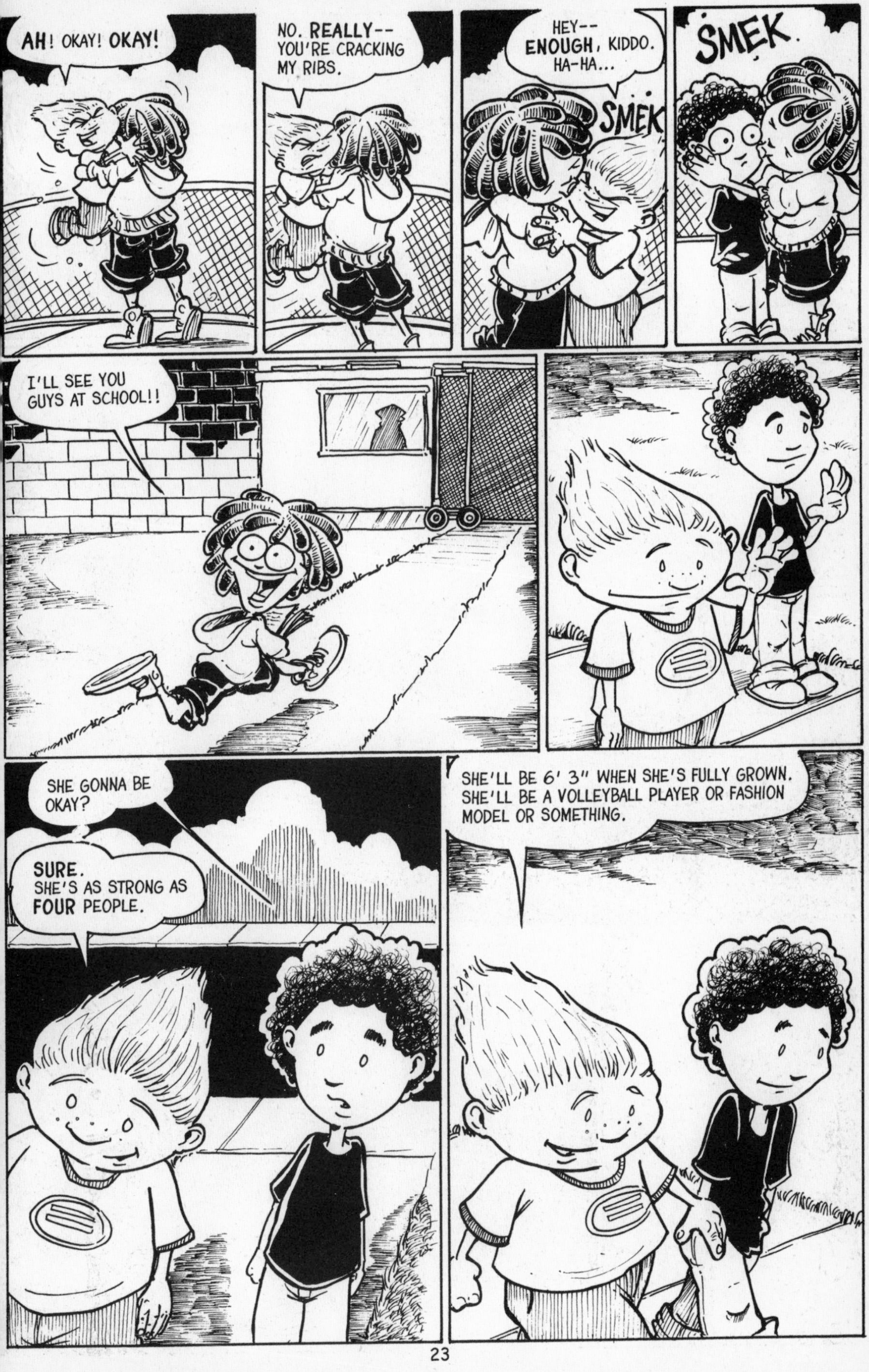
AH! OKAY! OKAY!
NO. REALLY-- YOU'RE CRACKING MY RIBS.
HEY-- ENOUGH, KIDDO. HA-HA...
SMEK
SMEK
I'LL SEE YOU GUYS AT SCHOOL!!
SHE GONNA BE OKAY?
SURE. SHE'S AS STRONG AS FOUR PEOPLE.
SHE'LL BE 6' 3" WHEN SHE'S FULLY GROWN. SHE'LL BE A VOLLEYBALL PLAYER OR FASHION MODEL OR SOMETHING.

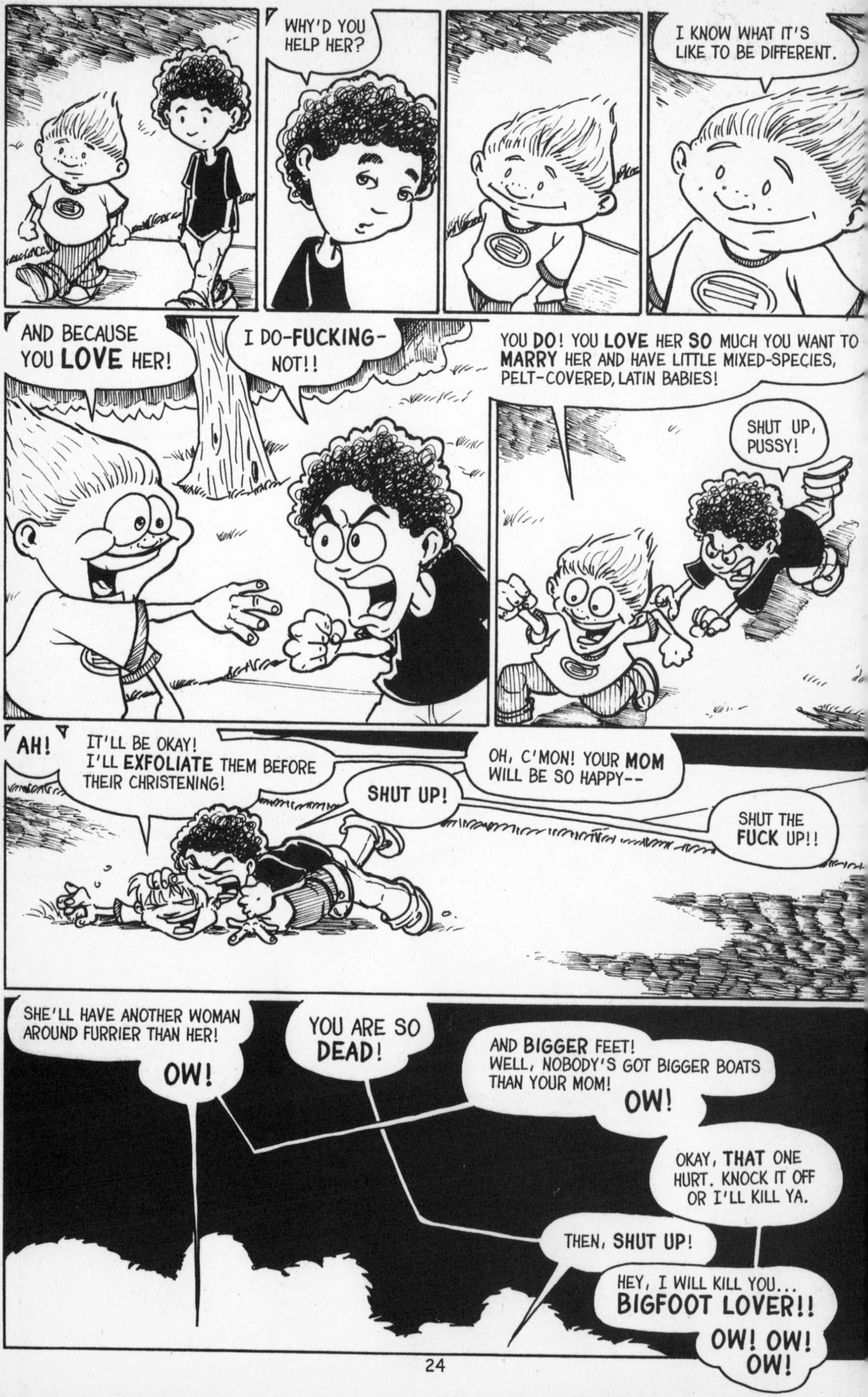
WHY'D YOU HELP HER?
I KNOW WHAT IT'S LIKE TO BE DIFFERENT.
AND BECAUSE YOU LOVE HER!
I DO-FUCKING-NOT!!
YOU DO! YOU LOVE HER SO MUCH YOU WANT TO MARRY HER AND HAVE LITTLE MIXED-SPECIES, PELT-COVERED, LATIN BABIES!
SHUT UP, PUSSY!
AH!
IT'LL BE OKAY! I'LL EXFOLIATE THEM BEFORE THEIR CHRISTENING!
OH, C'MON! YOUR MOM WILL BE SO HAPPY--
SHUT UP!
SHUT THE FUCK UP!!
SHE'LL HAVE ANOTHER WOMAN AROUND FURRIER THAN HER!
OW!
YOU ARE SO DEAD!
AND BIGGER FEET! WELL, NOBODY'S GOT BIGGER BOATS THAN YOUR MOM!
OW!
OKAY, THAT ONE HURT. KNOCK IT OFF OR I'LL KILL YA.
THEN, SHUT UP!
HEY, I WILL KILL YOU... BIGFOOT LOVER!!
OW! OW! OW!

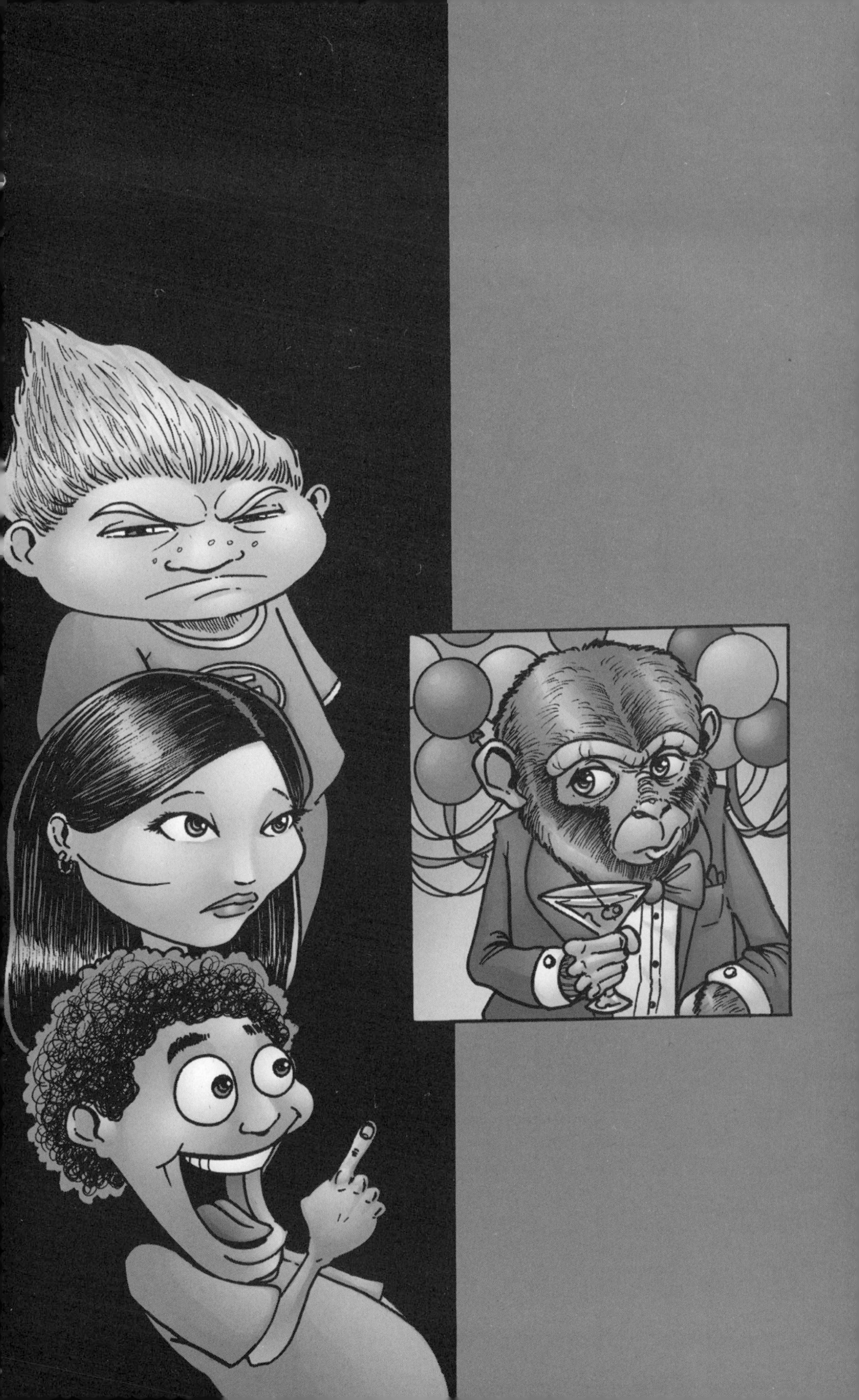

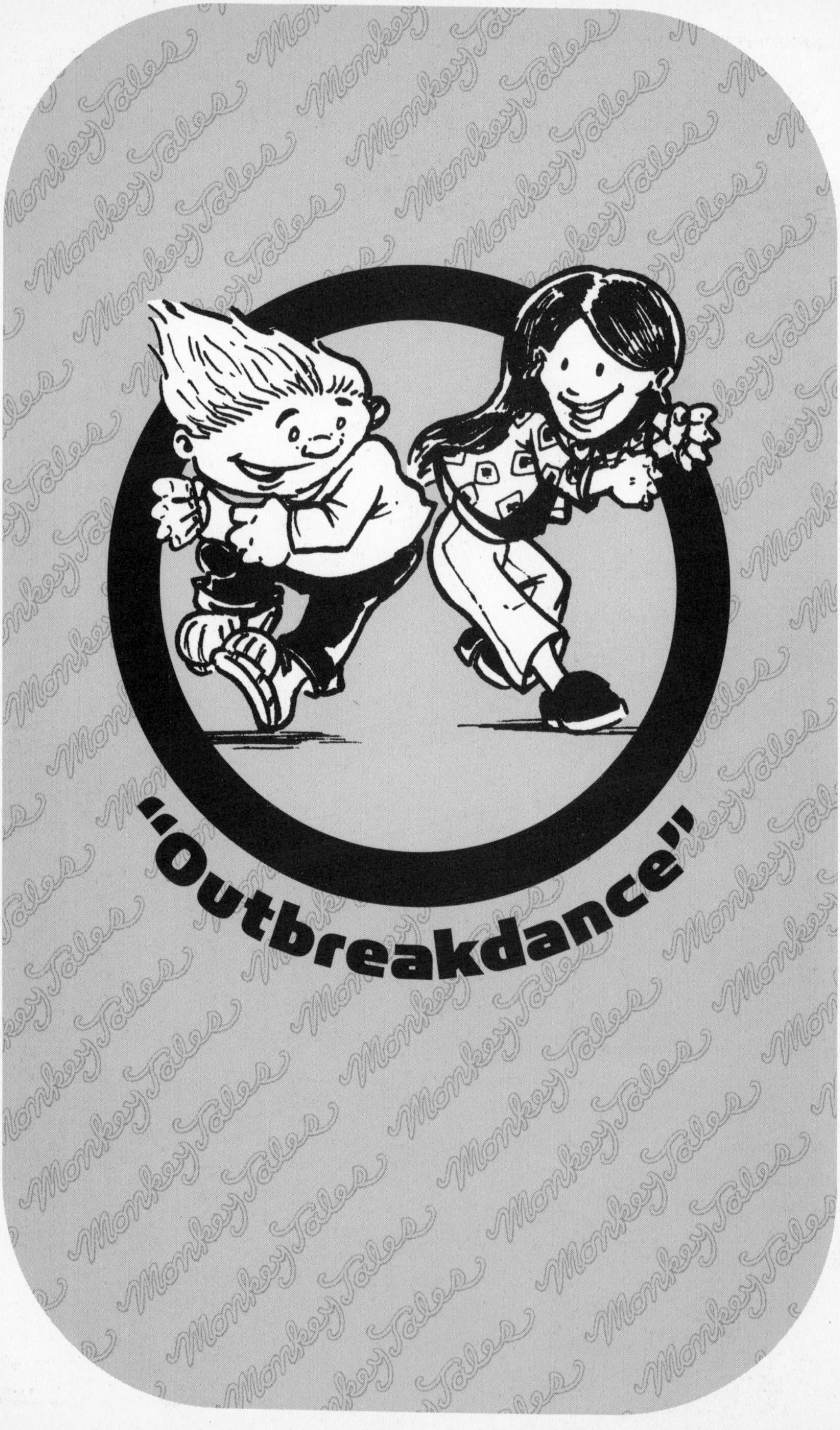
"Outbreakdance"

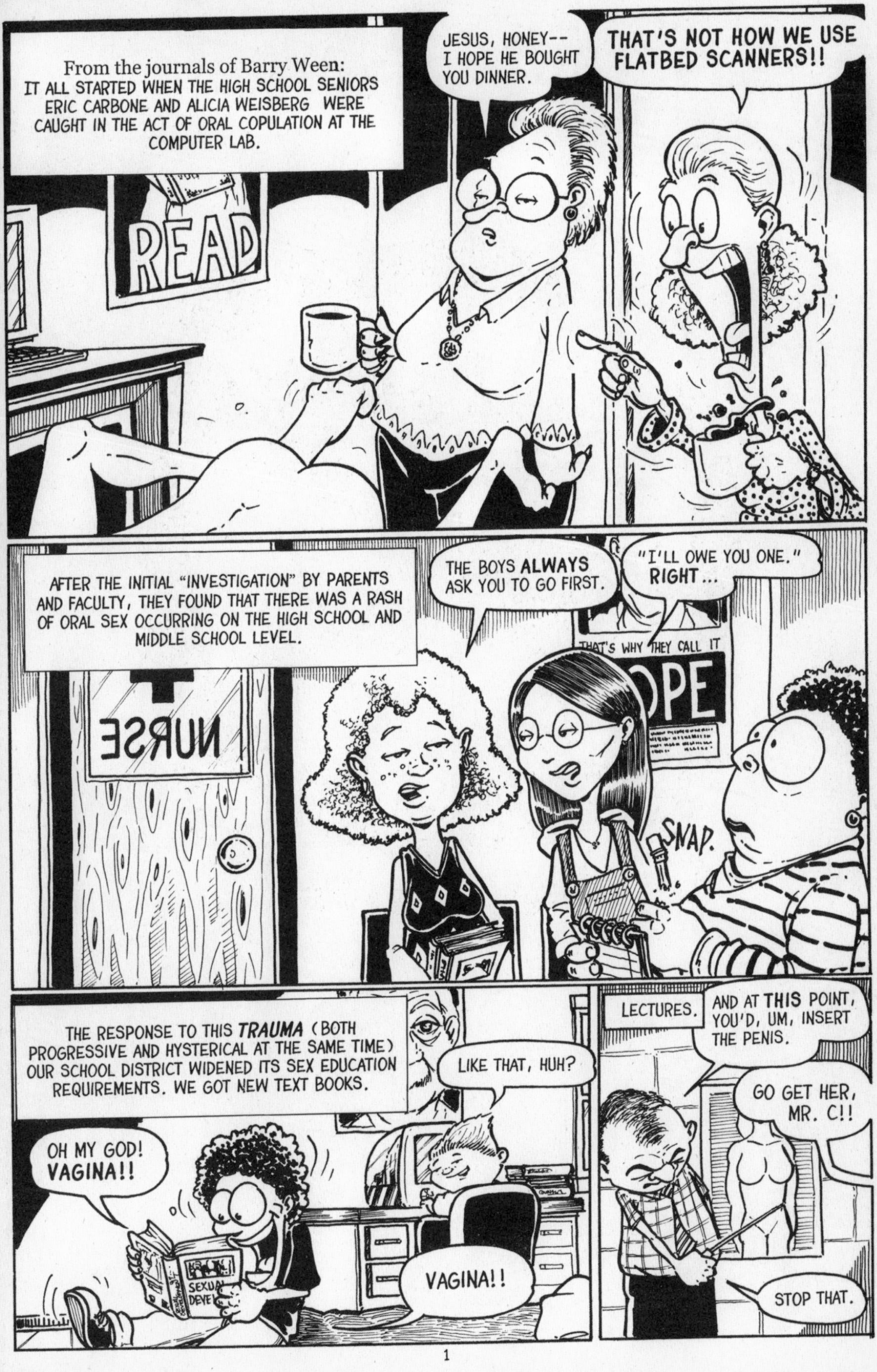
From the journals of Barry Ween:
IT ALL STARTED WHEN THE HIGH SCHOOL SENIORS ERIC CARBONE AND ALICIA WEISBERG WERE CAUGHT IN THE ACT OF ORAL COPULATION AT THE COMPUTER LAB.
READ
JESUS, HONEY-- I HOPE HE BOUGHT YOU DINNER.
THAT'S NOT HOW WE USE FLATBED SCANNERS!!
AFTER THE INITIAL "INVESTIGATION" BY PARENTS AND FACULTY, THEY FOUND THAT THERE WAS A RASH OF ORAL SEX OCCURRING ON THE HIGH SCHOOL AND MIDDLE SCHOOL LEVEL.
NURSE
THE BOYS ALWAYS ASK YOU TO GO FIRST.
"I'LL OWE YOU ONE." RIGHT...
THAT'S WHY THEY CALL IT
OPE
SNAP.
THE RESPONSE TO THIS TRAUMA (BOTH PROGRESSIVE AND HYSTERICAL AT THE SAME TIME) OUR SCHOOL DISTRICT WIDENED ITS SEX EDUCATION REQUIREMENTS. WE GOT NEW TEXT BOOKS.
LIKE THAT, HUH?
OH MY GOD! VAGINA!!
SEXUAL DEVE
VAGINA!!
LECTURES.
AND AT THIS POINT, YOU'D, UM, INSERT THE PENIS.
GO GET HER, MR. C!!
STOP THAT.

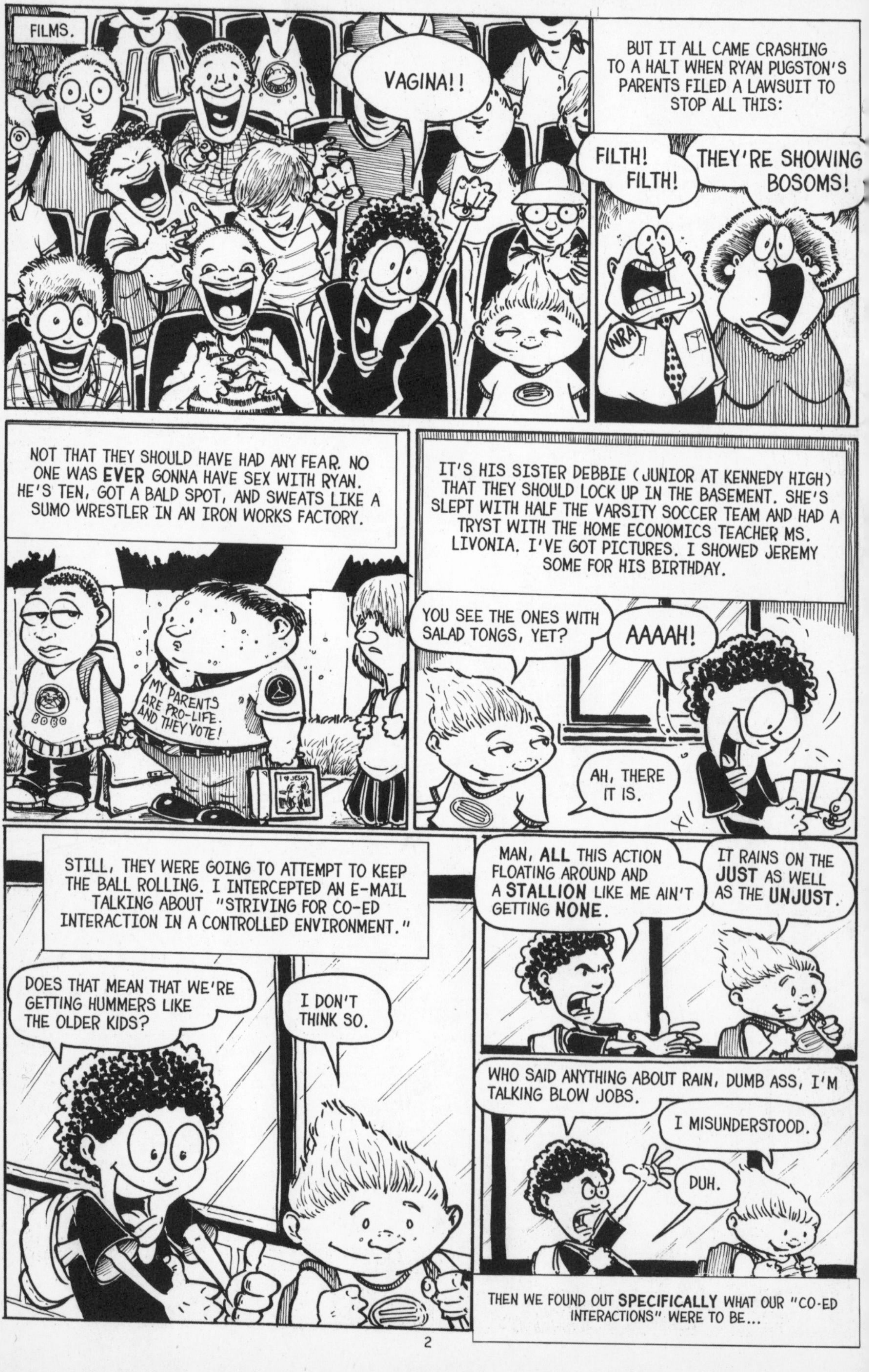
FILMS.
VAGINA!!
BUT IT ALL CAME CRASHING TO A HALT WHEN RYAN PUGSTON'S PARENTS FILED A LAWSUIT TO STOP ALL THIS:
FILTH! FILTH!
THEY'RE SHOWING BOSOMS!
NRA
NOT THAT THEY SHOULD HAVE HAD ANY FEAR. NO ONE WAS **EVER** GONNA HAVE SEX WITH RYAN. HE'S TEN, GOT A BALD SPOT, AND SWEATS LIKE A SUMO WRESTLER IN AN IRON WORKS FACTORY.
BOBO
MY PARENTS ARE PRO-LIFE. AND THEY VOTE!
I ♥ JESUS
IT'S HIS SISTER DEBBIE (JUNIOR AT KENNEDY HIGH) THAT THEY SHOULD LOCK UP IN THE BASEMENT. SHE'S SLEPT WITH HALF THE VARSITY SOCCER TEAM AND HAD A TRYST WITH THE HOME ECONOMICS TEACHER MS. LIVONIA. I'VE GOT PICTURES. I SHOWED JEREMY SOME FOR HIS BIRTHDAY.
YOU SEE THE ONES WITH SALAD TONGS, YET?
AAAAH!
AH, THERE IT IS.
STILL, THEY WERE GOING TO ATTEMPT TO KEEP THE BALL ROLLING. I INTERCEPTED AN E-MAIL TALKING ABOUT "STRIVING FOR CO-ED INTERACTION IN A CONTROLLED ENVIRONMENT."
DOES THAT MEAN THAT WE'RE GETTING HUMMERS LIKE THE OLDER KIDS?
I DON'T THINK SO.
MAN, **ALL** THIS ACTION FLOATING AROUND AND A **STALLION** LIKE ME AIN'T GETTING **NONE**.
IT RAINS ON THE **JUST** AS WELL AS THE **UNJUST**.
WHO SAID ANYTHING ABOUT RAIN, DUMB ASS, I'M TALKING BLOW JOBS.
I MISUNDERSTOOD.
DUH.
THEN WE FOUND OUT **SPECIFICALLY** WHAT OUR "CO-ED INTERACTIONS" WERE TO BE...

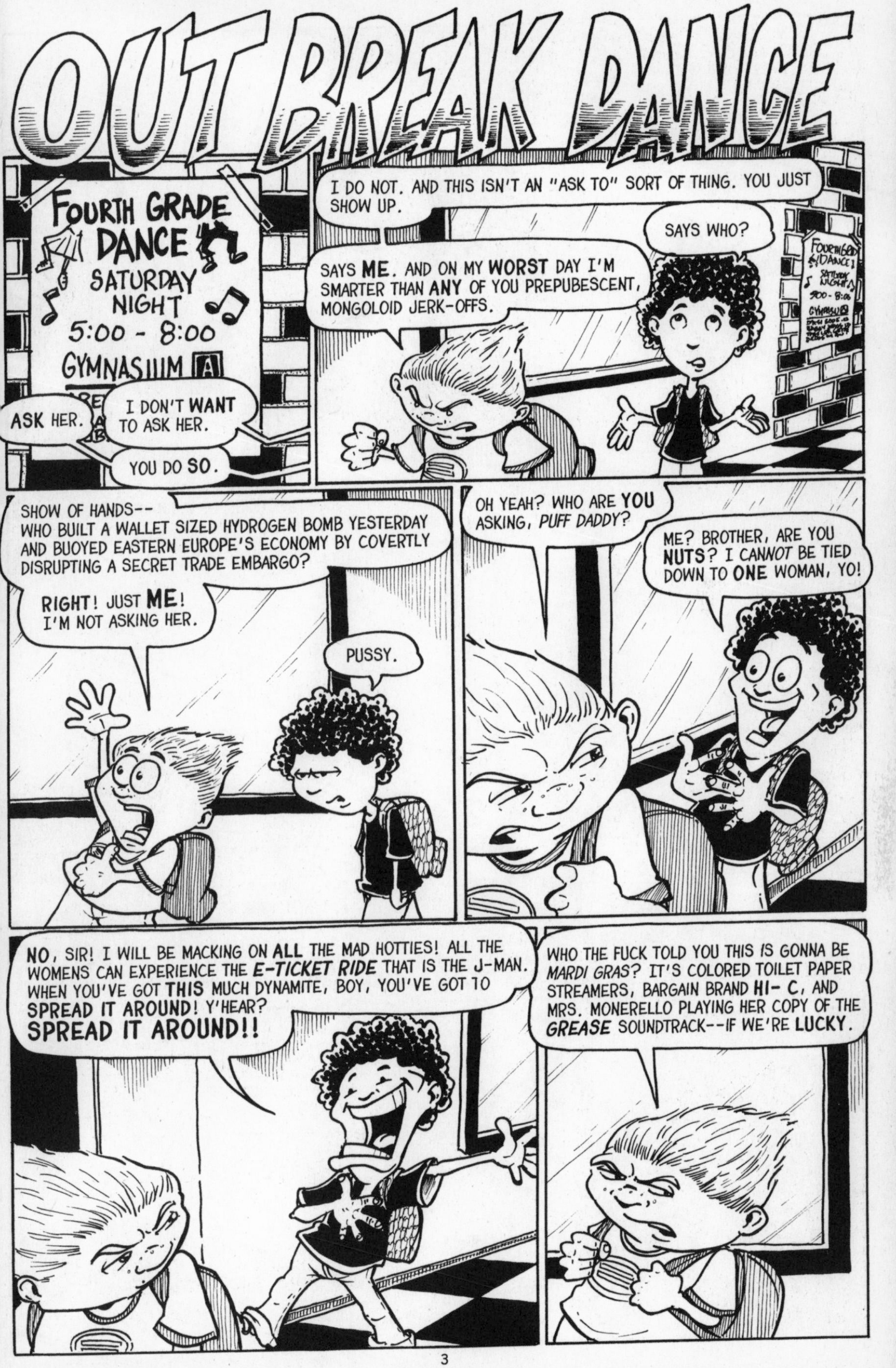
OUT BREAK DANCE
FOURTH GRADE DANCE SATURDAY NIGHT 5:00 - 8:00 GYMNASIUM A
ASK HER.
I DON'T WANT TO ASK HER.
YOU DO SO.
I DO NOT. AND THIS ISN'T AN "ASK TO" SORT OF THING. YOU JUST SHOW UP.
SAYS WHO?
SAYS ME. AND ON MY WORST DAY I'M SMARTER THAN ANY OF YOU PREPUBESCENT, MONGOLOID JERK-OFFS.
SHOW OF HANDS-- WHO BUILT A WALLET SIZED HYDROGEN BOMB YESTERDAY AND BUOYED EASTERN EUROPE'S ECONOMY BY COVERTLY DISRUPTING A SECRET TRADE EMBARGO?
RIGHT! JUST ME! I'M NOT ASKING HER.
PUSSY.
OH YEAH? WHO ARE YOU ASKING, PUFF DADDY?
ME? BROTHER, ARE YOU NUTS? I CANNOT BE TIED DOWN TO ONE WOMAN, YO!
NO, SIR! I WILL BE MACKING ON ALL THE MAD HOTTIES! ALL THE WOMENS CAN EXPERIENCE THE E-TICKET RIDE THAT IS THE J-MAN. WHEN YOU'VE GOT THIS MUCH DYNAMITE, BOY, YOU'VE GOT TO SPREAD IT AROUND! Y'HEAR? SPREAD IT AROUND!!
WHO THE FUCK TOLD YOU THIS IS GONNA BE MARDI GRAS? IT'S COLORED TOILET PAPER STREAMERS, BARGAIN BRAND HI- C, AND MRS. MONERELLO PLAYING HER COPY OF THE GREASE SOUNDTRACK--IF WE'RE LUCKY.

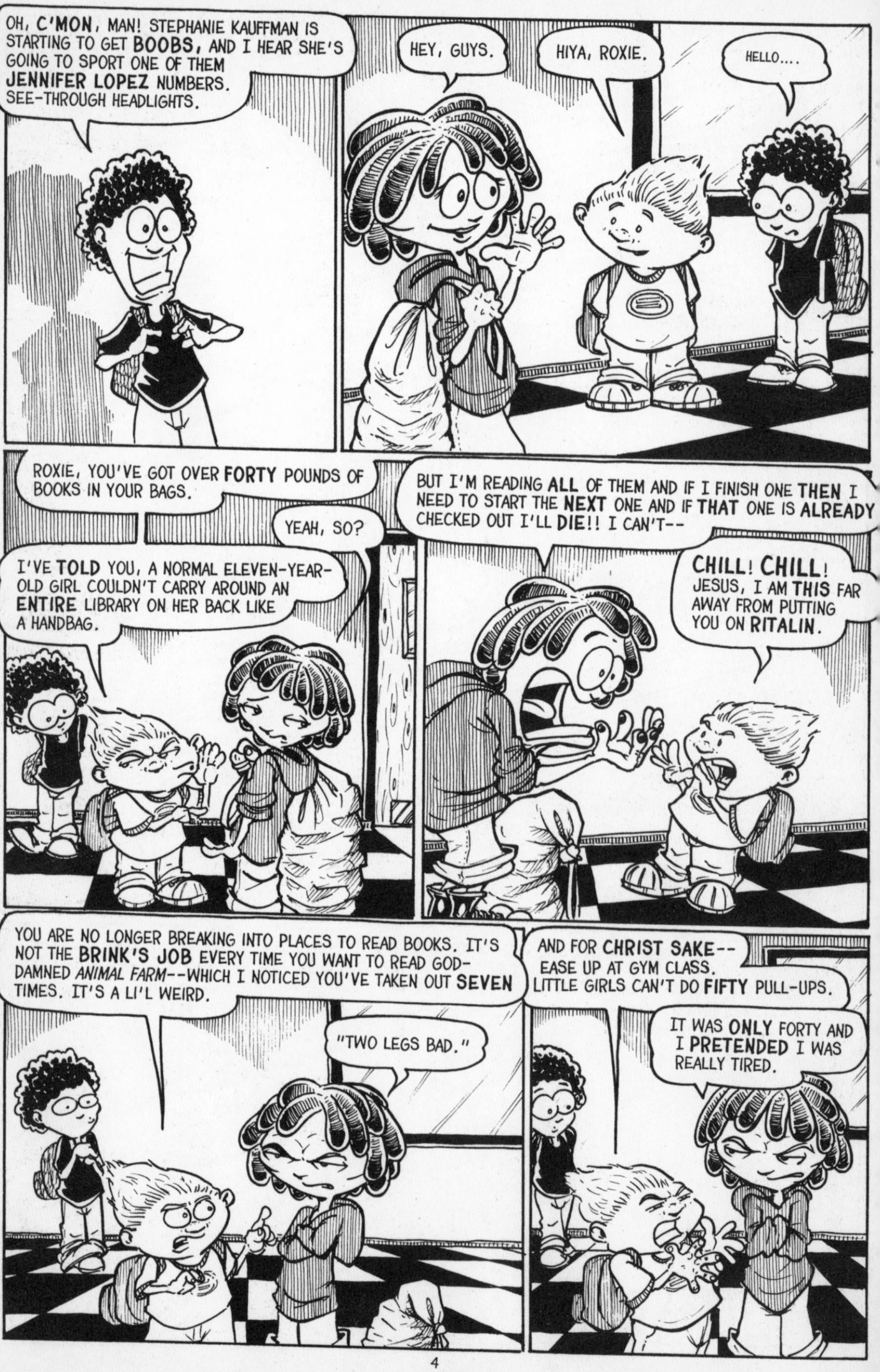
OH, C'MON, MAN! STEPHANIE KAUFFMAN IS STARTING TO GET BOOBS, AND I HEAR SHE'S GOING TO SPORT ONE OF THEM JENNIFER LOPEZ NUMBERS. SEE-THROUGH HEADLIGHTS.
HEY, GUYS.
HIYA, ROXIE.
HELLO....
ROXIE, YOU'VE GOT OVER FORTY POUNDS OF BOOKS IN YOUR BAGS.
YEAH, SO?
I'VE TOLD YOU, A NORMAL ELEVEN-YEAR-OLD GIRL COULDN'T CARRY AROUND AN ENTIRE LIBRARY ON HER BACK LIKE A HANDBAG.
BUT I'M READING ALL OF THEM AND IF I FINISH ONE THEN I NEED TO START THE NEXT ONE AND IF THAT ONE IS ALREADY CHECKED OUT I'LL DIE!! I CAN'T--
CHILL! CHILL! JESUS, I AM THIS FAR AWAY FROM PUTTING YOU ON RITALIN.
YOU ARE NO LONGER BREAKING INTO PLACES TO READ BOOKS. IT'S NOT THE BRINK'S JOB EVERY TIME YOU WANT TO READ GOD-DAMNED ANIMAL FARM--WHICH I NOTICED YOU'VE TAKEN OUT SEVEN TIMES. IT'S A LI'L WEIRD.
"TWO LEGS BAD."
AND FOR CHRIST SAKE-- EASE UP AT GYM CLASS. LITTLE GIRLS CAN'T DO FIFTY PULL-UPS.
IT WAS ONLY FORTY AND I PRETENDED I WAS REALLY TIRED.

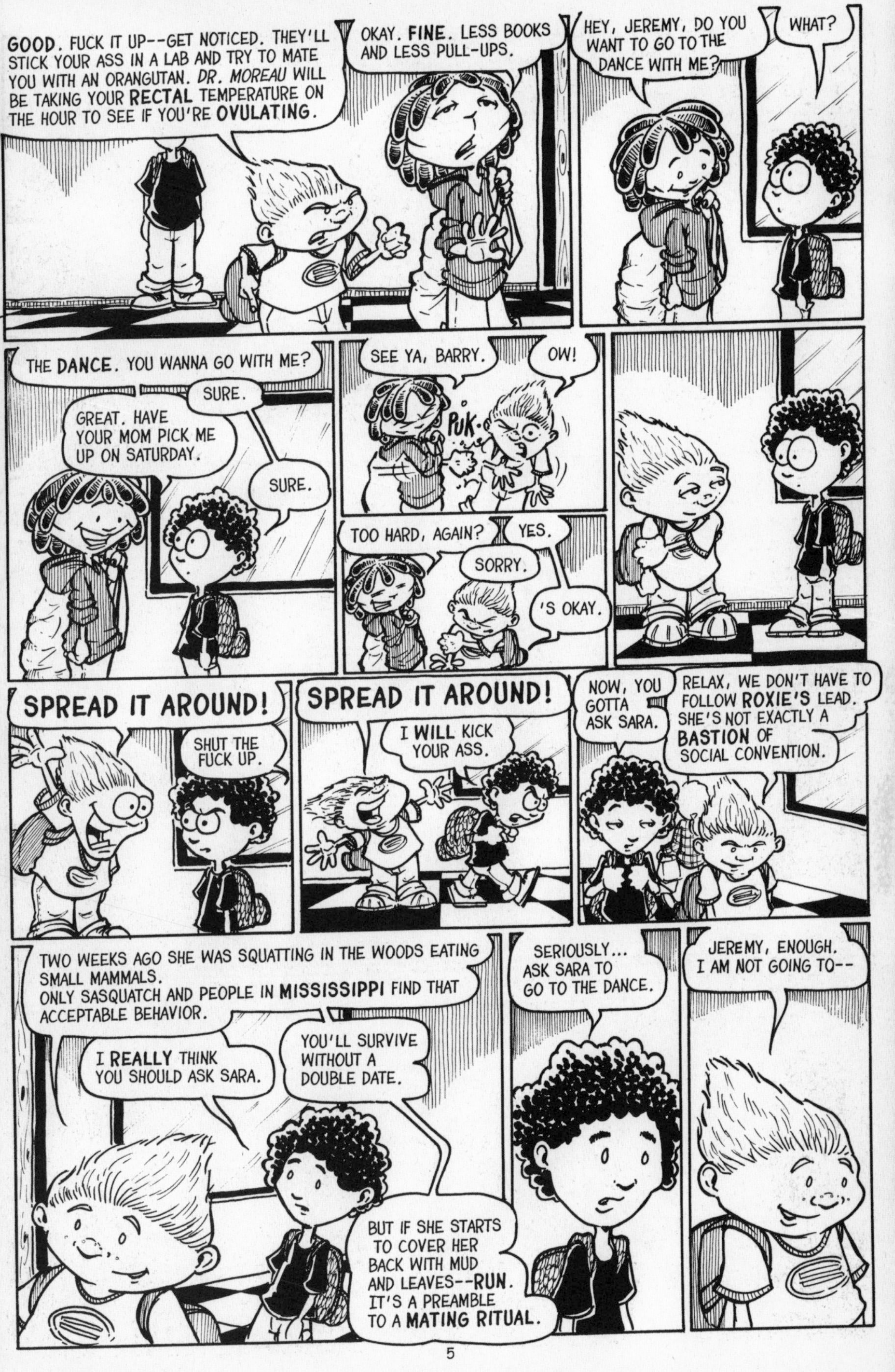
GOOD. FUCK IT UP--GET NOTICED. THEY'LL STICK YOUR ASS IN A LAB AND TRY TO MATE YOU WITH AN ORANGUTAN. DR. MOREAU WILL BE TAKING YOUR RECTAL TEMPERATURE ON THE HOUR TO SEE IF YOU'RE OVULATING.
OKAY. FINE. LESS BOOKS AND LESS PULL-UPS.
HEY, JEREMY, DO YOU WANT TO GO TO THE DANCE WITH ME?
WHAT?
THE DANCE. YOU WANNA GO WITH ME?
SURE.
GREAT. HAVE YOUR MOM PICK ME UP ON SATURDAY.
SURE.
SEE YA, BARRY.
OW!
PUK
TOO HARD, AGAIN?
YES.
SORRY.
'S OKAY.
SPREAD IT AROUND!
SHUT THE FUCK UP.
SPREAD IT AROUND!
I WILL KICK YOUR ASS.
NOW, YOU GOTTA ASK SARA.
RELAX, WE DON'T HAVE TO FOLLOW ROXIE'S LEAD. SHE'S NOT EXACTLY A BASTION OF SOCIAL CONVENTION.
TWO WEEKS AGO SHE WAS SQUATTING IN THE WOODS EATING SMALL MAMMALS.
ONLY SASQUATCH AND PEOPLE IN MISSISSIPPI FIND THAT ACCEPTABLE BEHAVIOR.
I REALLY THINK YOU SHOULD ASK SARA.
YOU'LL SURVIVE WITHOUT A DOUBLE DATE.
BUT IF SHE STARTS TO COVER HER BACK WITH MUD AND LEAVES--RUN. IT'S A PREAMBLE TO A MATING RITUAL.
SERIOUSLY... ASK SARA TO GO TO THE DANCE.
JEREMY, ENOUGH. I AM NOT GOING TO--

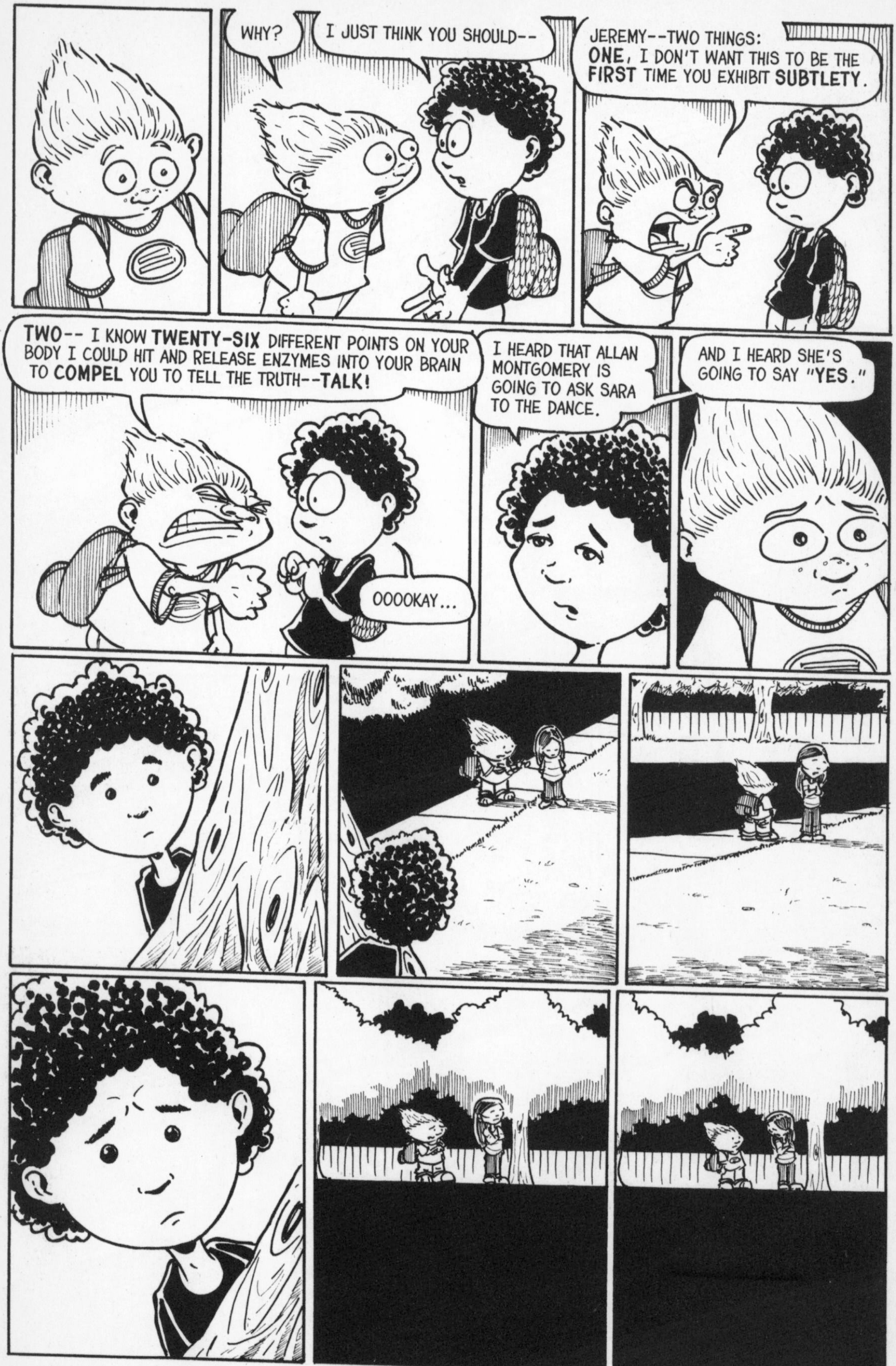

WHY?
I JUST THINK YOU SHOULD--
JEREMY--TWO THINGS: ONE, I DON'T WANT THIS TO BE THE FIRST TIME YOU EXHIBIT SUBTLETY.
TWO-- I KNOW TWENTY-SIX DIFFERENT POINTS ON YOUR BODY I COULD HIT AND RELEASE ENZYMES INTO YOUR BRAIN TO COMPEL YOU TO TELL THE TRUTH--TALK!
OOOOKAY...
I HEARD THAT ALLAN MONTGOMERY IS GOING TO ASK SARA TO THE DANCE.
AND I HEARD SHE'S GOING TO SAY "YES."

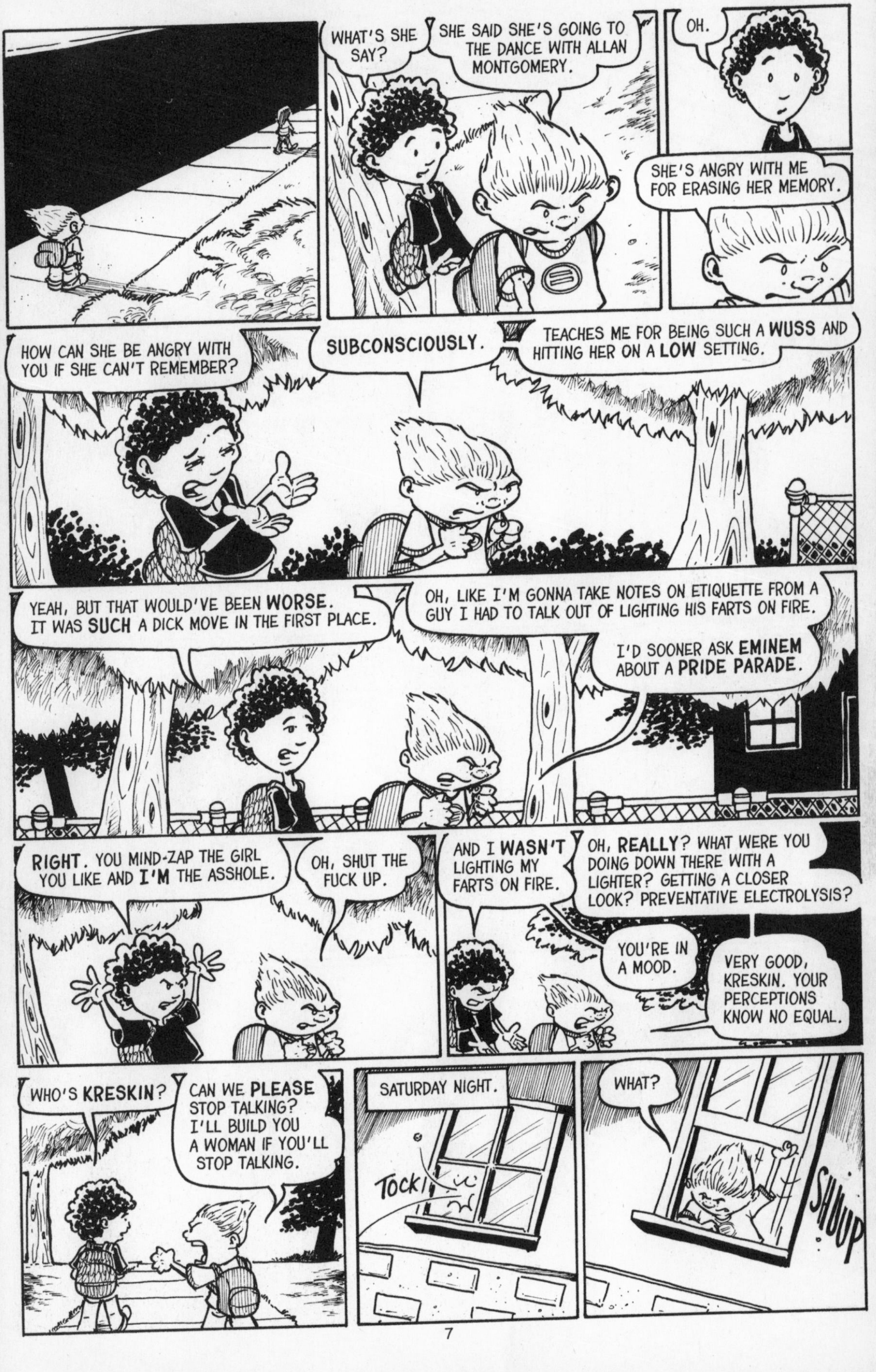
WHAT'S SHE SAY?
SHE SAID SHE'S GOING TO THE DANCE WITH ALLAN MONTGOMERY.
OH.
SHE'S ANGRY WITH ME FOR ERASING HER MEMORY.
HOW CAN SHE BE ANGRY WITH YOU IF SHE CAN'T REMEMBER?
SUBCONSCIOUSLY.
TEACHES ME FOR BEING SUCH A WUSS AND HITTING HER ON A LOW SETTING.
YEAH, BUT THAT WOULD'VE BEEN WORSE. IT WAS SUCH A DICK MOVE IN THE FIRST PLACE.
OH, LIKE I'M GONNA TAKE NOTES ON ETIQUETTE FROM A GUY I HAD TO TALK OUT OF LIGHTING HIS FARTS ON FIRE.
I'D SOONER ASK EMINEM ABOUT A PRIDE PARADE.
RIGHT. YOU MIND-ZAP THE GIRL YOU LIKE AND I'M THE ASSHOLE.
OH, SHUT THE FUCK UP.
AND I WASN'T LIGHTING MY FARTS ON FIRE.
OH, REALLY? WHAT WERE YOU DOING DOWN THERE WITH A LIGHTER? GETTING A CLOSER LOOK? PREVENTATIVE ELECTROLYSIS?
YOU'RE IN A MOOD.
VERY GOOD, KRESKIN. YOUR PERCEPTIONS KNOW NO EQUAL.
WHO'S KRESKIN?
CAN WE PLEASE STOP TALKING? I'LL BUILD YOU A WOMAN IF YOU'LL STOP TALKING.
SATURDAY NIGHT.
TOCK!
WHAT?
SHUUP

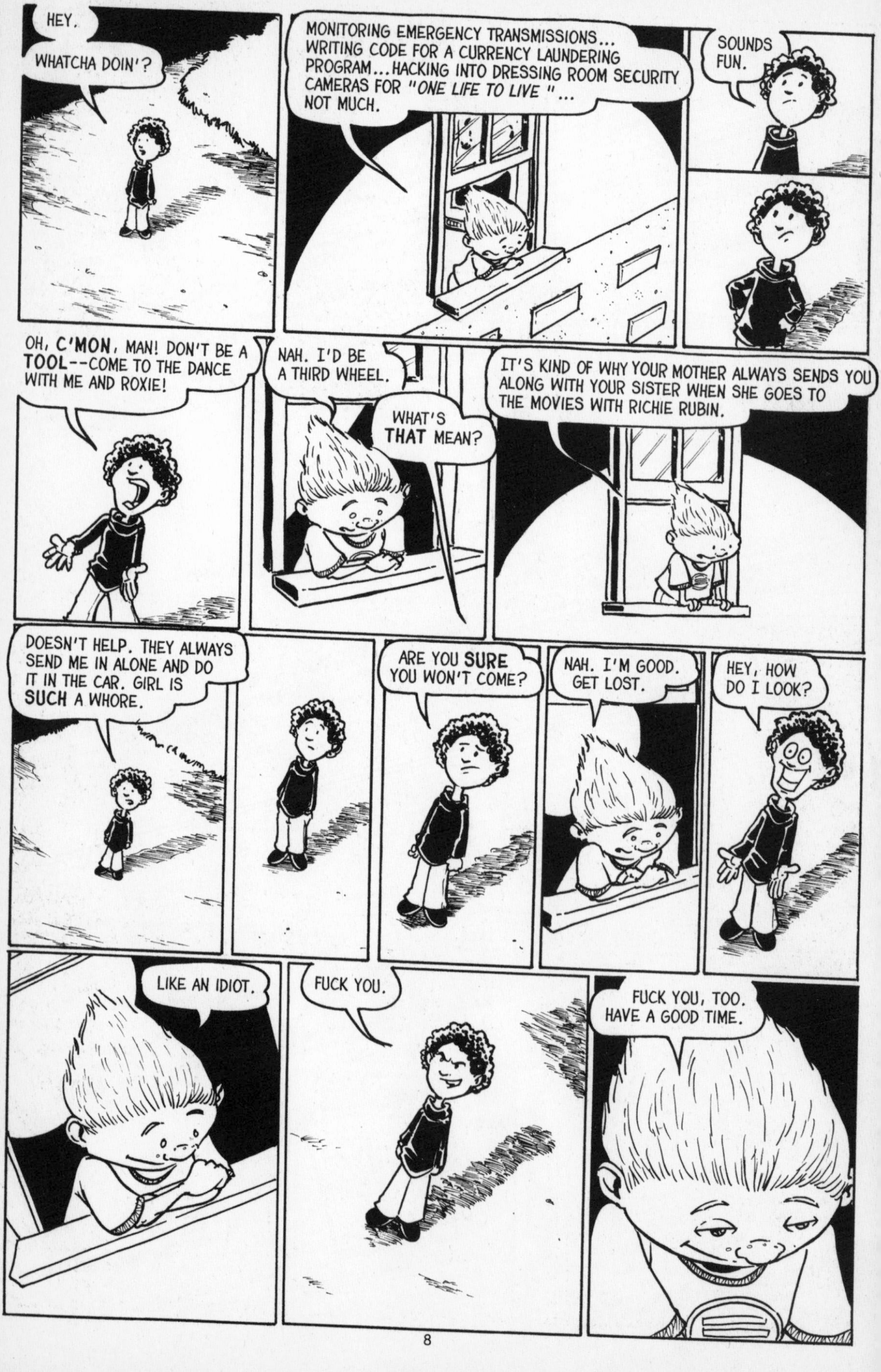
HEY.
WHATCHA DOIN'?
MONITORING EMERGENCY TRANSMISSIONS... WRITING CODE FOR A CURRENCY LAUNDERING PROGRAM... HACKING INTO DRESSING ROOM SECURITY CAMERAS FOR "ONE LIFE TO LIVE"... NOT MUCH.
SOUNDS FUN.
OH, C'MON, MAN! DON'T BE A TOOL--COME TO THE DANCE WITH ME AND ROXIE!
NAH. I'D BE A THIRD WHEEL.
WHAT'S THAT MEAN?
IT'S KIND OF WHY YOUR MOTHER ALWAYS SENDS YOU ALONG WITH YOUR SISTER WHEN SHE GOES TO THE MOVIES WITH RICHIE RUBIN.
DOESN'T HELP. THEY ALWAYS SEND ME IN ALONE AND DO IT IN THE CAR. GIRL IS SUCH A WHORE.
ARE YOU SURE YOU WON'T COME?
NAH. I'M GOOD. GET LOST.
HEY, HOW DO I LOOK?
LIKE AN IDIOT.
FUCK YOU.
FUCK YOU, TOO. HAVE A GOOD TIME.

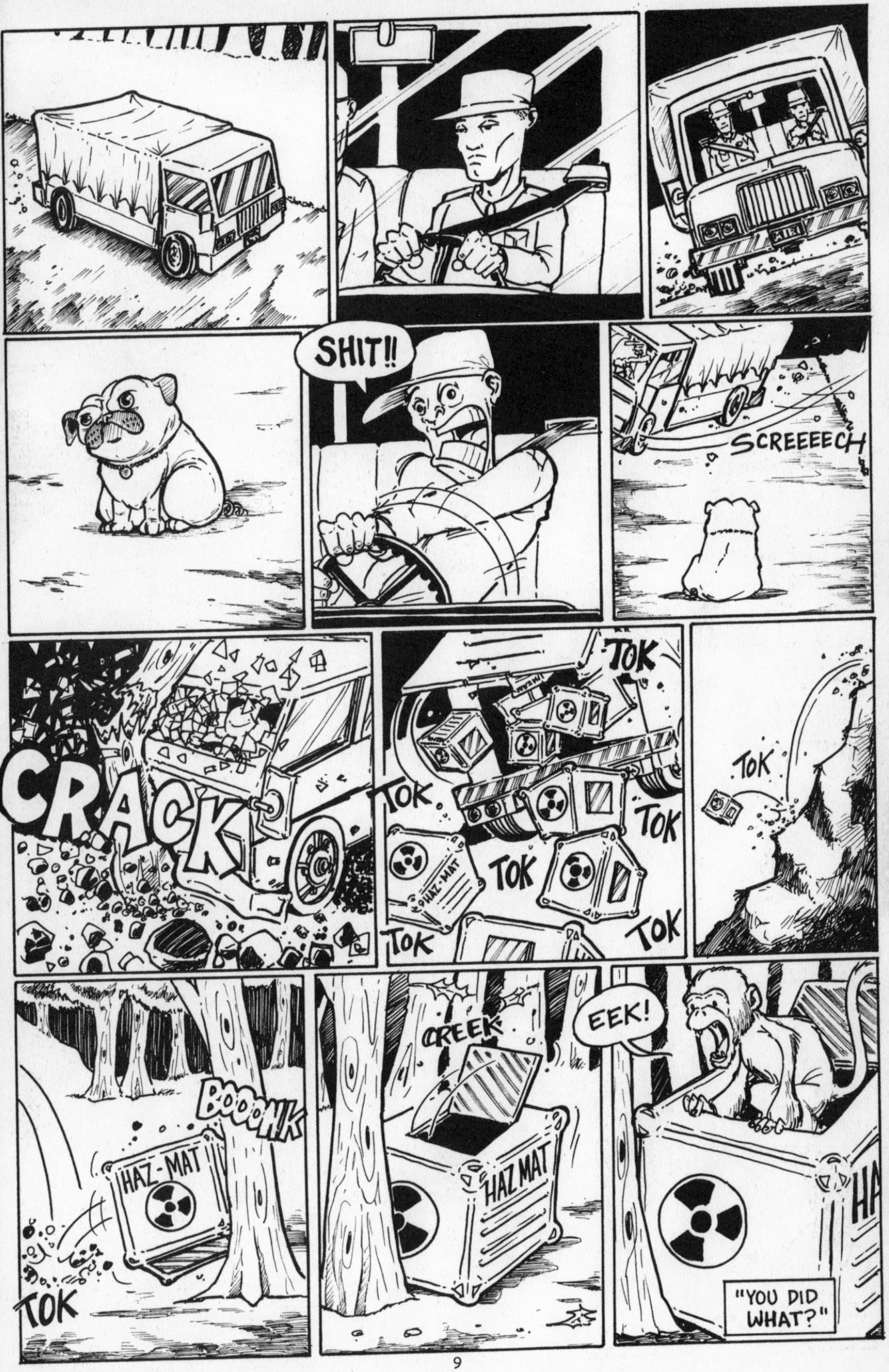
SHIT!!
SCREEEECH
CRACK
TOK
TOK
TOK
TOK
HAZ-MAT
TOK
TOK
TOK
BOOONK
HAZ-MAT
TOK
CREEK
HAZ MAT
EEK!
"YOU DID WHAT?"

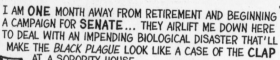

I AM **ONE** MONTH AWAY FROM RETIREMENT AND BEGINNING A CAMPAIGN FOR **SENATE**... THEY AIRLIFT ME DOWN HERE TO DEAL WITH AN IMPENDING BIOLOGICAL DISASTER THAT'LL MAKE THE *BLACK PLAGUE* LOOK LIKE A CASE OF THE **CLAP** AT A SORORITY HOUSE--

AND I FIND OUT IT'S BECAUSE **THIS** LITTLE PISSIN'-HER-PANTIES FUCK OF A **GIRL** UNDER YOUR COMMAND SWERVED TO **MISS A CHIPMUNK!!**

IT WAS A **PUG**, SIR.

I DON'T CARE IF **J. EDGAR HOOVER** WEARING A CHENILLE GOWN AND BLOWING A ROW OF CHORUS BOYS IS BLOCKING THE ROAD--
YOU MOW HIS DEAD, CLOSETED, GAY ASS OVER!!

WERE YOU **DRUNK**?! JERKING YOUR **JIMMY**?! LISTENING TO THE RADIO AND ENSNARED BY THE SCORCHING RHYTHMS OF A HOMOSEXUAL BOY BAND?!!

I--

SHUT UP!!

WHERE'S THAT FUCKING MONKEY?!

THE TRACKING CHIP HAS IT HEADING EAST, SIR.

GO GET IT.

" AND KILL ANY LIVING THING IT HAS CONTACT WITH..."

BEEP

CLICK
CLICK
CLICK
CLICK

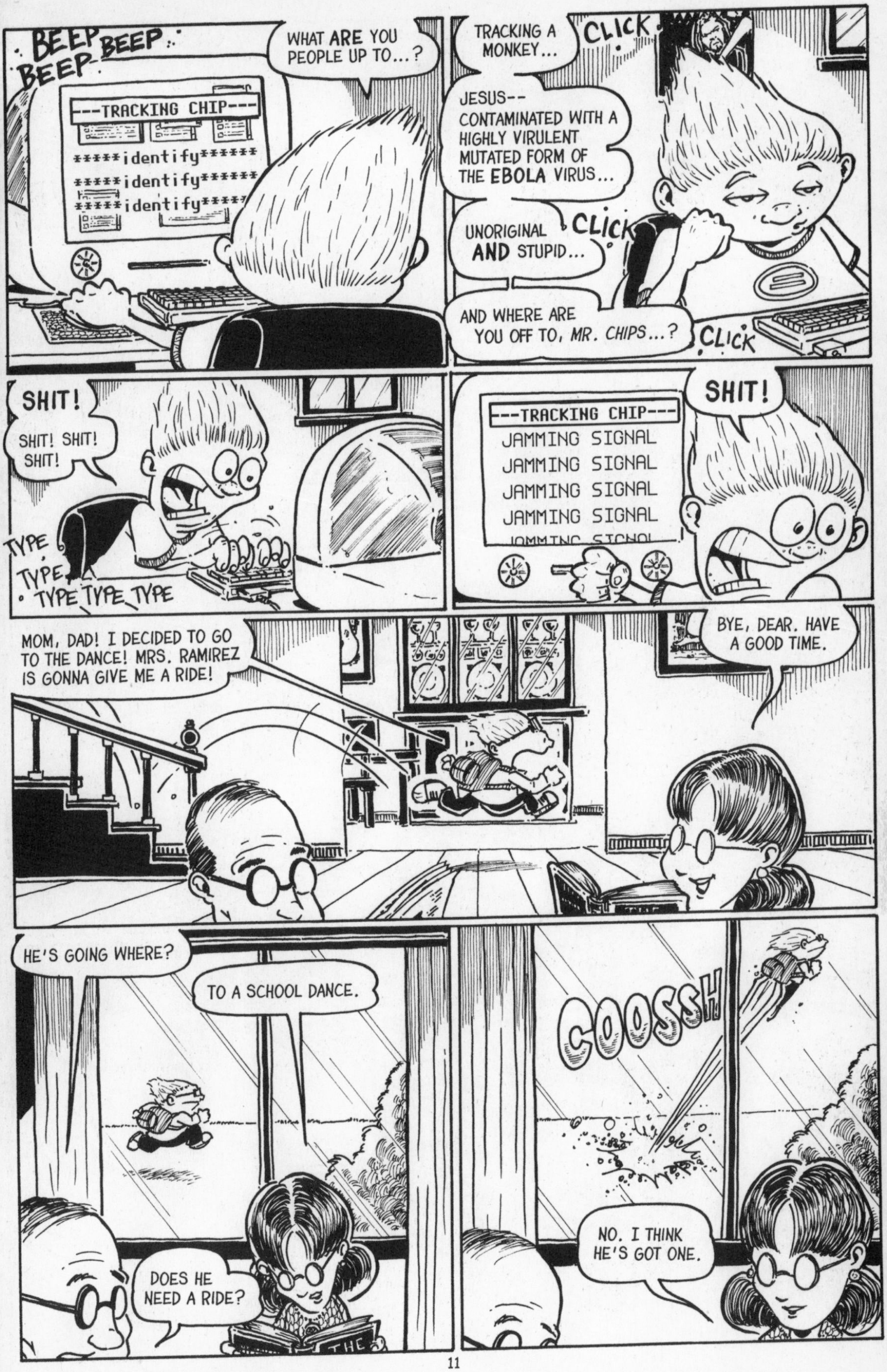
BEEP BEEP BEEP
---TRACKING CHIP---
*****identify******
*****identify******
*****identify*****
WHAT ARE YOU PEOPLE UP TO...?
TRACKING A MONKEY...
CLICK
JESUS-- CONTAMINATED WITH A HIGHLY VIRULENT MUTATED FORM OF THE EBOLA VIRUS...
UNORIGINAL AND STUPID...
CLICK
AND WHERE ARE YOU OFF TO, MR. CHIPS...?
CLICK
SHIT!
SHIT! SHIT! SHIT!
TYPE TYPE TYPE TYPE TYPE
---TRACKING CHIP---
JAMMING SIGNAL
JAMMING SIGNAL
JAMMING SIGNAL
JAMMING SIGNAL
SHIT!
MOM, DAD! I DECIDED TO GO TO THE DANCE! MRS. RAMIREZ IS GONNA GIVE ME A RIDE!
BYE, DEAR. HAVE A GOOD TIME.
HE'S GOING WHERE?
TO A SCHOOL DANCE.
DOES HE NEED A RIDE?
COOSSH
NO. I THINK HE'S GOT ONE.

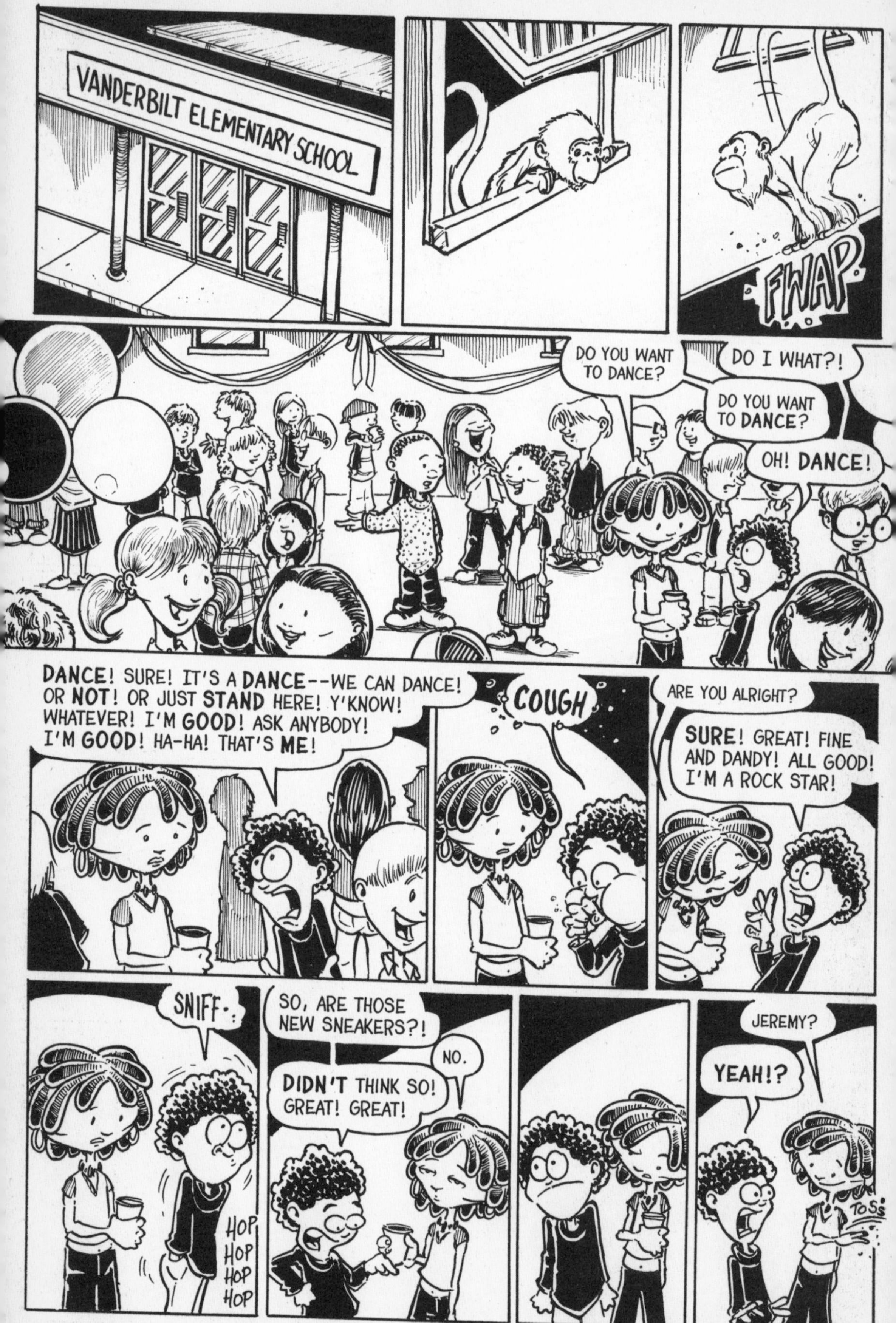
VANDERBILT ELEMENTARY SCHOOL
FWAP
DO YOU WANT TO DANCE?
DO I WHAT?!
DO YOU WANT TO DANCE?
OH! DANCE!
DANCE! SURE! IT'S A DANCE--WE CAN DANCE! OR NOT! OR JUST STAND HERE! Y'KNOW! WHATEVER! I'M GOOD! ASK ANYBODY! I'M GOOD! HA-HA! THAT'S ME!
COUGH
ARE YOU ALRIGHT?
SURE! GREAT! FINE AND DANDY! ALL GOOD! I'M A ROCK STAR!
SNIFF
HOP HOP HOP HOP
SO, ARE THOSE NEW SNEAKERS?!
NO.
DIDN'T THINK SO! GREAT! GREAT!
JEREMY?
YEAH!?
TOSS

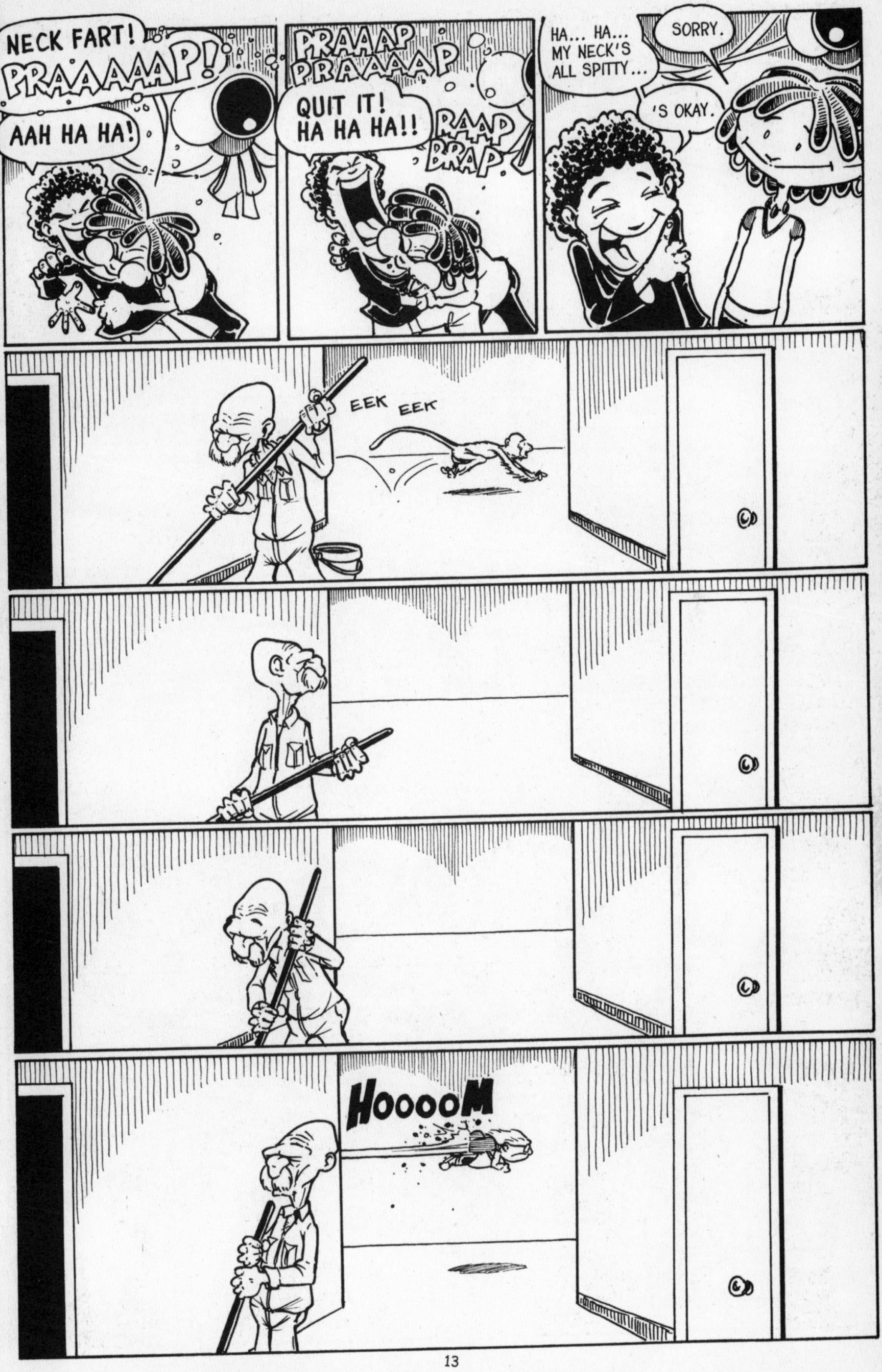
NECK FART!
PRAAAAAP!
AAH HA HA!
PRAAAP
PRAAAAAP
QUIT IT! HA HA HA!!
RAAP
BRAP
HA... HA... MY NECK'S ALL SPITTY...
SORRY.
'S OKAY.
EEK
EEK
HOOOOM

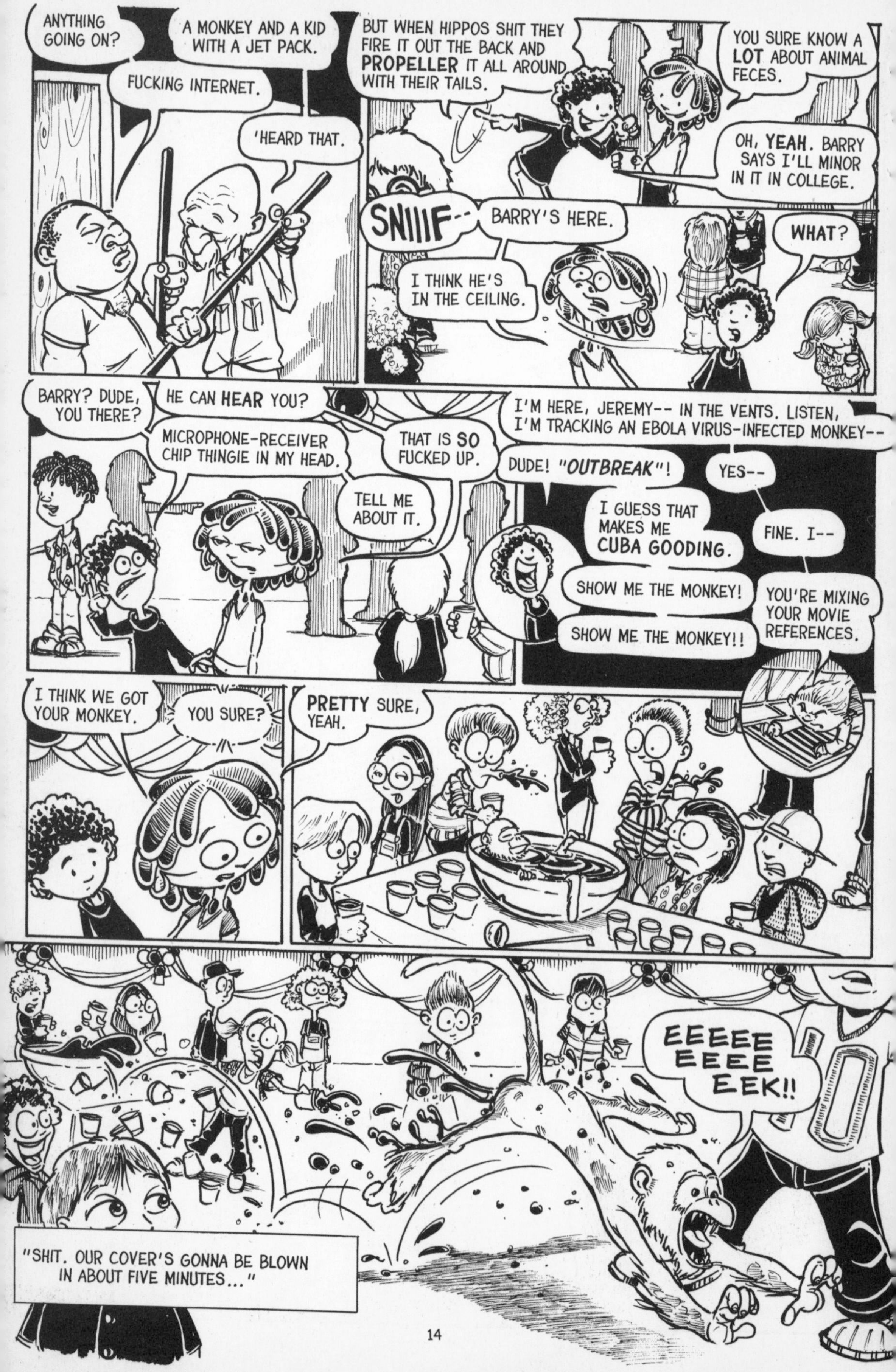
ANYTHING GOING ON?
A MONKEY AND A KID WITH A JET PACK.
FUCKING INTERNET.
'HEARD THAT.
BUT WHEN HIPPOS SHIT THEY FIRE IT OUT THE BACK AND PROPELLER IT ALL AROUND WITH THEIR TAILS.
YOU SURE KNOW A LOT ABOUT ANIMAL FECES.
OH, YEAH. BARRY SAYS I'LL MINOR IN IT IN COLLEGE.
SNIIIIF--
BARRY'S HERE.
I THINK HE'S IN THE CEILING.
WHAT?
BARRY? DUDE, YOU THERE?
HE CAN HEAR YOU?
MICROPHONE-RECEIVER CHIP THINGIE IN MY HEAD.
THAT IS SO FUCKED UP.
TELL ME ABOUT IT.
I'M HERE, JEREMY-- IN THE VENTS. LISTEN, I'M TRACKING AN EBOLA VIRUS-INFECTED MONKEY--
DUDE! "OUTBREAK"!
YES--
I GUESS THAT MAKES ME CUBA GOODING.
FINE. I--
SHOW ME THE MONKEY!
SHOW ME THE MONKEY!!
YOU'RE MIXING YOUR MOVIE REFERENCES.
I THINK WE GOT YOUR MONKEY.
YOU SURE?
PRETTY SURE, YEAH.
EEEEE EEEE EEK!!
"SHIT. OUR COVER'S GONNA BE BLOWN IN ABOUT FIVE MINUTES..."

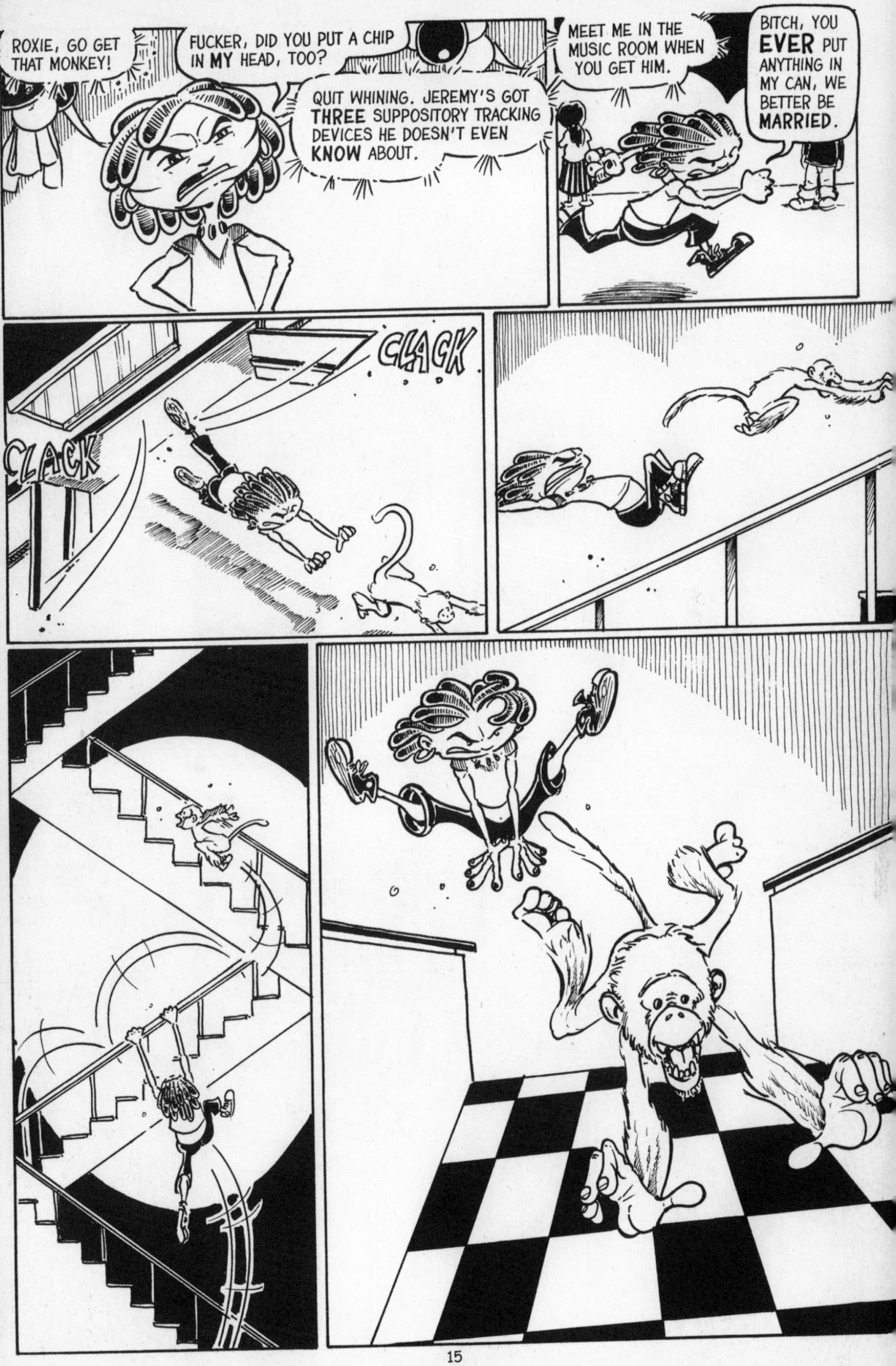
ROXIE, GO GET THAT MONKEY!
FUCKER, DID YOU PUT A CHIP IN MY HEAD, TOO?
QUIT WHINING. JEREMY'S GOT THREE SUPPOSITORY TRACKING DEVICES HE DOESN'T EVEN KNOW ABOUT.
MEET ME IN THE MUSIC ROOM WHEN YOU GET HIM.
BITCH, YOU EVER PUT ANYTHING IN MY CAN, WE BETTER BE MARRIED.
CLACK
CLACK

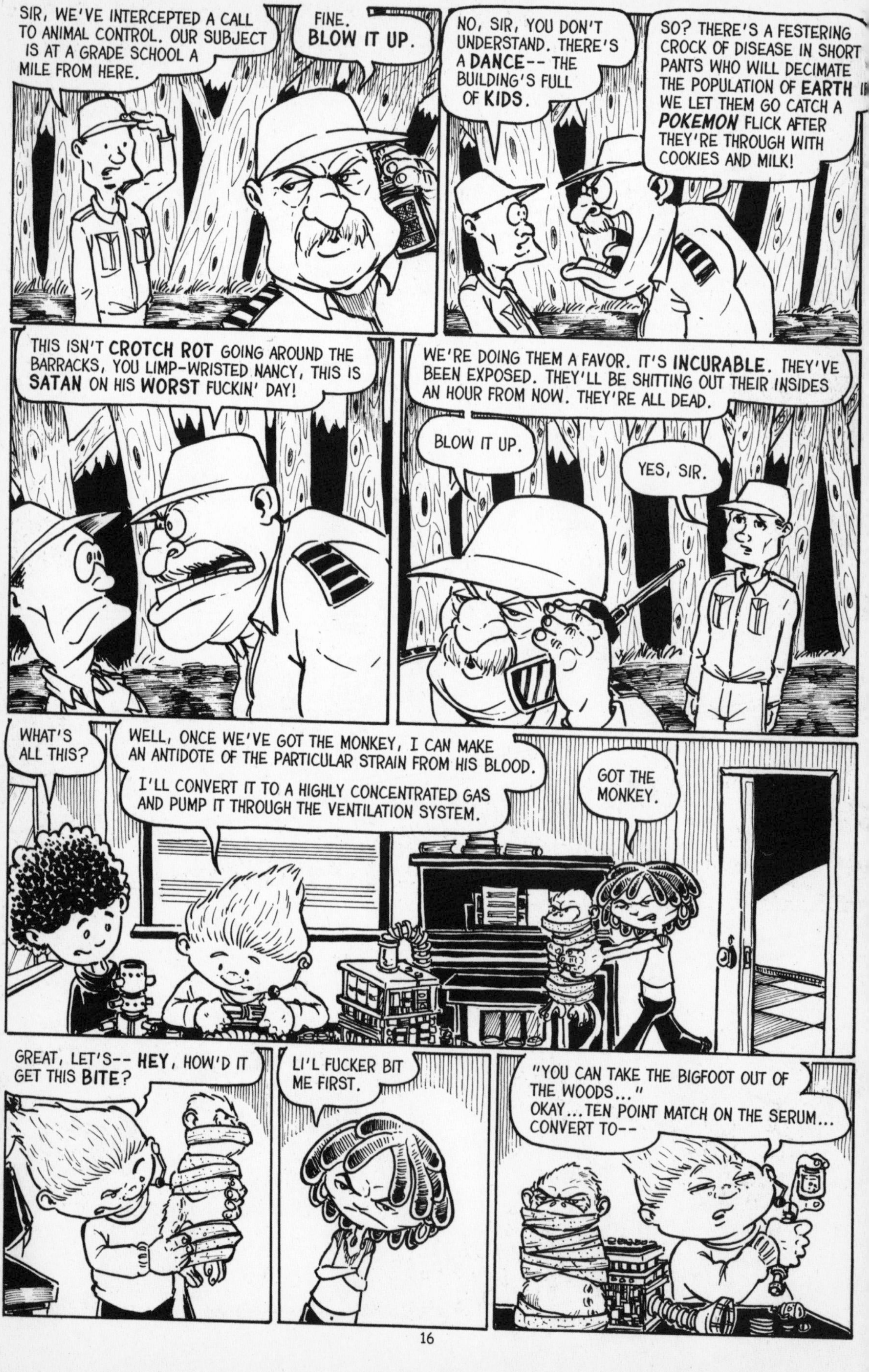
SIR, WE'VE INTERCEPTED A CALL TO ANIMAL CONTROL. OUR SUBJECT IS AT A GRADE SCHOOL A MILE FROM HERE.
FINE. BLOW IT UP.
NO, SIR, YOU DON'T UNDERSTAND. THERE'S A DANCE-- THE BUILDING'S FULL OF KIDS.
SO? THERE'S A FESTERING CROCK OF DISEASE IN SHORT PANTS WHO WILL DECIMATE THE POPULATION OF EARTH IF WE LET THEM GO CATCH A POKEMON FLICK AFTER THEY'RE THROUGH WITH COOKIES AND MILK!
THIS ISN'T CROTCH ROT GOING AROUND THE BARRACKS, YOU LIMP-WRISTED NANCY, THIS IS SATAN ON HIS WORST FUCKIN' DAY!
WE'RE DOING THEM A FAVOR. IT'S INCURABLE. THEY'VE BEEN EXPOSED. THEY'LL BE SHITTING OUT THEIR INSIDES AN HOUR FROM NOW. THEY'RE ALL DEAD.
BLOW IT UP.
YES, SIR.
WHAT'S ALL THIS?
WELL, ONCE WE'VE GOT THE MONKEY, I CAN MAKE AN ANTIDOTE OF THE PARTICULAR STRAIN FROM HIS BLOOD.
I'LL CONVERT IT TO A HIGHLY CONCENTRATED GAS AND PUMP IT THROUGH THE VENTILATION SYSTEM.
GOT THE MONKEY.
GREAT, LET'S-- HEY, HOW'D IT GET THIS BITE?
LI'L FUCKER BIT ME FIRST.
"YOU CAN TAKE THE BIGFOOT OUT OF THE WOODS..."
OKAY...TEN POINT MATCH ON THE SERUM... CONVERT TO--

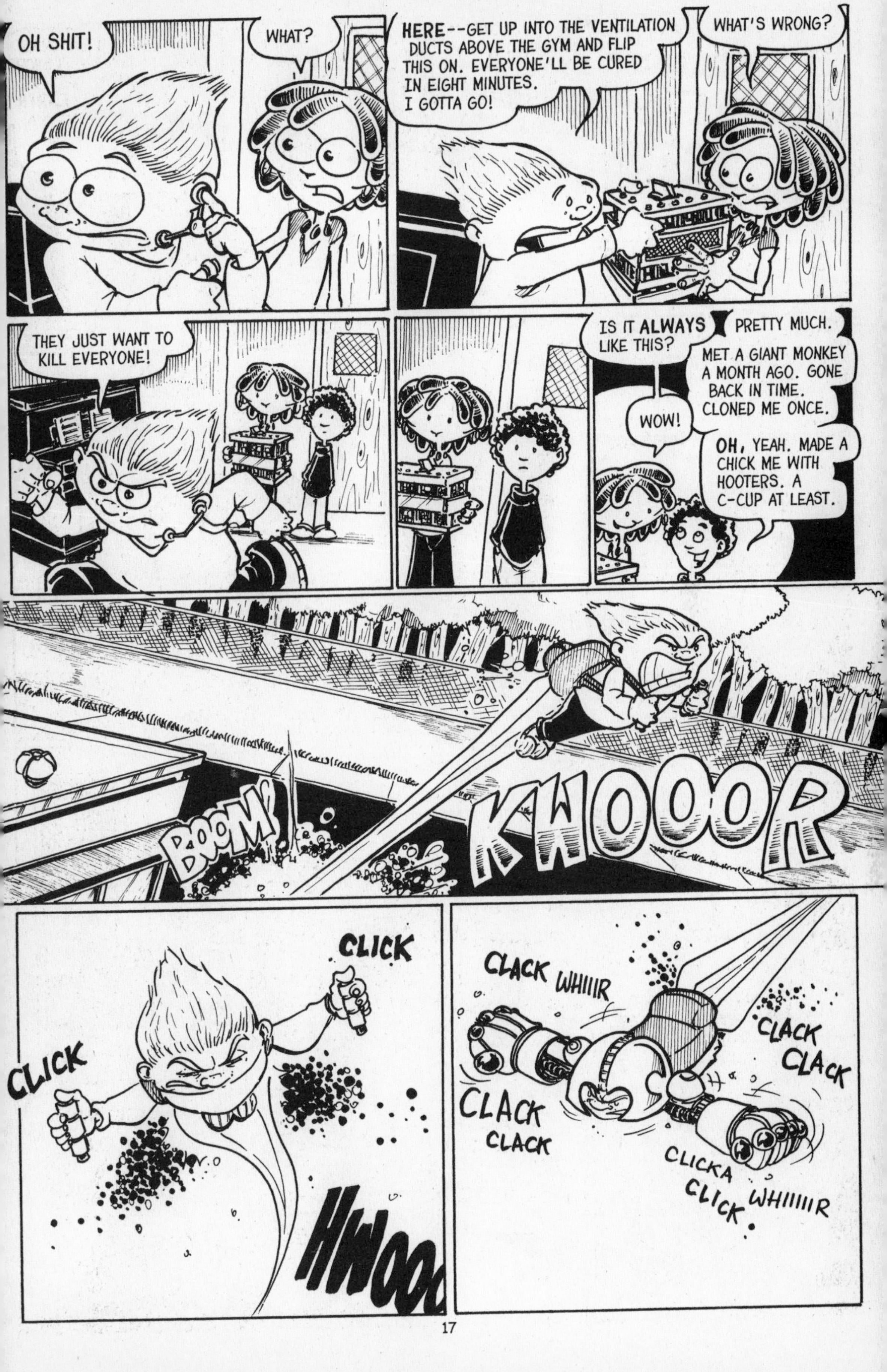
OH SHIT!
WHAT?
HERE--GET UP INTO THE VENTILATION DUCTS ABOVE THE GYM AND FLIP THIS ON. EVERYONE'LL BE CURED IN EIGHT MINUTES. I GOTTA GO!
WHAT'S WRONG?
THEY JUST WANT TO KILL EVERYONE!
IS IT ALWAYS LIKE THIS?
PRETTY MUCH.
MET A GIANT MONKEY A MONTH AGO. GONE BACK IN TIME. CLONED ME ONCE.
WOW!
OH, YEAH. MADE A CHICK ME WITH HOOTERS. A C-CUP AT LEAST.
BOOM!
KWOOOR
CLICK
CLICK
HWOO
CLACK WHIIIR
CLACK CLACK
CLACK CLACK
CLICKA CLICK
WHIIIIIR

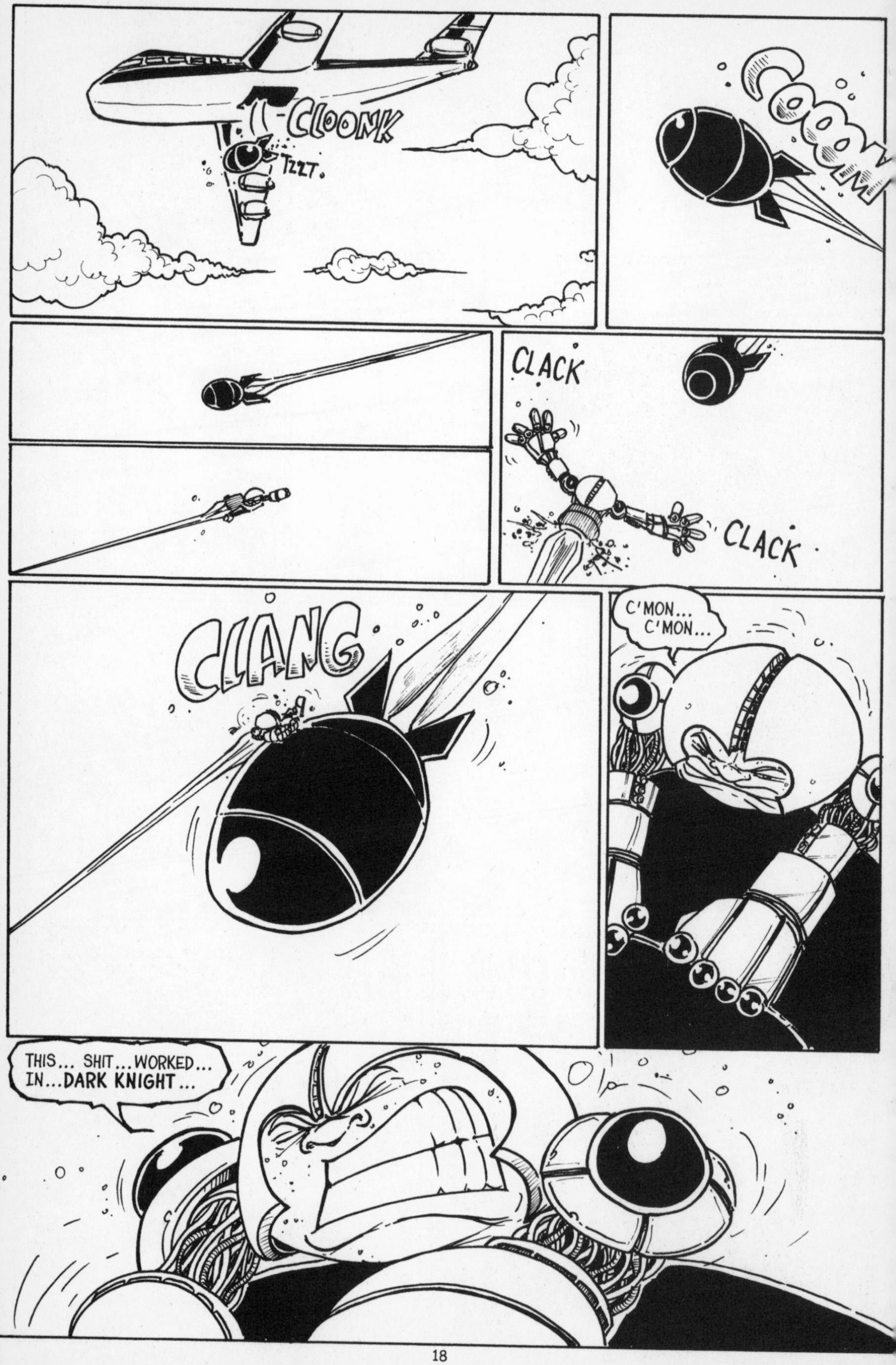
CLOONK
TZZT
COOOOM
CLACK
CLACK
CLANG
C'MON... C'MON...
THIS... SHIT...WORKED... IN...DARK KNIGHT...

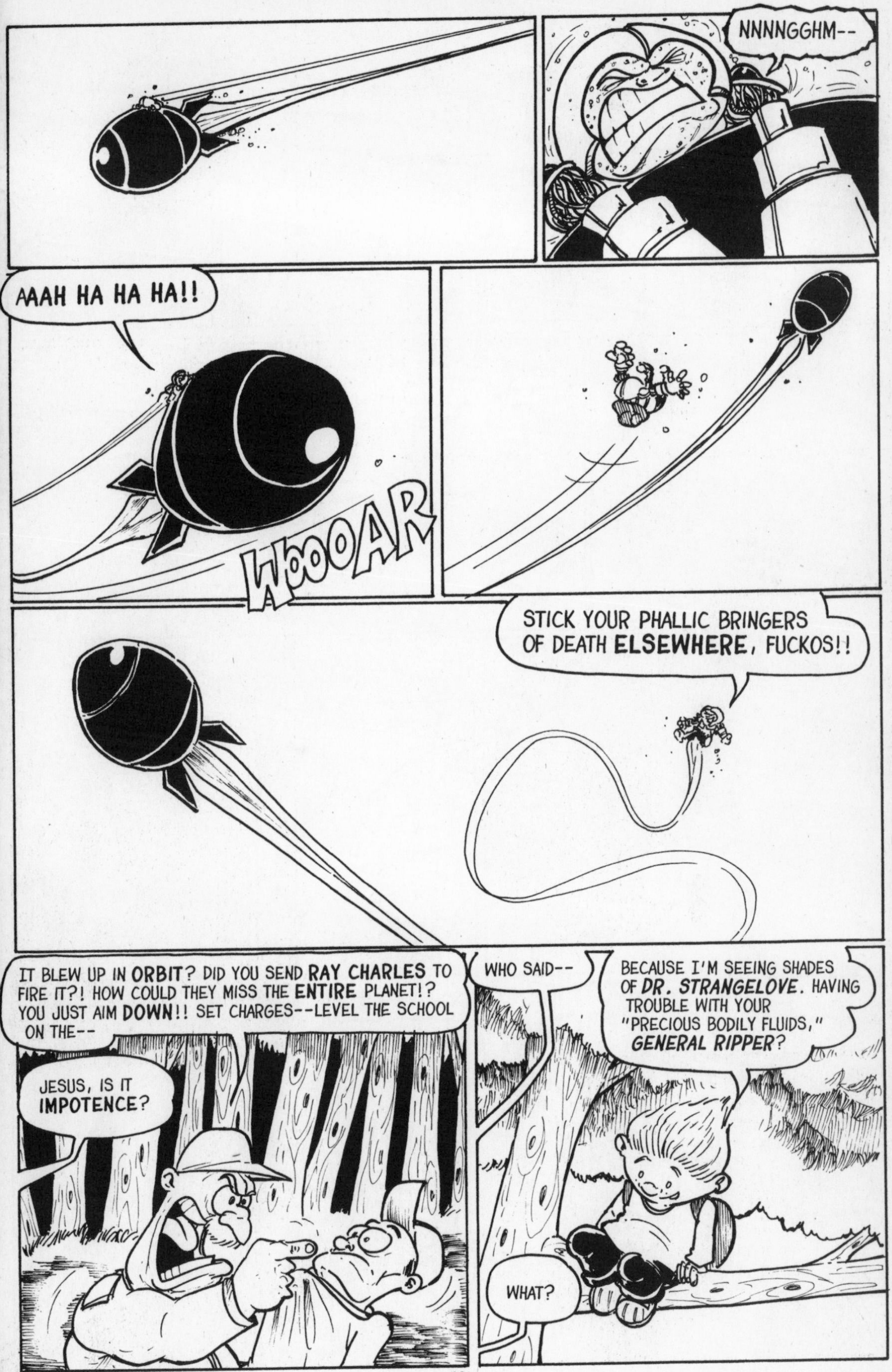
NNNNGGHM--
AAAH HA HA HA!!
WOOOAR
STICK YOUR PHALLIC BRINGERS OF DEATH ELSEWHERE, FUCKOS!!
IT BLEW UP IN ORBIT? DID YOU SEND RAY CHARLES TO FIRE IT?! HOW COULD THEY MISS THE ENTIRE PLANET!? YOU JUST AIM DOWN!! SET CHARGES--LEVEL THE SCHOOL ON THE--
JESUS, IS IT IMPOTENCE?
WHO SAID--
BECAUSE I'M SEEING SHADES OF DR. STRANGELOVE. HAVING TROUBLE WITH YOUR "PRECIOUS BODILY FLUIDS," GENERAL RIPPER?
WHAT?

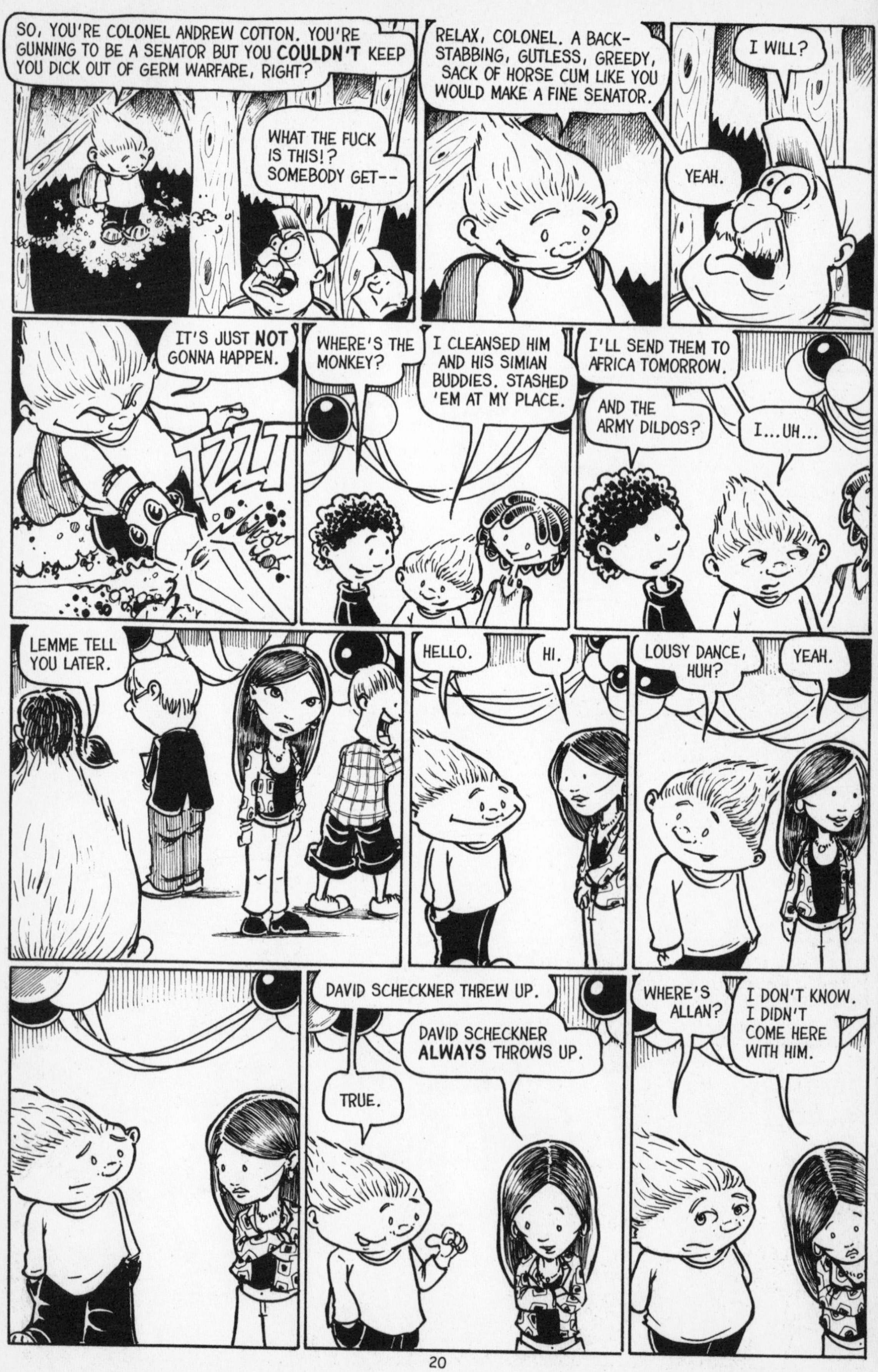
SO, YOU'RE COLONEL ANDREW COTTON. YOU'RE GUNNING TO BE A SENATOR BUT YOU COULDN'T KEEP YOU DICK OUT OF GERM WARFARE, RIGHT?
WHAT THE FUCK IS THIS!? SOMEBODY GET--
RELAX, COLONEL. A BACK-STABBING, GUTLESS, GREEDY, SACK OF HORSE CUM LIKE YOU WOULD MAKE A FINE SENATOR.
I WILL?
YEAH.
IT'S JUST NOT GONNA HAPPEN.
TZZZT
WHERE'S THE MONKEY?
I CLEANSED HIM AND HIS SIMIAN BUDDIES. STASHED 'EM AT MY PLACE.
I'LL SEND THEM TO AFRICA TOMORROW.
AND THE ARMY DILDOS?
I...UH...
LEMME TELL YOU LATER.
HELLO.
HI.
LOUSY DANCE, HUH?
YEAH.
DAVID SCHECKNER THREW UP.
DAVID SCHECKNER ALWAYS THROWS UP.
TRUE.
WHERE'S ALLAN?
I DON'T KNOW. I DIDN'T COME HERE WITH HIM.

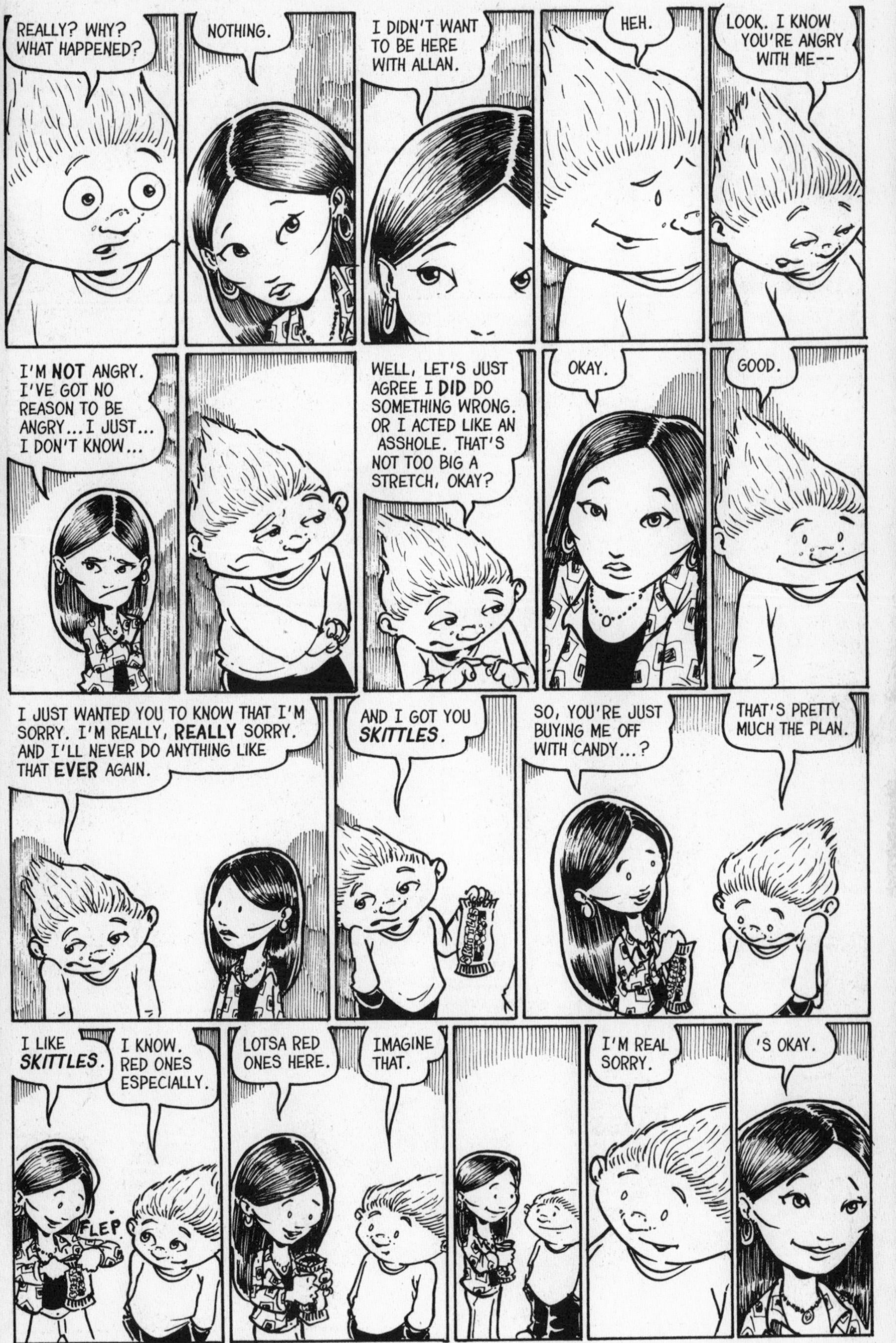
REALLY? WHY? WHAT HAPPENED?
NOTHING.
I DIDN'T WANT TO BE HERE WITH ALLAN.
HEH.
LOOK. I KNOW YOU'RE ANGRY WITH ME--
I'M NOT ANGRY. I'VE GOT NO REASON TO BE ANGRY... I JUST... I DON'T KNOW...
WELL, LET'S JUST AGREE I DID DO SOMETHING WRONG. OR I ACTED LIKE AN ASSHOLE. THAT'S NOT TOO BIG A STRETCH, OKAY?
OKAY.
GOOD.
I JUST WANTED YOU TO KNOW THAT I'M SORRY. I'M REALLY, REALLY SORRY. AND I'LL NEVER DO ANYTHING LIKE THAT EVER AGAIN.
AND I GOT YOU SKITTLES.
SO, YOU'RE JUST BUYING ME OFF WITH CANDY...?
THAT'S PRETTY MUCH THE PLAN.
I LIKE SKITTLES.
I KNOW. RED ONES ESPECIALLY.
FLEP
LOTSA RED ONES HERE.
IMAGINE THAT.
I'M REAL SORRY.
'S OKAY.

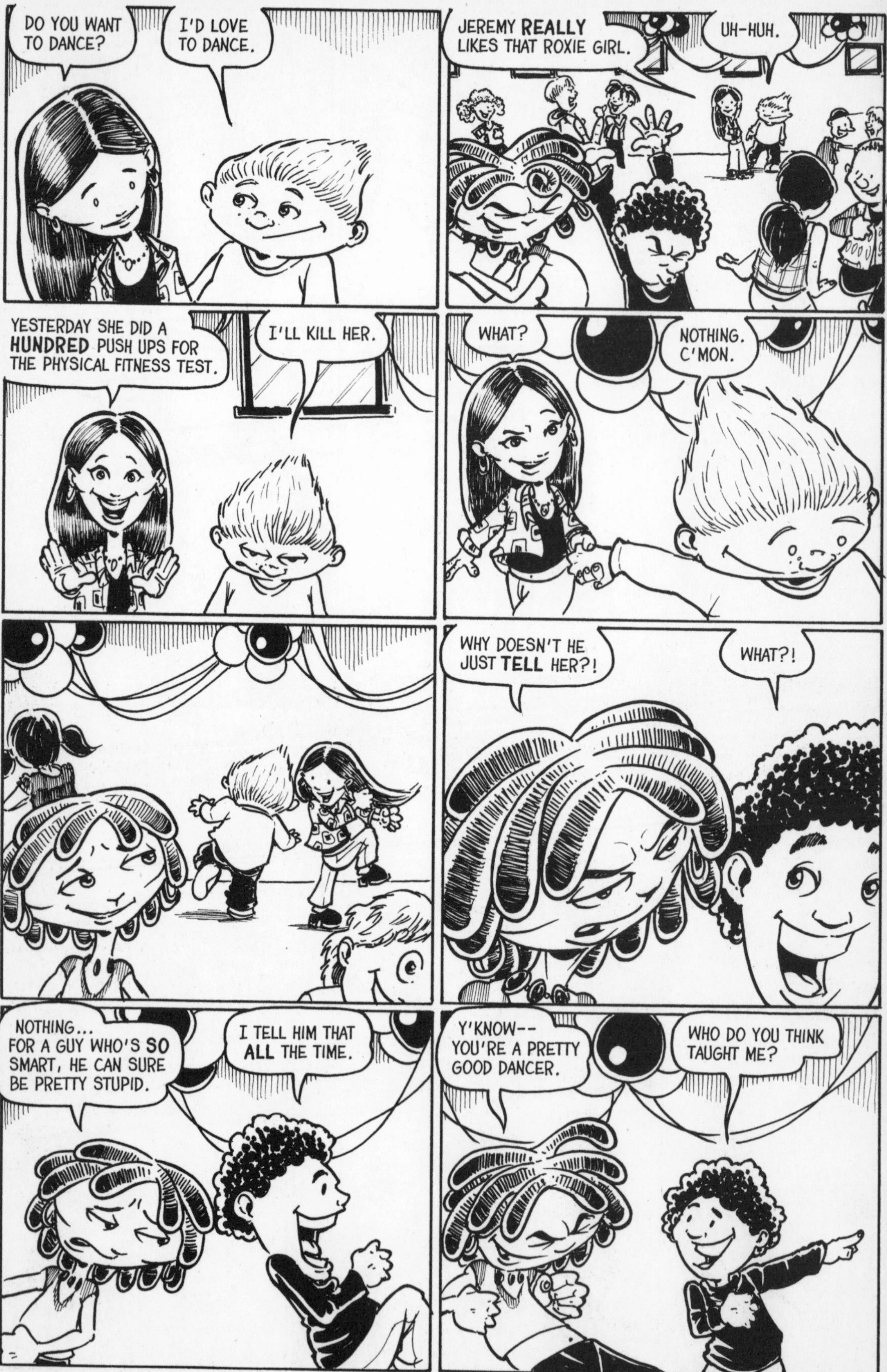
DO YOU WANT TO DANCE?
I'D LOVE TO DANCE.
JEREMY REALLY LIKES THAT ROXIE GIRL.
UH-HUH.
YESTERDAY SHE DID A HUNDRED PUSH UPS FOR THE PHYSICAL FITNESS TEST.
I'LL KILL HER.
WHAT?
NOTHING. C'MON.
WHY DOESN'T HE JUST TELL HER?!
WHAT?!
NOTHING... FOR A GUY WHO'S SO SMART, HE CAN SURE BE PRETTY STUPID.
I TELL HIM THAT ALL THE TIME.
Y'KNOW-- YOU'RE A PRETTY GOOD DANCER.
WHO DO YOU THINK TAUGHT ME?

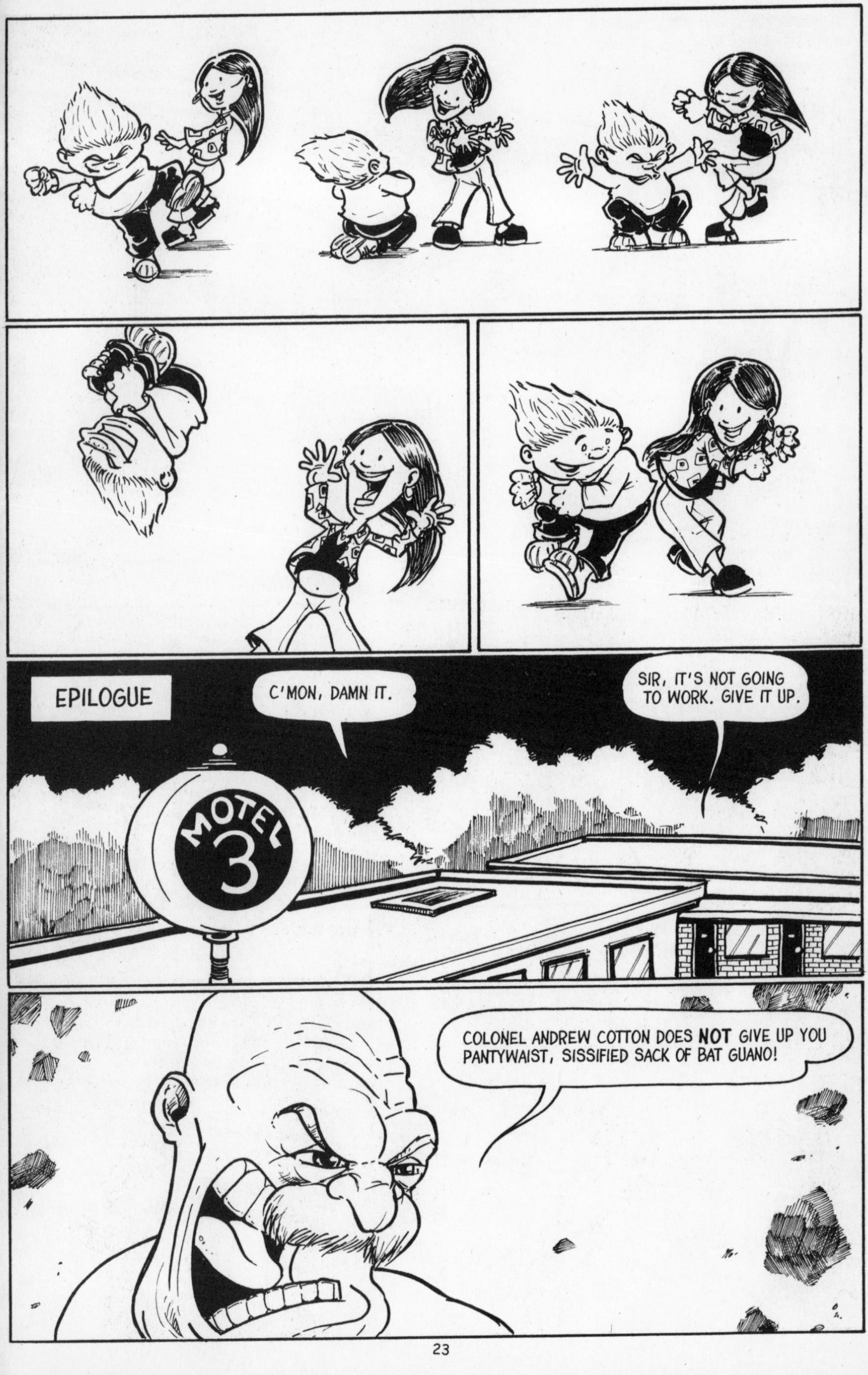
EPILOGUE
C'MON, DAMN IT.
SIR, IT'S NOT GOING TO WORK. GIVE IT UP.
MOTEL 3
COLONEL ANDREW COTTON DOES **NOT** GIVE UP YOU PANTYWAIST, SISSIFIED SACK OF BAT GUANO!

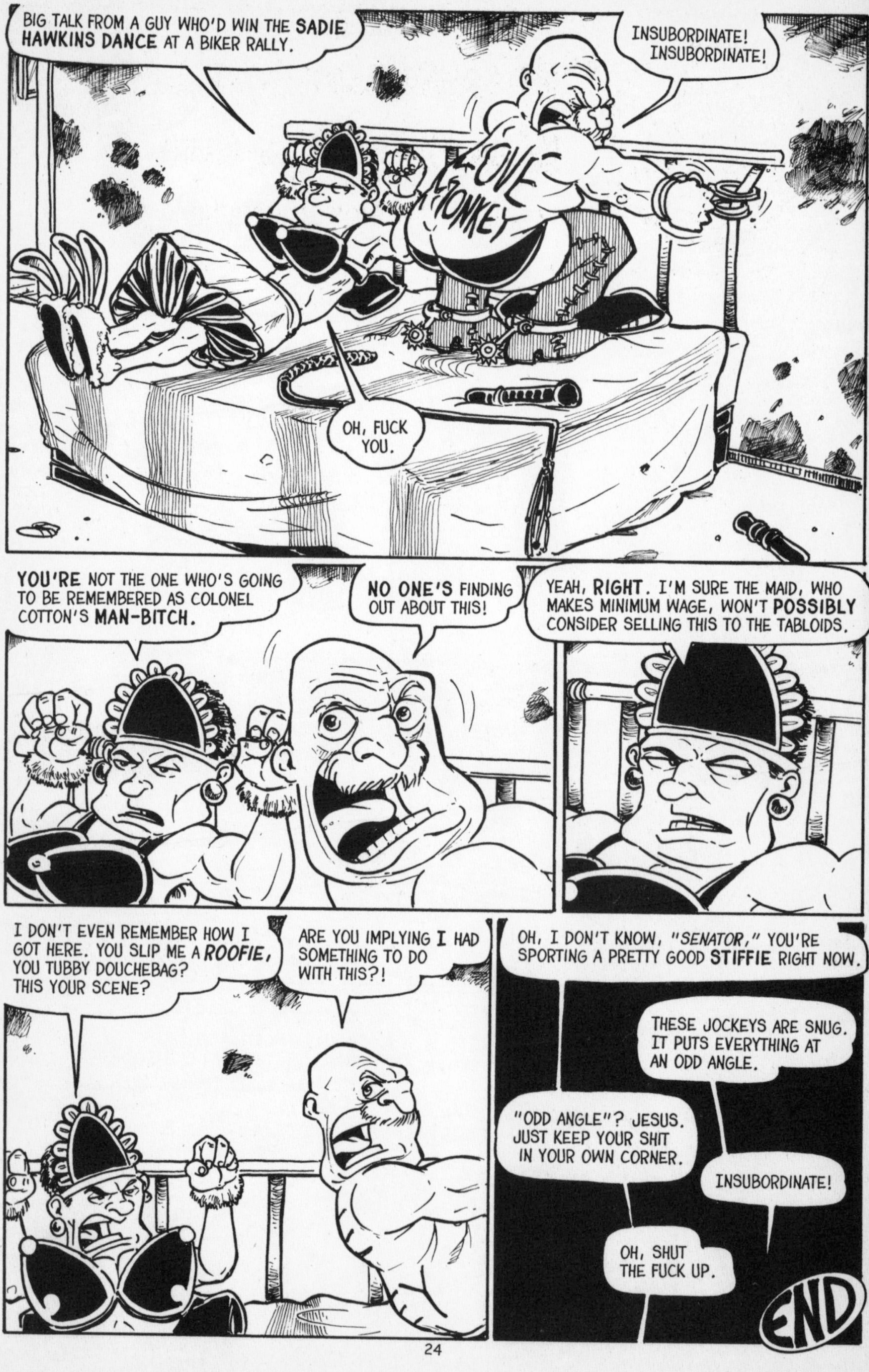

BIG TALK FROM A GUY WHO'D WIN THE SADIE HAWKINS DANCE AT A BIKER RALLY.
INSUBORDINATE! INSUBORDINATE!
OH, FUCK YOU.
YOU'RE NOT THE ONE WHO'S GOING TO BE REMEMBERED AS COLONEL COTTON'S MAN-BITCH.
NO ONE'S FINDING OUT ABOUT THIS!
YEAH, RIGHT. I'M SURE THE MAID, WHO MAKES MINIMUM WAGE, WON'T POSSIBLY CONSIDER SELLING THIS TO THE TABLOIDS.
I DON'T EVEN REMEMBER HOW I GOT HERE. YOU SLIP ME A ROOFIE, YOU TUBBY DOUCHEBAG? THIS YOUR SCENE?
ARE YOU IMPLYING I HAD SOMETHING TO DO WITH THIS?!
OH, I DON'T KNOW, "SENATOR," YOU'RE SPORTING A PRETTY GOOD STIFFIE RIGHT NOW.
THESE JOCKEYS ARE SNUG. IT PUTS EVERYTHING AT AN ODD ANGLE.
"ODD ANGLE"? JESUS. JUST KEEP YOUR SHIT IN YOUR OWN CORNER.
INSUBORDINATE!
OH, SHUT THE FUCK UP.
END

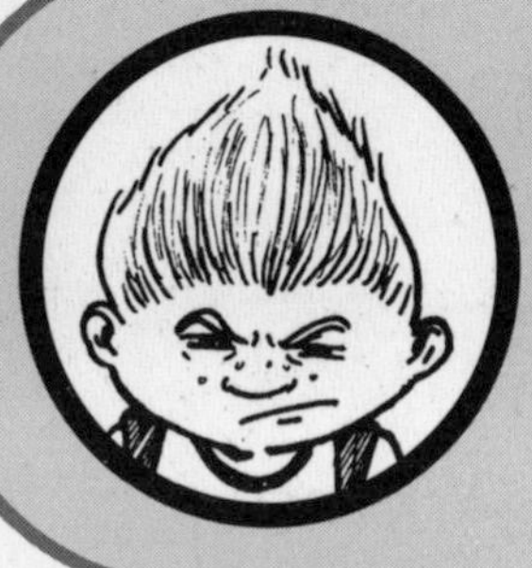

"How we make Barry Ween"

"A fairly serious look at something silly"

STEP ONE!
THE WRITIN'...

(1)

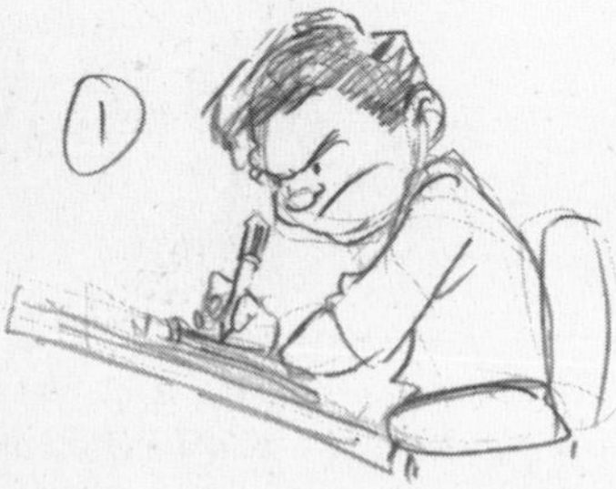

I'M NOT A "WAIT FOR THE MUSE TO HIT" KINDA GUY.

I PARK MY ASS IN A CHAIR AND I GET TO IT. MOST TIMES, IT DOESN'T START WELL.

(2)

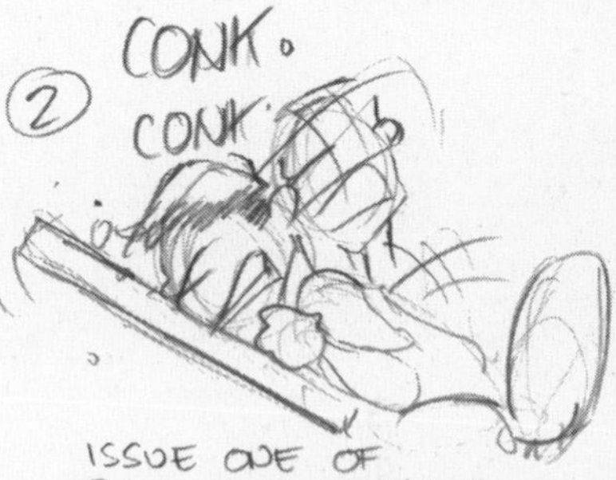
CONK.
CONK.

ISSUE ONE OF B.W.-MONKEY TALES HAD ME NEARLY SUICIDAL. ON THE OTHER HAND, ISSUE TWO POPPED OUT SO QUICK I GOT PARANOID.

(3) WHEN IT AIN'T WORKING, I LEAVE MY HOME STUDIO AND VENTURE OUTSIDE. I'LL SET UP CAMP AT AN INDEPENDANTLY OWNED COFFEE SHOP--

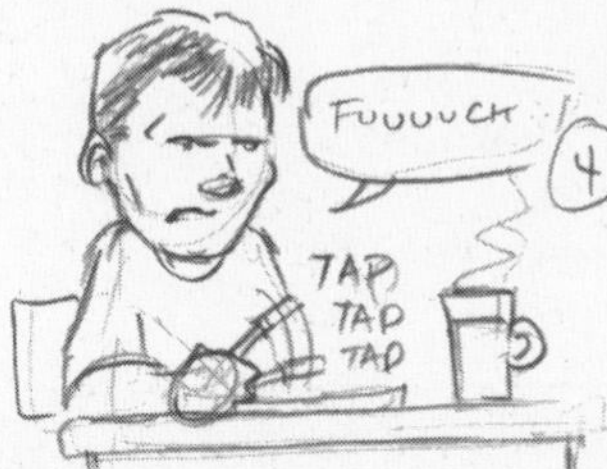
FUUUUCH...
TAP
TAP
TAP

(4) AND CONTINUE TO NOT WRITE VERY WELL...

THE IDEAS COME, THE PLOT FALLS INTO PLACE, BUT THE "REAL FUN" NEVER HAPPENS.

(5) THE BEST STUFF HITS ME LATER, NOT VERY LONG AFTER I PUT THE PEN DOWN.

IN THE CAR.

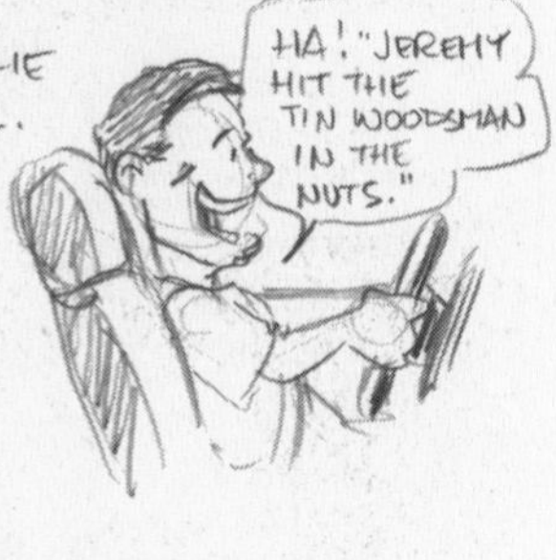
HA! "JEREMY HIT THE TIN WOODSMAN IN THE NUTS."

IN THE SHOWER.

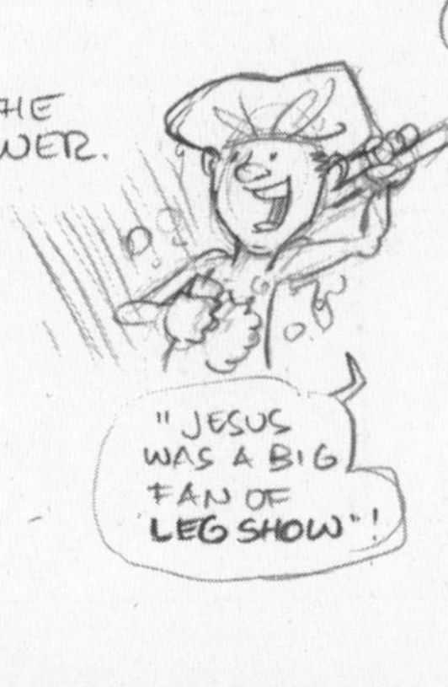
"JESUS WAS A BIG FAN OF LEG SHOW"!

(6)

I WAS UNAWARE UNTIL THE MOVIE AMERICAN BEAUTY THAT MEN ABUSE THEMSELVES IN THE SHOWER. I'M USUALLY WRITING. WHICH, IT COULD BE ARGUED IS ANOTHER FORM OF MASTURBATION, BUT I DIGRESS.

(7) BUT FINALLY, ALL THE STUFF IS
PUT DOWN ON PAPER. I WRITE IT
LONG HAND IN NOTEBOOKS. I
DON'T KNOW WHY BUT EVERYTHING
I WRITE AND DRAW BEGINS LIKE
THIS.

IT MOSTLY COMES OUT AS DIALOGUE.
I'LL WRITE IT AND REWRITE IT
UNTIL IT SOUNDS RIGHT TO ME.

IT'S MESSY AND CAN PROBABLY ONLY BE UNDERSTOOD
BY ME. HERE'S THE WRITTEN SCRIPT OF BARRY WEEN
MONKEY TALES # 4. PAGES EIGHT AND NINE (MOSTLY)

I DROP NON SEQUITURS ALL OVER THE PLACE. ON THIS
ONE THERE'S A RITALIN JOKE SCRAWLED IN THE CORNER,
A VERSION OF WHICH WAS ON PAGE TEN.

NON SEQUITURS USUALLY HIT ME WHEN I'M IN THE CAR,
SHOWERING, ETC. I THINK THEY'RE THE BACK BONE OF
THE BOOK.

- RELAX! YOUR MOTHER IS WATCHING
  BY NOW
BO DUKE SING "TRADITION" SHE'LL
NEVER KNOW.
- MOMMY SAYS THAT JESUS SEES
EVERYTHING AND HE'LL TELL HER.

- YOU'RE KIDDING? WHO ARE YOU,
LAURA INGELS? HAVE READ SOME
COMICS.
NOT ALLOWED. BAD STUFF.
IS THERE ANY GOD. WHAT ELSE
AREN'T YOU ALLOWED TO DO.
HANDS HIM LIST.
A LIST? LAMINATED. NO LESS.
NO VIDEO GAMES. NO COMICS. NO
TELEVISION OR VIDEOS. NO MUSIC. NO BOARD
GAMES WITH - WHAT - NEGATIVE
RELIGIOUS OR THEMES - WHAT
THE FUCK - CHUTES AND LADDERS
ARE BAGS ON CHRIST.
JOHNNY SLAPS HANDS OVER
MOUTH.
CURSING NO GOOD WITH MOMS &
J.C. AS WELL HUH?

"THEY PUT ME ON
RITALIN BUT I
STOPPED POOPING"

JOHNNY NODS.
NO SODA OR SUGAR BASED DRINKS...
ONLY AFTER FIRST ONE I AGREE WITH,
LIMITED DRINKING OF BEVERAGES.
ON OR PER TRIP
NO PEE PEE ACCIDENTS.
- I'M WEARING MY BIG BOY PANTS.
UH-HUH. NO CANDY, OR JUNK FOOD
OF ANY KIND.
NO ROUGH PLAY. NO CONTACT
SPORTS. NO "BAD TALK".

GREAT. SO FOUR HOURS STUCK WITH
ONE OF THE OSMONDS. HERE LOOK
AT THESE FOR AWHILE.

THESE ARE NAKED LADIES.
THEY ARE INDEED. IS THERE ANYTHING
ON YOU LIKE ABOUT LOOKING AT PICTURES
OF NAKED LADIES?
NOPE.
NOW WE'RE TALKING.
THEY'VE GOT HAIR DOWN THERE.
OH YEAH. THERE ARE MANY MYSTERIES
TO BE DISCOVERED.